CREATION AND THE PERSISTENCE OF EVIL

Creation
and the
Persistence
of
Evil

The Jewish Drama
of Divine Omnipotence

Jon D. Levenson

PRINCETON UNIVERSITY PRESS
PRINCETON, NEW JERSEY

Published by Princeton University Press, 41 William Street, Princeton, New Jersey 08540
In the United Kingdom: Princeton University Press, Chichester, West Sussex

Originally published in 1987 by Harper & Row Publishers, Inc., New York, N.Y.; reprinted in paperback by arrangement with HarperSanFrancisco, San Francisco, C.A.

Library of Congress Cataloging-in-Publication Data

Levenson, Jon Douglas.
  Creation and the persistence of evil : the Jewish drama of divine omnipotence / Jon D. Levenson.
    p.   cm.—(Mythos series)
  Previously published: 1st ed. San Francisco : Harper & Row, c1988.
  Includes bibliographical references and indexes.
    ISBN 0-691-02950-4
    1. Creation—Biblical teaching.   2. Bible. O.T. Genesis I–II, 3—
  Theology.   3. Covenants (Theology)—Biblical teaching.   4. Bible.
  O.T.—Theology.   I. Title.   II. Series.
  BS651.L377   1994
  296.3'4—dc20   94-31950

Grateful acknowledgment is given for use of excerpts from *Ancient Near Eastern Texts Relating to the Old Testament*, 3rd edition, with supplement by James B. Pritchard, ed. Copyright © 1969 by Princeton University Press. Reprinted by permission of Princeton University Press.

Unless otherwise noted, Scripture quotations contained herein are from *Tanakh*, copyright © 1985 and used through the courtesy of the Jewish Publication Society.

Princeton University Press books are printed on acid-free paper and meet the guidelines for permanence and durability of the Committee on Production Guidelines for Book Longevity of the Council on Library Resources

First Princeton Paperback printing, 1994
Printed in the United States of America

10 9 8 7 6

http://pup.princeton.edu

ISBN-13: 978-0-691-02950-4 (pbk.)

For Ruth, Judah, Daniel, and Noah
Ps. 128:3

Contents

Abbreviations

AB	Anchor Bible
Abot R. Nat.	Abot de Rabbi Nathan
An Bib	Analecta Biblica
ANET	*Ancient Near Eastern Texts Relating to the Old Testament,* 3rd ed., ed. James Pritchard (Princeton, N.J.: Princeton University, 1969)
AOAT	Alter Orient und Altes Testament
ASORDS	American Schools of Oriental Research Dissertation Series
b.	*Babylonian Talmud*
BASOR	*Bulletin of the American Schools of Oriental Research*
B. Bat.	*Baba Batra*
Ber.	*Berakot*
Ber. Rab.	*Bereshit Rabbah*
BHK	*Biblia Hebraica* (ed. Rudolf Kittel)
BHS	*Biblia Hebraica Stuttgartensia* (ed. K. Elliger and W. Rudolf)
BJS	Brown Judaic Series
BKAT	Biblischer Kommentar: Altes Testament
CBQ	*Catholic Biblical Quarterly*
CJ	*Conservative Judaism*
Comm	*Commentary*
CSHJ	Chicago Studies in the History of Judaism
CTA	*Corpus des tablettes en cunéiformes alphabétiques,* ed. A. Herdner (Paris: Imprimerie Nationale, 1963)
EB	*Encyclopaedia Biblica*
ET	English Translation
HAR	*Hebrew Annual Review*
HSM	ʾHarvard Semitic Monographs
HSS	Harvard Semitic Series
HTR	*Harvard Theological Review*
HTR HDR	Harvard Theological Review Harvard Dissertations in Religion
HUCA	*Hebrew Union College Annual*
IRT	*Issues in Religion and Theology*
JBL	*Journal of Biblical Literature*
JJS	*Journal of Jewish Studies*
JQR	*Jewish Quarterly Review*
JSS	*Journal of Semitic Studies*
JTC	*Journal for Theology and the Church*
JTS	*Journal of Theological Studies*
Jud	*Judaism*
LCL	Loeb Classical Library
Lev. Rab.	*Leviticus Rabbah*

LXX	Septuagint
m.	*Mishnah*
Meg.	*Megillah*
Mid	*Midstream*
MT	*Masoretic Text*
NJV	New Jewish Version
Num Sup	*Numen* Supplements
Or	*Orientalia*
OTL	Old Testament Library
Pesiq. R.	*Pesiqta Rabbati*
Pesiq. Rab. Kah.	*Pesiqta de Rab Kahana*
1QS	The community rule from Qumran, Cave 1
RB	*Revue Biblique*
REJ	*Revue des études juive*
Roš. Haš.	*Roš Haššanah*
Šabb.	*Šabbat*
SBLDS	Society of Biblical Literature Dissertation Series
SBT	Studies in Biblical Theology
SHR	Studies in the History of Religion
SNVAO	Skrifter utgitt av Det Norske Videnskaps-Akademi i Oslo
STDJ	Studies on the Texts of the Desert of Judah
Suk.	*Sukkah*
Tanḥ	*Tanḥuma'*
TB	Theologische Bücherei
Trad.	*Tradition: A Journal of Orthodox Jewish Thought*
TS	*Theological Studies*
TZ	*Theologische Zeitschrift*
UF	*Ugaritische Forschungen*
VT	*Vetus Testamentum*
VT Sup	Vetus Testamentum Supplements
WMANT	Wissenschaftliche Monographien zum Alten und Neuen Testament
ZAW	*Zeitschrift für die alttestamentliche Wissenschaft*

Acknowledgments

Two scholars were kind enough to read all or most of this book and share their expert judgment of it with me. Professors Robert L. Cohn and Wolfgang M. W. Roth deserve my thanks, though they bear no responsibility for any errors or wrongheadedness in the study. My thinking on the subject of creation in the ancient Near Eastern world has benefited greatly from discussions over the years with Professors Richard J. Clifford, I. Tzvi Abusch, and Baruch Halpern. Conversations with all five of these scholars have only deepened my conviction that true scholarship is a social and collegial activity. I am privileged to have had associations with colleagues of their stature.

I also owe a debt of thanks to Michelle Harewood, my secretary during 1985–1986, when I was composing the book. Her powers of decipherment would put many an accomplished epigrapher to shame. I also want to thank my student Michael C. Douglas for helping with the proofreading and preparing the indices.

I gratefully acknowledge the permission of the Jewish Publication Society of America to use their fine new translation of the *Tanakh* as the usual source for quotations from the Hebrew Bible.

Jon D. Levenson
Skokie, Illinois
5 Shevat, 5747
February 4, 1987

Note on the Text (1994)

This edition differs from the first in the appending of the new Preface and in the correction of typographical and other errors. For his diligent and meticulous work in the latter realm, I owe thanks to my student, teaching fellow, and research assistant, Larry L. Lyke. For typing the new Preface, I thank my omnicompetent secretary, Brian D. Murphy. Finally, I must express my appreciation to Deborah A. Tegarden of Princeton University Press for her expert work in seeing the new edition through to publication. Considering the argument of the book, it seems strangely appropriate that I should be finishing the second edition on the fiftieth anniversary of D-Day.

Newton, Massachusetts
27 Sivan, 5754
June 6, 1994

Preface (1994)

In the six years since the appearance of the first edition of *Creation and the Persistence of Evil: The Jewish Drama of Divine Omnipotence*, enough reactions have been registered to warrant a further definition of its central thesis and some additional reflections upon the relationship of the ancient Israelite theologies of creation to other intellectual currents, including some of our own era.

The basic idea of the book can perhaps be most readily communicated through a contrast with the problem of evil as it has been classically formulated by theologians and philosophers: If God is the sole author of all that is and he is good, how can there be evil in the world? Or, to put the question in terms a bit closer to the ancient Hebraic idiom, that is, in terms of justice: If God is omnipotent, omniscient, and benevolent, why do the innocent suffer and the wicked prosper? With this as the pressing question, my book could be understood as a *theodicy*, a vindication of God's justice in the face of the enormous suffering with which humanity seems forever cursed. And, indeed, some readers have so understood it, thinking that my vindication of God has entailed a notion of inherent limitation that prevents God from establishing the reign of perfect justice he so ardently desires. In these readers' minds, the mythic symbolization of the limitation upon God is the chaos monster of the combat myth, the persistent evil checking the creative labor of the great and good God.

In point of fact, however, I went out of my way to differentiate the biblical theologies that were my subject from the notion of a limited God. For example, on pp. 24–25 I wrote that "God is also *reproached* for his failure, told that it is neither inevitable nor excusable: no limited God here, no God stymied by invincible evil, no faithless resignation before the relentlessness of circumstance." More importantly,

I worked the expression "omnipotence" into my subtitle in part to encourage the thought that omnipotence was not being eliminated but redefined in ways more appropriate to the Hebrew Bible (as well as to ancient Judaism and earliest Christianity) than the classical definition has proven to be. Just as the title involves two elements in a paradoxical and problematic relationship ("creation" and "the persistence of evil"), so does the subtitle ("drama" and "omnipotence"). The operative dichotomy, thus, is not that between limitation and omnipotence, but that which lies between omnipotence as a static attribute and omnipotence as a dramatic enactment: the absolute power of God realizing itself in achievement and relationship. What this biblical theology of dramatic omnipotence shares with the theology of the limited God is a frank recognition of God's setbacks, in contrast to the classical theodicies with their exaggerated commitment to divine impassibility and their tendency to ascribe imperfection solely to human free will, the recalcitrance of matter, or the like. (The classical theodicy that ascribes evil to Satan and his wondrous powers is another matter altogether, one much closer to the biblical theologies.) But whereas the theology of the limited God provides exoneration of a sort for God's failures (for, in Kantian terms, how can we say God ought to do what he cannot?), the theology of omnipotence as a dramatic enactment allows people to *fault* God for the persistence of evil (including, on occasion, human evil) and to goad him into reactivating his primal omnipotence, which is never relinquished but often agonizingly, catastrophically dormant. One might call this latter position a theology of omnipotence *in potentia*, omnipotence recollected from the cosmogonic past and expected in the eschatological future but only affirmed in faith in the disordered present.

Why reality should be this way— why God does not simply exercise his sovereign will so as to reactivate his omnipotence and establish perfect justice—remains a crucial question in the philosophy of religion. I make no claim to have solved it or even to have addressed it, nor have I attempted the Miltonic task of justifying the ways of God to man. For this reason, I must decline both the praise of those who commend me for my theodicy and the censure of those who find it philosophically unpersuasive. My failure to address the problem of evil in the philosophical sense, however, rests on more than my own obvious inadequacies. It rests also on a point usually overlooked in discussions of theodicy in a biblical context: the overwhelming tendency of biblical writers as they confront undeserved evil is not to *explain* it away but to call upon God to *blast* it away. This struck me as a significant difference between biblical and philosophical thinking that had not been given its due either by theologians in general or by biblical theologians in particular.

Let me illustrate. No biblical text comes closer to the classical formulation of the problem of evil than Jeremiah 12:1–3, the passage that inspired Gerard Manley Hopkins's great poem, "Thou Art Indeed Just, Lord."

> [1]You will be in the right, o LORD, if I make claim against You,
> Yet I shall present charges against You:
> Why does the way of the wicked prosper?
> Why are the workers of treachery at ease?
> [2]You have planted them, and they have taken root,
> They spread, they even bear fruit.
> You are present in their mouths,
> But far from their thoughts.
> [3]Yet You, LORD, have noted and observed me;
> You have tested my heart, and found it with You.
> Drive them out like sheep to the slaughter,
> Prepare them for the day of slaying! (Jer. 12:1–3)[1]

The question is familiar: "Why does the way of the wicked prosper?" The answer, however—and please note that there *is* an answer here—is nothing like those rationalizations proposed by the philosophers: "Drive them out like sheep to the slaughter." The answer to the question of the suffering of the innocent is a renewal of activity on the part of the God of justice. In light of the answer, it becomes clear that the question is not an intellectual exercise but rather a taunt intended to goad the just God into action after a long quiescence. It is more like liturgy than philosophy. Though we do not know whether the taunt worked in this case, there are instances in Jeremiah in which it does, as in 15:21, which closes with the promise, "I will save you from the hands of the wicked / And rescue you from the clutches of the violent." If the answer seems inappropriate, it is only because we have mistaken the function of the question. The same holds, I maintain, for Job. Those who want the Book of Job to offer a theodicy have missed the point as badly as his comforters, who offer several. It is true that God never provides Job with an intellectually satisfying justification of his suffering. But in the book as we now have it, he does finally end his silence and, more to the point, he ends Job's suffering as well, restoring Job to his former blessed status. What the sufferer wants is not an explanation but a prescription, something that he can *do* to reactivate God after this painful quiescence or to augment the benevolent side of God at the expense of his malevolence, converting fury into favor. The prescription that works for Job is unqualified submission to the mysterious and unfathomable deity.

When God's silence and inactivity do not end, when the prescription does not come or does not work, several options appear. One is to continue the argument with him in the hope that he might yet be cajoled, flattered, shamed, or threatened into acting in deliverance. This is the tactic of the lament literature.[2]

It can be taken both by those who believe their suffering to be undeserved or excessive and by those who, like Job, think themselves innocent.[3] (The ancient Israelites felt that difference to be less than it seems to us.) Another option is to abandon YHWH, the God of Israel, and to direct one's service to another God, as some Judeans in exile in Egypt did when they made offerings to the Queen of Heaven on the grounds that when they had previously done so, "we had plenty to eat, we were well-off, and suffered no misfortune."[4] Still another approach appears in the mouths of Daniel's three friends when Nebuchadnezzar threatens to cast them into the fiery furnace for their refusal to worship his golden statue:

[16]Shadrach, Meshach, and Abed-nego said in reply to the king, "O Nebuchadnezzar, we have no need to answer you in this matter, [17]for if so it

must be, our God whom we serve is able to save us from the burning fiery furnace, and He will save us from your power, O king. [18]But even if He does not, be it known to you, O king, that we will not serve your god or worship the statue of gold that you have set up." (Dan. 3:16–18)

In this last example, it is strikingly clear that God's deliverance of his loyal worshipers is deemed neither unlikely nor inevitable, at least in this life. To Shadrach, Meshach, and Abed-nego, the possibility that he may *not* save them from the flames of the furnace is real, but it does not cause them to doubt his power or to divert their service away from him and toward his rivals. That God's saving will is unevenly effectuated here implies no impairment of his omnipotence or of his absolute claim upon devotion—a devotion, if need be, even unto death. The experience of deliverance is taken as normative and characteristic; the experience of continuing affliction, or even martyrdom—that is, a freely chosen death occasioned by service to God—is seen as real but aberrant nonetheless. Given the reality of *both* these moments, the ringing affirmation of God's power to save in v. 17 is not a static truism, but a quasiliturgical act: its sole context is a point of crisis in the engaged religious life. It is a confession of faith in the face of imminent destruction. To abstract the affirmation from the God-Israel relationship and to convert it into a timeless and universal truth of philosophy is not to translate it but to traduce it.

The central claim of *Creation and the Persistence of Evil* is that these same dynamics apply to most of the varieties of creation theology attested in the Hebrew Bible. The affirmation that God is the creator of the world is directed against the forces that oppose him and his acts of creation—the forces of disorder, injustice, affliction, and chaos, which are, in the Israelite worldview, one. The radical implication in this must be faced. To say that creation is directed against *something* might be taken as a denial of the venerable doctrine of *creatio ex nihilo*, that God created the world out of nothing. Depending on how one understands "nothing," this is certainly the case for most and perhaps all of the biblical creation texts. The contradiction between the later Jewish doctrine of *creatio ex nihilo* and the Hebrew Bible itself is already recognized in ancient midrash:

Rav said: . . . In human practice, when a king builds a palace in a place of sewers, dung, and garbage, if anyone comes and says, "This palace is built on sewers, dung, and garbage," does he not pronounce it defective? Therefore, if anyone comes and says, "This world was created out of chaos [*tōhû wābōhû*], does he not pronounce it defective? Rabbi Huna said in the name of Bar Qappara: If the thing were not in Scripture, it would be impossible to say it! "In the beginning God created heaven and earth." Out of what? "The earth was chaos [*tōhû wābōhû*]."[5]

The comment of Rav, an Amora of the early third century C.E., is intended to counter the claim that the wasteland called *tōhû wābōhû* in Gen 1:2 (usually rendered "without form and void," or the like, though the hendyadis is actually composed of two nouns) served as the substratum of creation. In Rav's mind, such a claim calls God's majesty and the goodness of his creation into doubt. Bar Qappara, a teacher of the previous generation, seems to agree in principle, but insists nonetheless that the theological doctrine cannot trump the Torah itself, which, in his view endorses the very claim that Rav would seek to anathematize. Whether Bar Qappara thinks that *tōhû wābōhû* is primordial or created is unclear. If we may presuppose the parable of the palace with which his comment now appears, we should conclude that just as the king made only the palace and not the sewers, dung, and garbage on which it is founded, so did God create only the world and not the chaos that is its substratum. Alternatively, though less likely, it may be that Bar Qappara regards both the world and the antecedent chaos as God's handiwork. But, either way, creation is a positive that stands in pronounced opposition to the harsh negative of chaos. The world is good; the chaos that it replaces or suppresses is evil. On either reading, the point of Bar Qappara's exegesis of Genesis 1:1–2 is that God did not create the good world out of nothing, but out of a malignant substratum.

If one equates the "nothing" from which God created the world with a void, as the traditional English translation of *tōhû wābōhû* implies, then the belief in a primordial, uncreated chaos is obviously a denial of the doctrine of creation out of nothing. The question remains, however, whether the ancient sources held this rather abstract conception of "nothing." It seems more likely that they identified "nothing" with things like disorder, injustice, subjugation, disease, and death. To them, in other words, "nothing" was something—something negative. It was not the privation of being (as evil is the privation of good in some theodicies), but a real, active force, except that its charge was entirely negative. When order emerges where disorder had reigned unchallenged, when justice replaces oppression, when disease and death yield to vitality and longevity, this is indeed the creation of something out of nothing. It is the replacement of the negative by the positive every bit as much as is the erection of a majestic royal palace where there had once been only sewers, dung, and garbage. This crucial point will be lost on us if we follow the long-standing philosophical tradition of identifying God with perfect being, so that his opposite is non-being, or "nothing" in the sense of a void. It will equally be lost if we draw a sharp distinction between creation and redemption.

Among most who study the Hebrew Bible theologically, it has long been agreed that the God of Israel is better understood in relational than in classical philosophical terms. Think, for example, of the prominence given that most relational aspect of biblical theology, "covenant," over the last six decades. When it comes to creation, however, there remains a strange but potent tendency to resort to static affirmations of God's total power. Consider this statement from a book with a similar title to my own, Bernhard Anderson's *Creation versus Chaos*:

Israel's faith stressed the sovereignty of [YHWH's] will to such an uncompromising extent that it refused to allow the control to slip into the hand of some rival power, whether a good demon or an evil demon. Men believed that [YHWH] was the sole source of good and evil, of light and darkness, of life and death.[6]

Now it is true that the Hebrew Bible generally portrays its God as unwilling to allow other powers to *retain* control, but if, as Anderson thinks, those "rival power[s]" never *acquire* control, never pose a serious challenge to YHWH's sovereign will, then why the ecstatic jubilation at the thought of his vanquishing them? Indeed, why must they be vanquished at all? Elsewhere in the same volume, Anderson argues that the expression YHWH *mālāk* should not be translated "YHWH is king" because "in contrast to Marduk's and Baal's dominion, [YHWH's] kingship is not subject to the seasonal cycle of summer barrenness and fertility, of death and resurrection."[7] This apologetic distinction between the gods of nature and the God of history is not, in my judgment, germane to the Hebrew Bible, to which the dichotomy of nature and history is foreign. But even if we were to grant the notion that the Hebrew Bible has transposed divine activity from nature to history, it still would not follow that YHWH's control was conceived as constant and invariable. Instead, one would then still have to ask what the *historical* analogue is to the natural phenomenon of summer barrenness that allegedly negates Marduk's and Baal's dominion. What in Israel's experience gives them the perception that YHWH is as inactive as a dying and rising god between his death and his resurrection? Psalm 44 suggests that Israel's experience of their own undeserved suffering—suffering even unto death—could lead them to believe that God is not dead, to be sure, but close to it; for example, dangerously, irresponsibly asleep:

> [18]All this has come upon us,
>> yet we have not forgotten You.
>> or been false to Your covenant.
> . . . .
> [23]It is for Your sake that we are slain all day along,
>> that we are regarded as sheep to be slaughtered.
> [24]Rouse Yourself; why do You sleep, O Lord?
>> Awaken, do not reject us forever!
> [25]Why do You hide Your face,
>> ignoring our affliction and distress?
> [26]We lie prostrate in the dust;
>> our body clings to the ground.
> [27]Arise and help us,
>> redeem us, as befits Your faithfulness. (Ps 44:18, 23–27)

What provokes that troubling exhortation is the awareness that history, no less than nature, slips out of God's control and into the hands of obscure but potent forces of malignancy that oppose everything he is reputed to uphold. The jubilation that follows the announcement "YHWH *mālāk*" in those enthronement psalms[8] strongly commends the translation, "YHWH *has become* king," for it argues for the reality of the contrast between the grave situation before the announcement and the happy time that follows it. The worshiping community does not burst into song because they have suddenly recalled the uniform, uninterrupted truth that God is in control. Rather, their excitement is owing to the perception that he is at last about to redeem them as befits his faithfulness. The possibility of an interruption in his faithfulness is indeed troubling, and I repeat that I have ventured no explanation for it. I might add that I find it especially odd that scholars who lived through the years of the Holocaust and other unspeakable horrors of our century should have imagined that the Hebrew Bible consistently upheld a doctrine of God's uniform, uninterrupted kingship, in spite of ample textual evidence to the contrary.

Related to these obstacles to the proper understanding of creation in the Hebrew Bible is a certain conception of monotheism. Consider this definition of "radical monotheism" offered by the eminent liberal Protestant theologian, H. Richard Niebuhr:

It is the confidence that whatever is, is good, because it exists as one thing among the many which all have their origin and their being in the One—the principle of being which is also the principle of value. . . . Monotheism is less than radical if it makes a distinction between the principle of being and the principle of value . . . if, speaking in religious language, the Creator and the God of grace are not identified.[9]

Here Niebuhr takes certain terms that are completely alien to the ancient Hebrew vocabulary ("being" and "value") and asserts their identity, in part by reference to the very Hebraic notions of creation and grace. I wonder, however, what interpretation his conception of radical monotheism yields for these familiar verses:

[3]God said, "Let there be light,"; and there was light. [4]God saw that the light was good, and God separated the light from the darkness. (Gen. 1:3–4)

The effect of Niebuhr's "radical monotheism," it seems to me, is to remove that crucial separation, that crucial boundary, between light and darkness, as if the scripture had actually read:

God said, "Let there be darkness and light"; and there were darkness and light, and God saw that both darkness and light were good.

By removing that boundary, Niebuhr sets up a new one, the boundary between creation and moral struggle. No longer is God set against the darkness, even if only by reputation. Instead, he affirms everything because he creates everything. Whether Niebuhr intends this conclusion or not, according to his typology, we have to say that biblical monotheism is *not* radical, for it refuses to attribute value to everything that exists. Some things exist that ought not to, and these deserve to be blasted from the world. Not everything that exists in nature is good or conforms to God's highest intentions. Some of what is, is not yet good. Darkness is a case in point; recall that in some prophetic eschatologies, it is to disappear altogether.[10] I should add that even when it is asserted, as in Isaiah 45:7, that YHWH has indeed created darkness and woe, the point is not to endow these with value but to assert his absolute mastery over them, his power to obliterate them at will. That he has created them does not entail that they are good and should endure forever, but rather that they are under his control and thus unable to resist him when he reactivates his omnipotence. Here, too, creation is positive because it is an instance of God's active opposition to the negative.

Similar to Niebuhr's thinking, though in a rather different idiom, is the position of his Jewish contemporary, Abraham Joshua Heschel. Heschel, like his Hasidic sources, sought to affirm the principal "All is God" by reference to the doctrine of *creatio ex nihilo*. "The miracle of coming into being out of nothing is only possible through the continual action of God," Heschel wrote. "His power is constantly present within all His creations, and were He to remove Himself for a

moment they would revert to their natural state, which is nothingness."[11] This notion of the God who sustains all things, though derived from some common biblical affirmations, is difficult to
reconcile with the old mythological image of the divine warrior at
combat with the inimical forces.[12] Indeed, the great alternative to
God in Heschel's statement is only nothingness. The image of God's
creating out of nothing leads rather easily to a conception of God as
against nothing: there is nothing he is against. This, in turn, leads one
to wonder whether there is evil at all in a world in which, as Heschel
and his Hasidic source put in, "all is God." Thus Heschel, though
anxious to differentiate his position from pantheism, seems, like pantheism, unable to coordinate the God of morality with the God of
cosmogony. In this, his thought, like Niebuhr's, has broken with the
biblical pattern, for better or worse.

I have now discussed three related intellectual tendencies that
have historically led scholars away from a proper understanding of
creation in the Hebrew Bible and related literature: the residue of the
static Aristotelian conception of deity as perfect, unchanging being;
the uncritical tendency to affirm the constancy of divine action; and
the conversion of biblical creation theology into an affirmation of the
goodness of whatever is. In my view, the overall effect of these three
ways of thinking has been to trivialize creation by denying the creator a worthy opponent. Creation becomes self-referential, a tautol-
ogy, a truism: no serious alternative can be entertained, since chaos
or cosmic evil has been identified with non-being and unreality.
Thus, the language of combat, victory, and enthronement that is
prominent in so many biblical creation texts is not given its due, and
neither is the victorious warrior God, since it is no great accomplish-
ment to have triumphed over a non-entity or proven superior to
one's own handiwork. Similarly, the creation and maintenance of
boundaries, which I have argued is essential to the Priestly (P) conception of creation, is downplayed and ignored, since on the far side
of the boundary there lies either nothing or something just as good as
that which lies on this side. Either way, that all-important boundary
becomes unimportant, in fact silly.

One of the themes of *Creation and the Persistence of Evil* is that liturgy in the broad sense of the word was thought to mediate between the chaotic present and the ordered past and future, or, if you prefer spatial to temporal language, between this disordered world and the ordered ideal world (which I believe was most often identified with the Temple). In this theology, liturgy realizes and extends creation through human reenactment of cosmogonic events, such as the divine repose on the seventh day or the process of distinction making and boundary maintenance. Liturgy also realizes and renews creation by reactivating the slumbering benevolent elements in the Godhead through such things as genuine repentance, the cries and the taunts of the lament, or the offering of sweet-smelling sacrifices, which in the J account of Noah's flood, for example, move YHWH to vow never again to turn the world back to chaos.[13] If this is so, then a prime desideratum today is an appreciation of the *theurgic* character of religious acts in the Hebrew Bible, the way these affect God and move him from one stance to another. Here a principal obstacle, alongside the Aristotelian conception of God as unmoved, perfect being, is the classical Reformation notion of grace and its corollary, the fear of "works righteousness." Carried to an extreme, as it often has been, this theology of grace deprives the deeds of human beings of any role in the cosmogonic-soteriological drama: the cultic community is reduced to the status of a passive beneficiary of God's arbitrary and unmotivated action rather than a junior partner in his continual ordering of the world. On this point, if I may continue to use the Christian typology (which I know is too simple), we need to shift a bit from a Protestant to a Catholic understanding of liturgy and to reckon seriously with the ancient belief in the capacity of liturgy to effect substantive change in external reality. By liturgy, I mean not only prayer and sacrifice, but also the observance of purity laws, the performance of covenant stipulations in general, and much else. Only as the dignity and efficaciousness of these things are recognized can the true role of humanity in the ordering of the world in the Hebrew Bible be appreciated. That recognition is much aided by serious study of the theology of the commandments in rabbinic Judaism and especially in Qabbalah, where observance contributes, as it were, to healing the catastrophic rifts within God himself. Although biblical, rabbinic, and Qabbalistic thinking on these issues should not be equated, they do throw a much-needed light on each other—light that neither the classical philosophical nor the classical Protestant formulation has generated.

The identification of "nothing" with a void rather than with chaos has certain affinities with the extreme forms of the theology of grace. Both have the indirect effect of denying the *moral* and *interactive* character of God's action. When God creates something in a void, his act of creation is no longer a victory for justice and right order, nor can it be continued or reenergized by human action. The cosmology that affirms creation from the void has, in turn, certain affinities with modern science, which seeks to relate items such as space, time, matter, and light but certainly not morality or the justice of the political order. Here, too, the moral dimension is downplayed. In fact, the tendency in modern scientific society has increasingly been to think of this dimension as only a cultural or social construct or as an expression of emotion or private preference. The detachment of the physical world from the moral and spiritual worlds (and the casting of the reality of the nonphysical realm into doubt) has been a hallmark of modern Western thought. It is also a point that is now being revisited from a number of directions. One of my goals in composing *Creation and the Persistence of Evil* was to show that this detachment is not consonant with the theologies of creation in the Hebrew Bible. The latter offer, in my judgment, a rich resource for contemporary reflection if only they are not pressed into alien molds, philosophical, religious, or scientific. The very point that has been seen as a weakness of these biblical conceptions of creation may prove to be an outstanding asset—their deep engagement with the problem of evil and their inseparability from the engaged religious life.

NOTES TO PREFACE (1994)

1. I have used the NJV's alternate reading, "be in the right," over its preferred reading, "win," in the first clause in order to highlight the forensic context.

2. E.g., Lamentations 3:49–66.

3. See, e.g., Exodus 32:11–13 and Job 19:21–29.

4. Jeremiah 44:17.

5. *Ber. Rab.* 1:5. I have departed from the NJV in the rendering of Genesis 1:1–2 here in order to do justice to Bar Qappara's understanding.

6. Bernhard W. Anderson, *Creation versus Chaos* (Philadelphia: Fortress, 1987), 151. See also p. 167.

7. Ibid., 102.

8. E.g., Psalm 97:1.

9. H. Richard Niebuhr, *Radical Monotheism and Western Culture* (New York: Harper and Row, 1943), 32.

10. See, e.g., Isaiah 60:14–20.

11. Abraham Joshua Heschel, *Man's Quest for God* (New York: Scribner's Sons, 1954), 73, n. 43.

12. There is room to wonder, however, whether those affirmations of God's continual solicitude and protection of his loyal worshipers, too, are not often theurgic rather than static and simply descriptive. My suspicion is that they often constitute a hopeful pledge of allegiance to YHWH's ideal reputation rather than the Pollyannaish reporting of empirical fact that they seem to be.

13. Genesis 8:20–22.

Preface

"The making of books is without limit,"[1] and studies about creation in the Hebrew Bible being no exception, the reader is entitled to know in advance what dissatisfactions have led me to produce another. These can be summarized in three specific points and two general ones. I will discuss the specific points, and then the general ones.

First, although it is now generally recognized that *creatio ex nihilo,* the doctrine that God produced the physical world out of nothing, is not an adequate characterization of creation in the Hebrew Bible, the legacy of this dogmatic or propositional understanding lives on and continues to distort the perceptions of scholars and laypersons alike. In particular, a false finality or definitiveness is ascribed to God's act of creation, and, consequently, the fragility of the created order and its vulnerability to chaos tend to be played down. Or, to put the point differently, the formidability and resilience of the forces counteracting creation are usually not given their due, so that the drama of God's exercise of omnipotence is lost, and a static idea of creation then becomes the cornerstone of an overly optimistic understanding of the theology of the Hebrew Bible.

Next, although critical scholars are nearly universal in ascribing Genesis 1:1–2:3 to P, the Priestly source in the Pentateuch, the affinities of this crucial text with the Priestly theology of the cultus have not been sufficiently explored. In particular, the connection of this cosmogony with ancient Near Eastern temple building has generally been missed. This failure to reckon with the sacral or cultic aspect of Genesis 1:1–2:3 has, in turn, led generally to a neglect of the role of humanity in forming and sustaining the world order therein described. This neglect has helped obscure the fact that this text too deals in large part with the question of how to neutralize the powerful and ongoing threat of chaos.

Finally, the vast amount of overlap between the idea of God as creator and the idea of God as lord in covenant needs to be exposed and explored. Indeed, properly understood, many of the ancient texts about the creation of the world testify to the limited consensual basis of royal authority, which is fundamental to the biblical concept of covenant in most of its manifestations. The role of human beings in ratifying the royal claim of the creator/suzerain through confederation and, conversely, the dependence of the creator/suzerain upon his would-be confederates, have generally been missed. The old separation of creation from the history of redemption *(Heilsgeschichte)* has been eroding in recent decades, but the full measure of congruence between the two needs attention.

These three dissatisfactions are the basis for the three parts of the book, respectively. Two other, more general, points help explain my goal in writing it:

First, I believe that there is generally a lack of sophisticated theological reflection upon even such central and overworked aspects of the religion of Israel as creation and covenant. Although it is religious motivation that accounts for the existence of almost all biblical research, the theological significance of the discoveries that the researchers make is rarely assessed, and, conversely, those interested in theology and willing to admit it are often uninformed about philological research, especially into the religions of the ancient Near East. Too often the result is pedantic philology and anachronistic theology. One goal in undertaking this study has been to reassess the biblical theologies of creation in dialogue with the philologists and their discoveries. In so doing, I have tried to avoid the technical jargons of both communities of scholars and to produce a theological study that can be read by any layperson conversant with the humanities.

Second, the tendency to draw a hard line between the Hebrew Bible and the literature of Rabbinic Judaism, Talmud and midrash, has obscured in the minds of scholars of both periods the degree of continuity between these two literatures. This, in turn, has obscured the fact that so many ideas that originated in the ancient Israelite cult survived the multiple interruptions of that cult, including its destruction by the Romans in 70 C.E., and became, so to speak, free-floating theological ideas, though often concretized in specific practices. Just as I have tried to maintain a conversation with the study of the Near Eastern antecedents of biblical Israel, so have I tried to cast a glance at her Rabbinic successor. My use of Rabbinic materials has necessarily been selective and subordinated to the discussion of the Hebrew Bible, and I have made here no effort to do justice to the mediating period of the late Second Temple. My discussion should demonstrate, however, that despite vast changes in the historical situation and the theological idiom, the biblical theologies at point had a continuing relevance in Rabbinic Judaism. This explains my use of the term "Jewish" rather than "biblical" in the subtitle, *The Jewish Drama of Divine Omnipotence.*

My method is historical inasmuch as the cultural connections of the texts are deemed essential to understanding them. My goal, however, was not to write a history of the idea of creation in ancient Judaism. Much as I would like to read such a study, I do not believe that the theological task can await its appearance. The sad fact is that increasing uncertainty about the relative and absolute chronologies alike of most of the texts in question makes such a historical investigation highly problematic. In a period of less than two decades since I left graduate school, the old verities that we learned have mostly been shaken, and no new historical consensus has emerged. This is not, as some would have it, a warrant for a thoroughly ahistorical approach to Scripture, but it does argue for a method that is more typological or phenomenological than diachronic in the classic mode.

Unless otherwise noted, all biblical citations are taken from the recent translation undertaken by the Jewish Publication Society and generally known among scholars as the "New Jewish Version" (NJV).[2] As in the NJV, chapter and verse follow the Hebrew enumeration rather than the English where there is a divergence. It is a point of Jewish law not to write "YHWH," the tetragram or four-letter proper name of the God of Israel, with its vowels. I have therefore removed the vowels even in quoting authors who retained them. In the NJV, the tetragram appears as LORD.

Jon D. Levenson
Skokie, Illinois
29 Tammuz, 5746
August 5, 1986

He puts no trust in His holy ones;
The heavens are not guiltless in His sight;
What then of one loathsome and foul,
Man, who drinks wrongdoing like water!

JOB 15:15–16

Power as such is a *relational* concept and requires relation.

HANS JONAS

I. THE MASTERY OF GOD AND THE VULNERABILITY OF ORDER

He puts no trust in His holy ones. . . .

1. The Basic Idea of Israelite Religion?

We can capture the essence of the idea of creation in the Hebrew Bible with the word "mastery." The creation narratives, whatever their length, form, or context, are best seen as dramatic visualizations of the uncompromised mastery of YHWH, God of Israel, over all else. He alone is "the Lord of all the earth,"[1] and when the cosmogonic events are complete, his lordship stands beyond all doubt. He reigns in regal repose, "majestic on high,"[2] all else subordinate to him.

Yehezkel Kaufmann (1889–1963), one of the great Jewish biblical scholars of modern times, went a step further. He considered the concept that I am calling mastery to be more than merely the essence of creation: he deemed it "the basic idea of Israelite religion"[3] and the factor that differentiates absolutely between that religion and "paganism," that is, all religions that are not derived from it. Whereas the "pagan" believes "that there exists a realm of being prior to the gods and above them, upon which the gods depend, and whose decrees they must obey,"[4] for Israel "there is no realm above or beside YHWH to limit his absolute sovereignty."[5] But even for Kaufmann it is in the stories of creation that one sees so markedly the differences wrought by this most fundamental of Israelite beliefs. Whereas "pagan" creation stories display "the idea of a primeval realm out of which the gods have emerged and within which they operate,"[6] "the idea of a supreme deity who is above any natural connection with his creation found expression in the image of Genesis 1: a deity who creates by fiat."[7]

The Babylonian creation story, *Enuma elish,* is an instructive and often cited contrast to Genesis 1.[8] In the *Enuma elish,* "creation," if we may call it that, begins with the mingling of the subterranean fresh waters, Apsu, and the saline waters of the oceans, Tiamat. From these emerge new gods, whose clamor is so disruptive that Apsu resolves to annihilate them. But Ea, one of the intended victims, succeeds in anaesthetizing Apsu with a spell, despoiling him of his kingship, and then killing him. This so enrages Apsu's wife, Tiamat, that she is easily persuaded to declare war on the other gods, appointing Kingu her field marshal. In the pantheon there is only great disconsolation, as god after god proves inadequate to the challenge. Finally Marduk, Ea's son, undertakes to do combat with the sea goddess's formidable hosts. But Marduk exacts his price—that he be proclaimed supreme among the gods and the command of his lips unalterable. The other gods submit, they acclaim him king, and in a horrific battle he overwhelms his foes. Marduk then proceeds to create the familiar world out of the body of Tiamat, which he has split in half. He fixes a crossbar and posts guards over the half from which the heavens were made, so that their waters might not escape and threaten his victory. Out of Kingu he creates humanity, to relieve the gods of some of their drudgery. In gratitude, a delegation of gods asks whether they might repay their debt to Marduk by building him a palace, or temple, and when he assents, they construct Esagila, the terraced Marduk temple in Babylon. The *Enuma elish* closes with the gods' hymnic recitation of the glorious fifty names of Marduk, their hero, savior, lord, and king.

Like other scholars, Kaufmann cited the *Enuma elish* as a parade example of "paganism,"[9] and it is not hard to see why. Marduk is not primordial; like the other younger gods, he emerges at a certain point in time. The two who are primordial, Apsu and Tiamat, fail to transcend nature. One never forgets their physical basis, water, and each of them dies, so that the primordial gods are no more, and Tiamat is now at best only the matter out of which Marduk has shaped the world.[10] Marduk's own mastery is not inherent, but something others—the members of the pantheon— have conveyed to him. The collegial basis of his authority has not been eradicated from memory. And although his commands are efficacious, he does not create *ex nihilo,* but exerts his creative word upon a powerful preexistent material substratum. All of this suggests a different and more qualified concept of mastery than one finds in Genesis 1.

On the other hand, we must be careful about overdrawing the contrast. Nowhere in the seven-day creation scheme of Genesis 1 does God create the waters; they are most likely primordial. The traditional Jewish and Christian doctrine of *creatio ex nihilo* can be found in this chapter only if one translates its first verse as "In the beginning God created the heaven and the earth" and understands it to refer to some comprehensive creative act on the first day. But that translation, subject to doubt since the Middle Ages,[11] has fallen into disfavor among scholars,[12] and the rest of the chapter indicates that the heaven was created on the second day to restrain the celestial water (vv. 7–8), and the earth on the third day (vv. 9–10). It is true—and quite significant—that the God of Israel has no myth of origin. Not a trace of a theogony can be found in the Hebrew Bible.[13] God has no nativity. But there do seem to be other divine beings in Genesis 1, to whom God proposes the creation of humanity, male and female together: "Let us make man in our image, after our likeness" (v. 26).[14] When were these other divine beings created? They too seem to have been primordial. Whether their existence should be interpreted as a qualification upon God's mastery in Genesis is impossible to determine. Because they do not dissent from his proposal to create humanity in his and their image, we cannot say whether God's authority, like Marduk's, involved some element of collegiality. From other biblical accounts of the divine assembly in session,[15] it would appear that these "sons of God/gods" played an active role and made fresh proposals to God, who nonetheless retained the final say. In short, like the other gods at the *close* of the *Enuma elish,* they are thought to be real and important, but also subordinate and not very individualized.

The placement of Genesis 1 first in the Bible makes a theological statement that must not be evaded.[16] Nonetheless, it is possible to overstress that chapter, as occurs when scholars present it as the only Israelite creation story or, worse, as the quintessence of ancient Hebrew theology. On the basis of Genesis 1, one must say, as does Kaufmann, that the God of Israel has no origin and his mastery has no origin: he has always reigned supreme. It is likely that it was just such a theology that the compilers of the Torah sought to make by beginning with this passage. But it is characteristic of the Hebrew Bible that some of the alternatives that the Torah tries to suppress have been preserved and can yet be examined.

Psalm 82 is a case in point. It begins when

> [1]God takes his stand in the assembly of El;
> among the gods He pronounces judgment.[17]

The judgment is a reaction to their injustice, their failure to favor the unfortunate of society.

> [6]I had said, "You are gods,
> sons of Elyon all of you,
> [7]But you shall die like a man,
> fall like a prince." (Ps. 82:6–7)

The psalm closes with a plea that God rule, that he take possession of all nations.

One can interpret Psalm 82 according to the traditional theology represented in our discussion by Kaufmann's critical restatement of it. In that case, "God" (ʾĕlōhîm), El, and Elyon will all be seen to refer to the same deity. The "gods" (also ʾĕlōhîm) will be interpreted as only angels or, less plausibly but more traditionally, as human judges.[18] On this reading, Psalm 82 represents nothing more than God's death sentence upon corrupt and insensitive underlings. If, however, "God" and El are not to be identified here, and if ʾĕlōhîm is taken at face value, then Psalm 82 commemorates the moment that God assumed the commanding position in the pantheon (perhaps replacing El or Elyon, probably two names for one deity[19]) and eliminated his colleagues. If this interpretation is correct, then the theology of the poem bears a striking resemblance to that of the *Enuma elish:* both celebrate the assumption of mastery by the supreme deity of the society. In neither case is the deity's mastery primordial. Although on either interpretation there is still no theogony in Psalm 82, on the second one, we should have to doubt Kaufmann's unnuanced claim of an absolute distinctiveness to Israel. Just as the *Enuma elish* proclaims and celebrates Marduk's mastery, so does Psalm 82 proclaim and celebrate YHWH's. In neither case is the mastery that of the unchallenged sovereign ruling from all eternity in splendid solitude. Rather, it is the mastery of the deity whose special excellence comes to entitle him to supremacy. The recitation of the *Enuma elish* during the Babylonian New Year's festival[20] suggests that Marduk's celebrated mastery was not a simple given, but something that had to be renewed and reactualized periodically. The closing plea of Psalm 82—"Arise, God, and rule the world/Take possession of all peoples" (v. 8)[21]—likewise implies that God's assumption of mastery is not complete and that the demise of the dark forces in opposition to him lies in the uncertain future. Kaufmann's "basic idea of Israelite religion" is an accurate description of the *hope* of Psalm 82 but not of the *current reality* that the psalmist experiences. Kaufmann has mistaken the volitive for the indicative, the visionary world of liturgy for a description of quotidian reality.

Whatever mythological ideas may underlie Psalm 82, the drama of YHWH's ascent to cosmic mastery that predominates in the Hebrew Bible is one that nicely parallels the story of combat with the sea found in the *Enuma elish* and its analogues:

> [12]O God, my king from of old,
>   who brings deliverance throughout the land;
>   [13]it was You who drove back the sea with Your might,
>   who smashed the heads of the monsters in the waters;
>   [14]it was You who crushed the heads of Leviathan,
>   who left him as food for the denizens of the desert;
>   [15]it was You who released springs and torrents,
>   who made mighty rivers run dry;
>   [16]the day is Yours, the night also;
>   it was You who set in place the moon[22] and the sun;
>   [17]You fixed all the boundaries of the earth;
>   summer and winter—You made them. (Ps. 74:12–17)

The immediate background of this passage is a Canaanite myth, well attested in the literary remains of the city of Ugarit from the Late Bronze Age (ca. 14th century B.C.E.), in which the god Baal defeated the ocean, there conceived as masculine and known variously as Prince Yamm ("Sea"), Judge River, Lotan (the biblical "Leviathan"), the twisting seven-headed dragon, and "Tannin," some other sort of monster.[23] Each of these words occurs in some form in the passage just quoted. Without the Ugaritic literature, these allusions would remain tantalizing obscurities, for the Bible offers no connected narrative of primordial divine combat, only poetic snippets, usually within a hymnic or plaintive context. Having the Ugaritic and similar materials, we are able to get a sense of the full dimensions of the old myth and its continuing vitality in Israel—as well as the failed efforts of some circles to suppress it.

Aware of the Canaanite parallels to passages such as that just quoted, Kaufmann falls back upon the argument that in Israel we are dealing not with creation but with a rebellion against YHWH by some of his own creatures. In support of this he refers to those texts that explicitly state the creatureliness and subordination of the monstrous adversaries to YHWH.[24] Those texts are important, and our discussion of the scope of YHWH's mastery in the Hebrew Bible will reckon with them. But may we harmonize them with passages that contain no hint of the creaturely origin of YHWH's aquatic adversaries? May we assume that the *real* theology, the *essential* theology, is one of serene, divine supremacy, only temporarily and inconsequentially interrupted by a revolt of underlings of benign origin? To make this assumption, it seems to me, is to harmonize without warrant and to doom ourselves to miss the rich interplay of theologies and the historical dynamics behind the biblical text. For the truth is that in Psalm 74:12–17, we find *none* of the language of rebellion and *no* indication that the monsters whose demise is there memorialized had come into existence through the creative labors of the psalmist's lord.

The language of our passage strongly suggests that the context is indeed one of creation, provided we do not restrict our understanding of the term to the traditional, but postbiblical, doctrine of *creatio ex nihilo*. The second word of the phrase *malki miqqedem* ("my king from of old") may well denote primordial times, the era in which God *(ĕlōhîm)* attained to kingship. Certainly vv. 16–17, with their references to divine mastery over day and night, sun and moon, the boundaries of the Earth, and summer and winter ("You made them"), must be taken as explicit references to creation. The fact that the affirmation of creation by God follows directly the account of his defeat of the sea monster cannot, in the light of the *Enuma elish,* be coincidence.[25] Psalm 74:12–17 attests eloquently to an Israelite myth of combat between God and aquatic beasts, followed by his triumphant act of world ordering. This is a myth that speaks of God's total mastery not as something self-evident, unthreatened, and extant from all eternity, but as something won, as something dramatic and exciting.

On one point Kaufmann seems to have been right: "The Ugaritic allusions do not indicate that these battles had cosmogonic significance (as did the battle of Marduk with Tiamat)."[26] In Ugarit, the "creator of creatures"[27] is not Baal, the hero of the combat with Yamm (under the various names), but El, the old god who still seems to retain supreme authority in the pantheon and who in the Bible is often identified with YHWH.[28] In other words, whereas in Babylonian tradition Marduk's combat results in his supplanting the older gods, depriving their authority of its ultimacy and subordinating the entire pantheon to himself, in Ugarit, the situation is more complicated, and a strong case (some would say a persuasive one) can be made for El's continuing supremacy even after Baal wins his battles and his temple.[29] As his name indicates, Baal is a "lord" or "master," but not necessarily the exclusive lord and master of heaven and earth, at least in the Ugaritic materials.[30] In this he is to be distinguished from Marduk and YHWH. Kaufmann's attempt to argue for a closer connection of the biblical materials with the Ugaritic than with the Babylonian epics must be given up. From a phenomenological point of view, YHWH, the God of Israel, has absorbed some of the roles of both Baal and El.[31] He does combat with the Sea, and he creates the world. But these roles are united also in the figure of Marduk. Creation that is *not* the consequence of combat is an element that ties YHWH (as seen in some biblical traditions) tightly but not exclusively to El. Creation that *is* the consequence of combat ties him to Marduk, although the names of the enemy and other features of the myth are reminiscent of Baal's noncosmogonic combat at Ugarit.

The separation of the *Chaoskampf* from cosmic creation in the narrowest sense, which we may find in the Ugaritic literature, goes along nicely with the claim that the challenge of the Sea in those texts is best seen as a rebellion from within the created order. The rebellion, however, if such it be, does represent an interruption of the positive and beneficent ordering that is creation in the broader sense. In short, if Baal does not create, he does renew creation. His victory is an act of salvation which enables the created order to endure. Here the parallel with the biblical materials is striking, for in the latter, too, YHWH's magisterial ordering of reality is usually seen as healing a recent rupture. This is not true of Genesis 1, but it is true of the closely related story of the Flood in chapters 6–9. Therein, humanity's injustice threatens to undo the work of creation, to cause the world to revert to the primordial aquatic state from which it had emerged:

> All the fountains of the great deep burst apart,
> And the floodgates of the sky broke open. (Gen. 7:11)

As a result the division of the waters above from the waters below disappears, and with it the dry land, whose existence it makes possible.[32] Although almost all people and animals perish in the deluge, life endures because of Noah, the only just and blameless man of his age. Through him the world is re-created, and upon him the primordial command to "be fertile and increase" is reenjoined.[33] In the story of the Flood, the recession of the waters and the emergence of a beneficent, anthropocentric order is very much a sign of divine salvation. Like Israel escaping Pharaoh, Noah and his family survive the lethal fury of the Sea and are then awarded a covenant.[34]

Although the Noahide Covenant includes God's oath not to flood the world again, it is common in the Hebrew Bible to invoke the memory of God's creative might in other situations in which, to all appearances, his mastery and benevolence have ceased to be real. A case in point appears in the words of an anonymous prophet who struggled to rekindle the faith of Israel during the dismal days of the Babylonian Exile:

> [9]Awake, awake, clothe yourself with splendor,
> O arm of the LORD!
> Awake as in days of old,
> As in former ages!
> It was you who hacked Rahab in pieces,
> That pierced the Dragon [tannîn].
> [10]It was you that dried up the Sea [yām],
> The waters of the great deep [těhôm];
> That made the abysses of the Sea
> A road the redeemed might walk.
> [11]So let the ransomed of the LORD return,
> And come with shouting to Zion,
> Crowned with joy everlasting.
> Let them attain joy and gladness,
> While sorrow and sighing flee. (Isa. 51:9–11)

Like the events mentioned in Psalm 74:12–17, these occurred in times "of old" (qedem). If this expression be taken to denote the primordial age, then we have here a comparable attestation to the association of the combat myth with creation. If it be taken to mean simply "long ago," then it becomes arguable that the combat myth here lacks the cosmogonic connection that it so clearly manifests in Psalm 74 and should be seen instead as having to do with a rebellion within the created order—that is, as conforming to the Baal pattern rather than the Marduk pattern. In other words, the Israelite purging of the Chaoskampf of its cosmogonic associations may be a continuation of trends begun long before, in Late Bronze Age Canaan. The patent cosmogonic references in Psalm 74:12–17, however, warn against interpreting the process as unilinear and developmental. If the association of creation with combat is the older model, then one is obliged to say that the older model survived even as others grew up around it.

The observation that the *Chaoskampf* can appear without an accompanying cosmogony is worth making because it counters the tendency of many scholars to conflate or homogenize texts and, in the process, to miss changes and developments in the history of the religion. But too much can be made of the distinction between the myth *with* creation and the myth *without* creation. Two and a half millennia of Western theology have made it easy to forget that throughout the ancient Near Eastern world, including Israel, the point of creation is not the production of matter out of nothing, but rather the emergence of a stable community in a benevolent and life-sustaining order.[35] The defeat by YHWH of the forces that have interrupted that order is intrinsically an act of creation. The fact that order is being restored rather than instituted was not a difference of great consequence in ancient Hebrew culture. To call upon the arm of YHWH to awake as in "days of old" is to acknowledge that those adversarial forces were not annihilated in perpetuity in primordial times. Rising anew, they have escaped their appointed bounds and thus flung a challenge at their divine vanquisher. As was the case in Noah's Flood, so here too creation has been reversed, only this time in defiance of God, not in obedience to his just will. In both instances the positive order of things associated with creation is not held to be *intrinsically* irreversible, as if the elements that threaten it, human evil or the sea dragon, have been definitively eradicated. The continuance of the positive order is possible only because of a special act of God, in Noah's case his covenantal oath not to destroy the world again, in Isaiah 51, his reactivation of his victorious might after a long slumber. Whatever the special act of God, in the Hebrew Bible nature is not autonomous and self-sufficient, but dependent upon God's special solicitude, his tender concern for the ordered world.

The endurance of that world testifies to his own might and benevolence:

> The heavens declare the glory of God,
> the sky proclaims His handiwork. (Ps. 19:2)

2. The Survival of Chaos After the Victory of God

Both the story of the Flood and passages such as Psalm 74:12–17 (and perhaps Isaiah 51:9–11) attest to a view of creation in which God's ordering of reality is irresistible, but not constant or inevitable. The conclusion of the Flood story includes a divine pledge to maintain creation, but the story itself manifests a profound anxiety about the givenness of creation, a keen sense of its precariousness. On the one hand, God vows to maintain the created order. On the other hand, he does so only after having ended a state of chaos that began with his announcing that he regretted having ever authored creation in the first place.[1] Between creation and chaos, life and death, there stands neither human righteousness (which continues to be deficient) nor God's intrinsic unchangeability (which this and many other biblical stories belie), but only God's covenantal faithfulness, his respect for the solemn pledge that he makes to Noah. Here again the endurance and stability of nature is not intrinsic; it is only a corollary of God's faithfulness. Should he in his freedom choose to dishonor his covenantal pledge, the created order would vanish. Humanity's only hope is that God will spurn that option, fail to exercise his freedom, and consider himself bound by his word to Noah. Creation has become a corollary of covenant.

In the case of creation through combat, the survival of the possibility of the return to chaos is more unqualified. The Sea is not always described as destroyed, hacked to pieces, never to rise again. On the contrary, often the waters of chaos are presented as surviving, only within the bounds that define creation:

6You made the deep cover the earth as a garment;
   the waters stood above the mountains.
7They fled at Your blast,
   rushed away at the sound of Your thunder,
   8—mountains rising, valleys sinking—
   to the place You established for them.
9You set bounds they must not pass
   so that they never again cover the earth. (Ps. 104:6–9)

Here we proceed from chaos—the waters submerging even the mountains[2]—to creation, which comes about when God's angry breath blasts the waters back into their appointed place. At times this assignment by God of the waters' bounds is narrated even more colorfully, even more mythologically:

8Who closed the sea behind doors
When it gushed forth out of the womb,
9When I clothed it in clouds,
Swaddled it in dense clouds,
10When I made breakers My limit for it,
And set up its bars and doors,
11And said, "You may come so far and no farther;
Here your surging waves will stop"? (Job 38:8–11)

In these texts we detect a position somewhere between the full-fledged combat myth of creation of Psalm 74:12–17 (and elsewhere) and the idea of creation through the unchallenged magisterial word of God that we find in Genesis 1. Here the Sea does not seem to be a many-headed monster whose destruction creation necessitates, but neither is it disenchanted and inanimate, as in the first chapter of the Torah. Rather, we have a sense of the Sea as a somewhat sinister force that, left to its own, would submerge the world and forestall the ordered reality we call creation. What prevents this frightening possibility is the mastery of YHWH, whose blast and thunder or whose craftmanship and commanding word force the Sea into its proper place, apparently without a struggle.[3] These texts share with the combat myth the notion of the challenge of the Sea and its defeat. They share with Genesis 1 the sense of the creation of the habitable world through the containment of the waters by the efficacious utterance of God. They share with the story of the Flood a conviction that the habitable, life-sustaining world exists now only because of God's continuing commitment to the original command. Absent that command, the sinister forces of chaos would surge forth again. The biblical drama of world order is defined by the persistence of those forces, on the one hand, and the possibility (or is it an inevitability?) that God will exercise his vaunted omnipotence to defeat them, on the other.

There is another way to affirm simultaneously the world-ordering triumph of YHWH and the enduring existence of his primal challenger. Some texts portray the great sea dragon Leviathan as captured by YHWH and thus perpetually available for his enjoyment:

> [25]Can you draw out Leviathan by a fishhook?
> Can you press down his tongue by a rope?
> [26]Can you put a ring through his nose,
> or pierce his jaw with a barb?
> [27]Will he plead with you at length?
> Will he speak soft words to you?
> [28]Will he make a covenant with you
> To be taken as your eternal servant?[4]
> [29]Will you play with him like a bird,
> And tie him down for your girls?
> [30]Shall traders traffic in him?
> Will he be divided up among merchants?
> [31]Can you fill his skin with darts
> Or his head with fish-spears?
> [32]Lay a hand on him,
> And you will never think of battle again. (Job 40:25–32)

These words of YHWH to Job are intended to contrast humanity's limited capacities with God's infinite powers. They seem to allude to a lost myth in which YHWH, instead of crushing Leviathan's heads and scattering his remains,[5] caught him like a fish and forced him to plead for his life and to accept eternal vassalage, the great monster becoming merely a plaything of his divine captor. Verse 29, in particular, recalls the mention in Psalm 104:26 of "Leviathan that You formed to sport with." It is possible that the psalmist has here sanitized the old myth of the *Chaoskampf* altogether, so that Leviathan appears *ab initio* as the plaything of YHWH (his "rubber duckey," as a student once put it). It is also possible and, in my judgment, more probable that, as has long been thought,[6] the play of God with the monster involves the activity described in Job 40:25–26, God's catching the great sea beast with a hook and line. If this be so, the survival of Leviathan in captivity parallels the psalmist's earlier statement that God set bounds that the primeval waters must not dare to cross.[7] In each case, the confinement of chaos rather than its elimination is the essence of creation, and the survival of ordered reality hangs only upon God's vigilance in ensuring that those cosmic dikes do not fail, that the bars and doors of the Sea's jail cell do not give way, that the great fish does not slip his hook. That vigilance is simply a variant of God's covenantal pledge in Genesis 9 never to flood the world again. Whatever form the warranty takes, it testifies both to the precariousness of life, its absolute dependence upon God, and to the sureness and firmness of life under the protection of the faithful master. The world is not inherently safe; it is inherently unsafe.[8] Only the magisterial intervention of God and his eternal vigilance prevent the cataclysm. Creation endures because God has pledged in an eternal covenant that it shall endure and because he has, also in an eternal covenant, compelled the obeisance of his great adversary.[9] If either covenant (or are they one?) comes undone, creation disappears.

The survival of the tamed agent of chaos, whether imagined as the Sea, Leviathan, or whatever, points to an essential and generally overlooked tension in the underlying theology of these passages. On the one hand, YHWH's unique power to defeat and subjugate his adversary and to establish order is unquestioned. On the other hand, those passages that concede the survival of the defeated enemy raise obliquely the possibility that his defeat may yet be reversed. They revive all the anxiety that goes with this horrific thought. It is true that so long as God continues to exercise his magisterial vigilance and his suzerain faithfulness, the reversal of the defeat of chaos is impossible. But the experience of this world sorely tries the affirmation of this ever vigilant, ever faithful God, and it was in these moments of trial that the unthinkable was thought. Ps. 74: 12–17, as we have seen, is the *locus classicus* of the idea that the God of Israel not only defeated the Sea and its monsters, but also dismembered Leviathan altogether and then created the familiar world. Surely no text would seem more imbued with Kaufmann's "basic idea of Israelite religion," that "there is no realm above or beside YHWH to limit his absolute sovereignty."[10] But the context of these verses belies the unqualified note of triumphalism in this theology. For the context of vv. 12–17 in Psalm 74 shows that the celebratory language of victory is invoked here precisely when conditions have rendered belief in God's mastery most difficult, as the verses on each side attest:

> [10]Till when, O God, will the foe blaspheme,
>   will the enemy forever revile Your name?
> [11]Why do You hold back Your hand, Your right hand?
>   Draw it out of Your bosom!
>
> [18]Be mindful of how the enemy blasphemes the LORD,
>   how base people revile Your name.
> [19]Do not deliver Your dove to the wild beast;
>   do not ignore forever the band of Your lowly ones.
> [20]Look to the covenant!
> For the dark places of the land are full of the haunts of
>   lawlessness. (Ps. 74:10–11, 18–20)

The context shows that God's primordial victory is recalled at the moment when he seems to be suffering defeat from a historical foe. The continuity between v. 11 and v. 18 strongly suggests that the hymn in vv. 12–17 has been interpolated. The origins of the hymnic verses may well lie in a connected poetic account of YHWH's primordial combat and his subsequent creation of the world, now lost to us. By excerpting these verses and interpolating them into a context of lament, the author or redactor of Psalm 74 has made a theological statement that is both exceedingly significant and easily missed. That statement is that God's mythic victory must be interpreted in the light of the historical experience of the torching of his cult sites, the absence of miracles, the blaspheming of his sacred name, the defeat of his partners in covenant, and the general collapse of his mastery over the world. In short, the composition of Psalm 74 expresses a theology that is reluctant to accept the hymnic language of primordial creation as a given, but instead honestly and courageously draws attention to the painful and yawning gap between the liturgical affirmation of God's absolute sovereignty and the empirical reality of evil triumphant and unchecked. The psalmist refuses to deny the evidence of his senses in the name of faith, to pretend that there is some higher or inner world in which these horrific events are unknown. But he also refuses to abandon the affirmation of God's world-ordering mastery, his power to defeat even the primeval personifications of chaos and to fashion the world as he sees fit. In short, the author or redactor of Psalm 74 acknowledges the reality of militant, triumphant, and persistent evil, but he steadfastly and resolutely refuses to accept this reality as final and absolute. Instead he challenges YHWH to act like the hero of old, to conform to his magisterial nature:

Rise, O God, champion Your cause;
be mindful that You are blasphemed by base men all day long.
(Ps. 74:22)

The events of the primordial era, God's defeat of the monster and creation of the world, are not locked away in the vanished past. They are still available. That power, that energy, that unassailable mastery is still needed. It can be reactivated yet. The enemy is now human and historical, but the challenge to YHWH is not new or different in essence from the challenge he met *in illo tempore.* It is yet another example of what he must surmount if his enthronement is to be secure and his "absolute sovereignty" is to become

again a reality rather than an increasingly hollow liturgical affirmation. If we may adopt the imagery of other passages, the Sea has
burst out of its appointed place, Leviathan has slipped his hook,
and the covenant that ensures order has been dishonored. All is
not lost, but the joyful and triumphant language of the old myth
has been transformed into the plaintive cry of those who live by
hope alone, hope conceived in myth and nurtured in liturgy.

The same dialectic of realism and hope underlies the use of the
Chaoskampf in Isaiah 51:9–11, cited and discussed earlier. In this
passage the author stands on the other side of the era of affliction.
His task is to awaken the faith of the exilic community to the as
yet invisible fact that a new aeon has indeed dawned. Again, the
verses on each side of the mythic allusion underscore by juxtaposition the jarring incongruity of the community's experience with
the great victory that the "arm of the LORD" won in primordial
times:

> 7Listen to Me, you who care for the right,
> O people who lay My instruction to heart!
> Fear not the insults of men,
> And be not dismayed at their jeers;
> 8For the moth shall eat them up like a garment,
> The worm shall eat them up like wool.
> But my triumph shall endure forever,
> My salvation through the ages.
>
> 12I, I am He who comforts you!
> What ails you that you fear
> Man who must die,
> Mortals who fare like grass?
> 13You have forgotten the LORD your Maker,
> Who stretched out the skies and made firm the earth!
> And you live all day in constant dread
> Because of the rage of the oppressor
> Who is aiming to cut [you] down.
> Yet of what account is the rage of the oppressor? (Isa. 51:7–8, 12–13)

The terrifying absence of the new aeon is underscored by the fact
that the intervening mythic section in vv. 9–11 calls upon the
"arm of the LORD" to "awake as in days of old." That YHWH will
triumph is predestined and inevitable. It is a corollary of his pri-

mordial defeat of the sea monster, and the very existence of creation testifies to its maker's ultimate power and the futility and absurdity of resistance to him by mortals. The rub is that at the moment, YHWH is failing to exercise his magisterial powers over the world, so that those who revere him suffer the taunts and jeers of those who do not. In this predicament the proper posture of a faithful YHWHist is to keep his eye upon the inevitability of the defeat of YHWH's adversaries and to wait patiently and confidently for his master's reactivation of his infinite power to deliver. The benevolent, world-ordering side of God may be eclipsed for a while, but it can never be uprooted or overthrown. The limit that the act of creation places upon the very real and continuing possibility of chaos is parallel to the limit that the covenant with Noah fixes upon the same malevolent forces. This analogy is explicit elsewhere in the writings of our anonymous exilic prophet:

> [7]For a little while I forsook you,
> But with vast love I will bring you back.
> [8]In slight anger, for a moment
> I hid My face from you;
> But with kindness everlasting
> I will take you back in love
> > —said the LORD your Redeemer.
> [9]For this is to Me like the waters of Noah:
> As I swore that the waters of Noah
> Nevermore would flood the earth,
> So I swear that I will not
> Be angry with you or rebuke you.
> [10]For the mountains may move
> And the hills be shaken,
> But My loyalty shall never move from you,
> Nor My covenant of friendship be shaken,
> > —said the LORD, who takes you back in love.
>
> (Isa. 54: 7–10)

Here, as in the story of Noah in the Torah, even the chaotic waters are at the beck of YHWH; they are the rod of his anger employed to punish the Israelites for their sins. The side of God that unleashes them, however, is checked by the side of him that loves and forgives. This latter, friendlier dimension of the divine personality is here articulated as God's covenantal oath to Noah, his sacred and inviolable pledge to maintain the created order. In the prophet's mind, the present adversity is an aberration brought about by a prior aberration, Israel's sinning.[11] The point of the Noah metaphor is to assert that although Israel's transgressions unleash the adversarial forces, they cannot award them a victory, for YHWH's "covenant of friendship" (*běrît šělômî,* v. 10) is eternal and unconditional. In this oracle we see in its tightest form the mutual reinforcement of creation and covenant. Creation means making chaos into order, and covenant, in this formulation, means the guarantee that the experience of chaos serves an orderly purpose and shall pass away when it is no longer needed. Only YHWH's great victory in primordial times enables him to make a covenantal pledge of this scope. Only that pledge ensures that the ancient victory continues to bear on the present sufferings, limiting their duration. The combat myth of creation and the eternal covenant are two ways to image forth the transiency of affliction.

The other eternal covenant to which our prophet refers is the Covenant with David. God's everlasting faithfulness to him shall now become the inheritance of the whole nation.[12] We shall later analyze theologically the interplay between covenants in the Hebrew Bible.[13] Here it suffices to note that the Davidic Covenant too displays connections with cosmogony. In Psalm 89, YHWH commits the containment of the waters to his favorite and viceroy, David:

> I will set his hand upon the sea,
>   his right hand upon the waters. (Ps. 89:26)

This pledge is only the most extreme of a series of promises to David in vv. 20–28—that he shall always know divine support, that no enemy shall ever defeat him, that he shall be YHWH's first-born son and therefore the sovereign of all earthly kings. That YHWH can make such breathtaking promises follows from his own cosmic mastery, depicted in vv. 10–15 in the familiar imagery of his defeat of the surging Sea, his dismemberment of Rahab, and his subsequent creation of the world. It is now the Davidic throne that guarantees cosmic stability, the continuation of the order established through primeval combat. In Psalm 89, as in the *Enuma elish,* the bond between the exaltation of the deity and the imperial politics of his earthly seat is patent. David is YHWH's vicar on Earth. This unique relationship is formalized as a covenant, one that guarantees the eternity of David's posterity and his throne.[14] In the Davidic Covenant, even more than the Noahide, the promissory aspect dominates. There are no conditions here, and the indefectibility of the covenant even in the face of Davidic sins is undeniably explicit. This makes it all the more remarkable that the context of the psalm as we presently have it is not one of Davidic triumph, but one of defeat and ignominy.[15] No sooner does the psalmist conclude the divine pledge to maintain the dynasty forever, a pledge sworn by God's very own holiness and thus sacrosanct, than we are jolted out of our rapture by this:

> [39]Yet You have rejected, spurned,
>   and become enraged at Your anointed.
> [40]You have repudiated the covenant with Your servant;
>   You have dragged his dignity in the dust.
>
> [50]O LORD, where is Your steadfast love of old
>   which You swore to David in Your faithfulness? (Ps. 89:30–40, 50)

As in Psalm 74 and Isaiah 51, so here we find a jarring juxtaposition of the hymnic affirmation of God's world-ordering power and endless faithfulness and the grim reality of historical experience. And again here the remarkable point is that the author or redactor refuses to choose between faith and realism or to beat one into the mold of the other. Indeed, as v. 50 shows, the speaking voice of the psalm dares to reproach God for the incongruity of the two. In a world in which YHWH crushed Rahab and swore an irrevocable oath to David, how can he allow his viceroy to suffer so?

In the three examples of the *Chaoskampf* that we have been discussing, the old myth is applied to historical events in the manner of a dialectical counterstatement. The exhilarating reminiscence of YHWH's primordial victory is set directly against the bitter defeat of those with whom he has announced a unique relationship, his special treasures. The idea of God's absolute sovereignty, Kauf-mann's "basic idea of Israelite religion," is not affirmed in an unqualified way. Rather, its inaccuracy in the light of historical experience is boldly proclaimed, not so as to promote skepticism, but so as to call upon God to close the gap between his reputation and his current behavior. Frank Moore Cross is undoubtedly right to speak of "the tendency to mythologize historical episodes to reveal their transcendent meaning."[16] But in these three texts, something more is happening. The contradiction between the God of the myth and the God of current historical experience has risen to the level of consciousness. The myth continues to provide the language of transcendence that the great act of deliverance de-mands and deserves. Yet the invocation of the myth can only underscore the absence of that act of deliverance. To acknowledge openly the ground for doubting the stirring affirmations of the religion has itself become a religious act.

The religious vision that emerges from this dialectic of myth and history, hymn and complaint, is subtle and nuanced. On the one hand, it avoids the cheery optimism of those who crow that "God's in his heaven -/ All's right with the world." God's visible victory over the enemies of order is in the past. The present is bereft of the signs of divine triumph. It is a formidable challenge to faith and a devastating refutation of optimism. On the other hand, the dialectic of this vision does not allow for an unqualified acceptance of the pessimism that attributes to innocent suffering the immovability of fate. The absence of the omnipotent and cosmocratic deity is not accepted as final, nor his primordial world-ordering deeds as confined to the vanished past. Present experience, which seems to confirm these propositions, is not seen as absolute. Rather, it is seen as a mysterious interruption in the divine life, an interruption that the supplications of the worship-ing community may yet bring to an end. The failure of God is openly acknowledged: no smug faith here, no flight into an other-worldly ideal. But God is also *reproached* for his failure, told that it is neither inevitable nor excusable: no limited God here, no God stymied by invincible evil, no faithless resignation before the relentlessness of circumstance. It is between the Scylla of simplistic faith and the Charybdis of stoic resignation that the lament runs its perilous course. The cognitive pressure on faith and realism to fly apart from each other is, in every generation, so intense that the conjunction of the two in these texts continues to astound. The *cri de coeur* of the complainants is unsurpassable testimony not only to the pain of their external circumstances, but also to the pain of their internal dissonance, which only the creator God of old can heal.

3. The Futurity and Presence of the Cosmogonic Victory

In the preceding section we discussed evidence for doubting that Yehezkel Kaufmann's "basic idea of Israelite religion" can be upheld in a straightforward way. The assertion of YHWH's absolute sovereignty is real, but it is more than rarely qualified by a jarring juxtaposition with a description of a situation that might lead one to believe that YHWH is now a *deus otiosus,* unable to equal his feats of yore. The theological implication of this juxtaposition is that neither Kaufmann's "basic idea" nor the complainant's baleful circumstance is to be accepted as a complete account of the divine–human relationship. Rather, that relationship includes the possibility that YHWH's congregation might activate their lord's dormant mastery through their cultic action and thus actualize those nearly discredited creative wonders. Here liturgy mediates the contradiction between the two theological affirmations, although only the hoped-for new/old divine deed will resolve it.

The deficiency of YHWH's present behavior in the laments can be associated with those texts that speak of the survival of the primordial adversary, Leviathan, the Sea *(Yām)*, or whatever, rather than his decimation *in illo tempore.* Those texts tell not of chaos eliminated, but of chaos circumscribed, subjugated against its will: YHWH now plays with Leviathan in a sanitized and domesticated reenactment of what other texts describe as a violent, gory, and by no means predetermined struggle. YHWH is like a victorious emperor who demonstrates to all that he has nothing to fear from the handcuffed foe he now proudly marches through the streets of his capital. Yet it would, as I have said, be a mistake to think that these strange texts testify in an unqualified way to YHWH's absolute and unconditional victory in primordial times.

Rather, his victory is only meaningful if his foe is formidable,[1] and his foe's formidability is difficult, perhaps impossible, to imagine if the foe has long since vanished. No emperor will achieve heroic status in the eyes of his subjects if all he forces to march through his streets is a sunken-chested weakling or, worse, if he has no one to force to march. If we imagine a continuum of divine power, with the unqualified combat myth at one extreme and the lament at the other, the texts that speak of the survival of the agent of chaos which we examined fall somewhere in between, although a bit closer to the brute myth: they portray YHWH's current mastery, but also concede the magnitude of the challenge to be surmounted and even its survival in vigilantly controlled conditions. Indeed, the reversion of creation to chaos at the divine command in Genesis 6–9 suggests that YHWH's control of the great foe is not always a blessing.

Another set of texts speaks of the slaying of the aquatic monster in the future tense. Consider, for example, this passage from the "Isaianic Apocalypse" (Isa. 24–27):

> In that day the LORD will punish
> With His great, cruel, mighty sword
> Leviathan the Elusive Serpent—
> Leviathan the Twisting Serpent;
> He will slay the Dragon [*tannin*] in the sea. (Isa. 27:1)

Here, we are surely entitled to say, to use an overworked expression, *Endzeit gleicht Urzeit,*[2] "the end time recapitulates the primal time." The ancient Canaanite and Mesopotamian combat myth of creation has been projected onto the onset of the future era. In fact, it has been demonstrated that the Isaianic Apocalypse displays numerous other close parallels with Ugaritic mythology.[3] For example, the conjunction in Isaiah 24:18–19 of a theophany with the opening of heavenly sluices *('rbwt)* is more than coincidentally reminiscent of a theophany of Baal which begins with his opening a lattice *('urbt).*[4] It has been noted that the phrasing of Isaiah 24:18 is reminiscent of the language that describes the onset of the great Flood in the Priestly stratum of Genesis[5]—another indication that not all sources knew of a Noahide Covenant that precludes categorically a recurrence of watery chaos, as the sources of Genesis did. John Day goes so far as to assert that the "everlasting covenant" whose breach is mentioned in Isaiah 24:5 "can only be the Noachic covenant" of Gen. 9:16 (cf. v. 12) and that therefore "Is. 24 has made the unconditional promise of Gen. 9 conditional, since the return of the flood contradicts Gen. 9:15."[6] He may be right, but the absence of explicit mention of Noah or even a prior flood[7] suggests that *běrît 'ôlām* in Isaiah 24:5 is better rendered "ancient covenant," as in the NJV,[8] and that we had best refrain from any attempt to reconstruct the unspecified conditions in which this covenant emerged. If so, then there is no reason to assume that the "ancient covenant" had ever been unconditional or that God was thought to have reneged upon his solemn oath never to deluge the world again. Rather, the background of Isaiah 24–27 lies in a complex of mythological conceits in which the powers of chaos have never been eliminated or altogether domesticated. These still threaten, and human evil can provoke a cataclysm.

Central to the eschatological vision of the Isaianic Apocalypse is the victory banquet of YHWH upon his mountain:

> [6]The Lord of Hosts will make on this mount
> For all the peoples
> A banquet of rich viands,
> A banquet of choice wines—
> Of rich viands seasoned with marrow,
> Of choice wines well refined.
> [7]And He will destroy on this mount the shroud
> That is drawn over the faces of all the peoples
> And the covering that is spread
> Over all the nations;
> [8]He will swallow Death [*hammāwet*] forever.[9]
> My Lord God will wipe the tears away
> From all faces
> And will put an end to the reproach of His people
> Over all the earth—
> For it is the Lord who has spoken. (Isa. 25:6–8)

These lines recall the session of the divine assembly in the *Enuma elish,* in which, having just accepted Marduk's terms, the gods merrily ate and drank:

[Their] bod[ies] swelled as they drank the strong drink.
Exceedingly carefree were they, their spirit was exalted;
For Marduk, their avenger, they decreed the destiny.
They erected for him a lordly throne-dais,
And he took his place before his fathers to (receive) sovereignty.[10]

In each case the feast celebrates a victory, either retrospectively or proleptically, and the victory is the means by which the deity earned his sovereignty and rescued those who now proudly proclaim him their lord and savior. "This mount" in Isaiah 25:6 is most likely "Mount Zion . . . in Jerusalem," where, according to 24:23, "the LORD of hosts will reign . . . And the presence will be revealed to His elders." In short, the ancient enthronement of YHWH in his Temple in Jerusalem, long celebrated and reenacted in the liturgy,[11] is here projected into the future. These verses recall as well the scene in Exodus 24:9–11, when Moses, having solemnly concluded the Covenant, ascends Mount Sinai with Aaron, two of the latter's sons, and the seventy elders, and is granted with them a vision of God himself: "They beheld God, and they ate and drank." Here, and probably in the *Enuma elish* and the Isaianic Apocalpyse too, the feast is not only a celebration, but also a ratification of the claim to sovereignty of the deity in question. He is the generous patron of the assembly, divine or human, and they are his willing subjects and allies. But the eschatological dimension of the victory feast in Isaiah 25:6–8 implies that whatever past triumphs YHWH may have had, his lordship and his mastery are as yet incomplete or, to put it positively, those past acts of redemption and patronage are only earnests of a coming consummation, which will dwarf them.

The adversary overcome in Isaiah 25:6–8 is not Leviathan under whatever name, but "Death." It is best to see in this term the name of a deity, because the same word *(mt)* denotes in Ugaritic the name of one of Baal's foes, Mot, the deadly son of El, who succeeds in swallowing Baal.[12] Fortunately, Baal's sister Anat is able to decimate Mot and thus effect a resurrection of her brother. The revivified deity then becomes involved in another struggle with Mot, his erstwhile master and vanquisher, pushing him to the ground and returning to his throne, only to fight Mot yet again. The lack of a definitive outcome to this struggle, the alternation between Mot's victories and Baal's, is best explained in Michael David Coogan's words, by the fact "that the defeat of the forces of sterility was not permanent. Drought could return, unpredictably and fiercely, once again destroying the fertility that Baal personified."[13]

In the biblical reflex of this myth in Isaiah 25:6–8, however, it is YHWH, like Baal associated with natural abundance and enhanced vitality, who swallows Death, rather than the reverse, and we have here no hint that this victory will ever be reversed. Indeed, YHWH swallows Death "forever" (*lāneṣaḥ,* v. 8): the life-sapping forces will at last be eliminated, as the living God celebrates his unqualified victory upon his Temple mount.

It is not altogether clear what this means empirically. Some would identify Death with a historical power and interpret YHWH's feast as a victory party after the enemy has fallen. It is hard to escape the fact that the victory here narrated in old mythological colors would have carried in Israel some historical reference, and the fall of a hostile and murderous empire is surely appropriately described as YHWH's defeat of Death. But I doubt that the reference to Mot in Isaiah 25:8 is to be interpreted in so strictly an allegorical fashion, as if Mot is only a cipher for a human political foe. Rather, it is much more likely that what is definitively defeated here is the personification of *all* life-denying forces, natural and historical, all the forces that make for misery, enervation, disease, and humiliation.[14] In support of this, I would draw attention to 26:19, in which YHWH's life-giving dew brings about a resurrection:

Oh, let Your dead revive!
Let corpses arise!
Awake and shout for joy,
You who dwell in the dust!—
For Your dew is like the dew on fresh growth;
You make the land of the shades come to life.

This resurrection of the dead here is best seen as the logical consequence of the defeat of Death predicted in 25:8. To be sure, the Isaianic Apocalypse cannot be interpreted as exemplifying a doctrine of general resurrection *(tĕhiyat hammētim)* of the sort that was later to become central to Judaism, Christianity, and Islam. We do not yet hear of the resurrection of individuals about to be judged and definitively assigned to their fit destiny.[15] But we do hear of a definitive victory of YHWH over Death and of the rich and joyous feast he provides to all nations in celebration of his long-awaited triumph. The resurrection of the dead is to be distinguished, both in origin and in implication, from the immortality of the soul, an idea attested poorly, if at all, in the biblical universe. The hoped-for resurrection originates in an eschatology whose roots lie in the Canaanite tradition of the enthronement of the life-enhancing deity after his victory over the powers of chaos, disease, and sterility.[16] Death, like the sea monster, must be defeated if life is to go on and the worshiping community is to survive. It is no wonder that the enthronement of YHWH stood at the center of that community's liturgical life.

Our discussion of the Isaianic Apocalypse shows it to be a richly evocative reworking of themes known from older Semitic mythologies, most directly those of Canaan in the Late Bronze Age. There is, however, a distinctive feature here—the eschatologization of the old myths of the slaying of the sea monster and Death himself. This is not merely a question of the recrudescence of myth in the sixth century B.C.E. or later, when Isaiah 24–27 is to be dated, for the myth seems to have been alive throughout the era of the monarchy. In fact, the battle with the Sea played an important role in the theology of the Temple and the House of David while the latter stood,[17] and it is reasonable to think that it was always central to the liturgy of the Jerusalem shrine. The distinctive note of the sixth century and the Second Temple period is the note of eschatological urgency that one finds in these texts. That urgency derives from the dissonance between the world affirmed in liturgy and the world experienced in quotidian life. In the former YHWH reigns in justice, unchallenged, and abundantly favoring his faithful and obedient votaries, whereas in the latter Israel is a small and threatened people, lacking sovereignty and often even the respect of those who hold her fate in their hands, and fidelity to her religion brings no temporal rewards, but many afflictions. And thus in a time like that of the Seleucid persecution, when Antiochus IV sought to destroy the traditional Jerusalem cult (167–164 B.C.E.), the old myth is again heard, as a horrific beast from the sea is killed, its body buried, and eternal kingship is given to an angelic savior.[18] It is the disjunction between the ideal world of liturgy and the real world of innocent suffering that this apocalyptic eschatology shares with laments such as Psalms 74 and 89. In each case faith and realism qualify each other in a delicate and nuanced way. In the case of the laments, as we have seen, the combat myth is invoked in hopes of reactivating the victorious God of yore, who seems to slumber as his chosen people or his adopted viceroy suffers. In the case of apocalyptic eschatology, the myth of victory is not abandoned, but projected onto an imminent future which stands in astonishing contradiction to the afflicted present. Both types of literature are defined by the tension between the ideal and the real and the refusal to jettison one in order to embrace the other wholeheartedly. Apocalyptic eschatology grew and flourished in an era in which the afflictions of the laments seemed endless and structural rather than temporary and isolated. Apocalyptic is, in large part, born of the contradiction between the rhetoric of the First Temple period and the reality of the Second.[19]

The continuing political heteronomy of Jewry, relieved in full only briefly during the Hasmonean period, provided fertile soil for the growth of the apocalyptic flower. In the latter half of the Second Temple period, the paucity of references to eschatological combat between God and the sea monster in the Hebrew Bible gives way to the almost psychedelic world of Jewish apocalyptic, in which the God of Israel is about to redeem his good name and the glory of his chosen people with great force. In Christian circles the eschatological combat myth is best known from the Apocalypse of John (Revelation),[20] with its eerie yet stirring vision of "a new heaven and a new earth" in which "the sea was no more."[21] It is for good reason that Jewish apocalyptic has been called "the mother of all Christian theology,"[22] for nowhere has the expectation of a violent end time and the glorification of the ostensibly helpless divinity been so consistently central as in the church.

Rabbinic Judaism is usually portrayed as the polar opposite of this apocalyptic perspective—balanced, orderly, conciliatory, compromising, absorbed with matters of law and ethics, collegial, suspicious of charisma, exoteric, and this-worldly. There is a large measure of truth in this description, and if one concentrates on the legal literature of the rabbis, the description will seem accurate, and the question of how Second Temple Judaism could have spawned both the Rabbinic movement and Jewish apocalyptic will prove baffling. This single-minded concentration on law has been characteristic of the world of the yeshivot for the past several centuries and has colored more than a few modern critical studies as well. It accounts for a tendency of some scholars to reconstruct an early Rabbinic Judaism that absolutizes stasis and equilibrium[23] or escapes the authoritarianism of law only when it resorts to a gnosticizing esotericism.[24] But what if we take the aggadic, or nonlegal, literature into account? The fact is that Rabbinic midrash continues the tradition of eschatological combat and displays a greater interest in the figure of Leviathan than does the Hebrew Bible.[25] For example, a midrash on Job 40:19, 25 states that the angel Gabriel will arrange a hunter's chase of Leviathan and defeat him only if God intervenes. Another midrash holds that God will make a banquet or build a protective booth for the just from the body of the slain Leviathan.[26] The notion of a banquet harks back to the ancient Near Eastern idea of a victory feast that the supreme god holds for his loyalists just before or after the cosmogonic combat. The use of the slain adversary's flesh as food may owe something to the Baal–Mot cycle, because Anat sows the pulverized remains of Mot in the fields,[27] presumably to provide soil or fertilizer for next season's crops. Here an imperfect but revealing parallel with a point in the Egyptian Osiris myth suggests itself, for the murdered god Osiris too is identified with the new grain.[28] In all these cases the struggle that results, in various ways, in a deicide leads also to a meal in which the dead god, indirectly or directly, provides the victuals. Out of death—life.[29] The Talmudic image of a banquet prepared from the flesh of Leviathan owes something also to the phrasing of Psalm 74:14, in which God "left him as food for the denizens of the desert." The booth that is to be made for the just from Leviathan's corpse recalls the creation of heaven and earth from the body of Tiamat in the *Enuma elish,* although it is more directly influenced by Zechariah 14:16–19, in which the celebration of YHWH's victory in eschatological combat is a pilgrimage of all nations to Jerusalem to observe the Feast of Booths. This midrash thus ties the combat and the feast even more tightly together:[30] the booths themselves are constructed from the cosmic foe's remains, and the universal kingship of YHWH, the theme of Zechariah 14:16–19, is acclaimed in the presence of the corpse of his great challenger.

Just as it is a mistake to imagine a legal, or halakhic, Judaism totally independent of aggadic concerns, so is it a mistake to imagine that the legal and ethical dimensions of Rabbinic thought cohere nicely with the eschatological aggadah that we have been examining. If, as I have been arguing, the use of the combat myth in eschatology is intended to represent a radical reversal of the present world order, in which triumphant evil is overthrown by the God whom it seemed to have neutralized (or by his agents), then we should expect a certain tension between Torah and the new age, between the divine dispensation for the present aeon and the events that herald its successor. In fact, precisely in the notion of a feast made of Leviathan's remains, we see an instructive example of that tension. In one midrashic discussion, the idea that Behemoth[31] and Leviathan will serve as the game in an eschatological hunter's chase of the just is opposed by a point of law. If Behemoth gores Leviathan with his horns in the great combat, and Leviathan stabs Behemoth with his fin,[32] then neither is fit (kosher) for Jewish consumption, because neither was slaughtered as the law requires. The answer of Rabbi Abba bar Kahana (late third century C.E., Palestine) plays on a verse in Isaiah, "For teaching *(tôrâ)* will go forth from Me."[33] "A *new* Torah will go forth from Me," remarked the rabbi, or "a *renewal* of Torah will go forth from Me."[34] Presumably the new Torah will allow, at least in this instance, for a feast composed of meats from improperly slaughtered beasts.[35] His contemporary, Rabbi Berechiah, specifies the relationship between observance of Torah and participation in the new order marked by the nonkosher banquet of the just: "Whoever has not eaten meat from an improperly slaughtered animal in this world is earning the right to eat it in the world-to-come." Rabbi Berechiah supports his principle with a verse from the Torah itself. "Fat from animals that died or were torn by beasts may be put to any use, but you must not eat it" *(wĕʾākōl lōʾ tōʾkĕlūhû).*"[36] His assumption seems to be that two forms of the verb *ʾākal* (to eat) appear in this verse, with only one of them in the negative, in order to signal that "if you don't eat it now, you will eat it then": in this way, the threatening opposition between the two dispensations falls away, and in its place there appears a relationship of mutual reinforcement. It is not in spite of observance of the Torah, but through it that one may participate in eschatological reality. The eschatological feast does not negate ordinary Jewish meals; it consummates them. In this theology the commandments *(miṣwôt,* commonly pronounced *mitsvot)* of the Torah are possessed of a special sacramental efficacy. They serve as the conduits through which a Jew may effect his entry into the promised world-to-come. The genius of Rabbi Berechiah's midrash on Leviticus 7:24 is that it upholds both the absolute normativity of the *mitsvot* and the radical reversal of the present order of things that is central to the apocalyptic heritage. The commandments of the Torah are neither valid *in toto* for all time nor dispensable in the currently unredeemed world. At least in the case of the

prohibition on eating meat from a torn animal, their current validity is inextricably associated with participation in an eschatological reality in which they will be suspended.

It is important to retain sight of the fact that in this midrashic
text about the demise of Behemoth and Leviathan, observance of
the law is not seen as *effecting* the victory over the two great monsters. They kill off *each other* here, although this is thought to be
providential, part of God's promise of ultimate redemption. In this
sense the victory is, to use the unhappy Pauline terminology, a
matter of "grace" rather than "works." But it must be noted that
in Rabbi Berechiah's theology, the human appropriation of the
eschatological victory, that is, the right to dine at the great banquet, is dependent upon observance of Torah. Both divine initia-
tive and human responsibility—grace *and* works—are central to
the vision of the eschatological feast. Neither dimension is allowed
to undercut the other. As in the *Enuma elish,* the table fellowship
is composed of the divine victor's loyal subordinates, those who
stand by their lord even when he seems unworthy of their fealty
and homage. Without them he would be a king without subjects,
a victor without acclaim. Through faithfulness to him they become servants of a gracious and generous patron in a world in
which cosmic evil has at last met its match.

These remarkable examples of continuity between late Rabbinic
eschatology and the use in apocalyptic of ancient Semitic myth
must not blind us to the difference in ambience between Rabbinic
literature and its apocalyptic forebears. It is telling that the eschatological combat and the ensuing banquet do not here appear
in free narrative, poetic or prosaic, but only in the form of midrash,
that is, in subordination to scripture. Rabbinic eschatological affirmations tend to be scholarly and exegetical; they lack the sustained passion and the wildly, even hysterically, proliferating visual imagery of apocalyptic. Much of this is owing to the
well-known fact that the rabbis of the Talmud usually did not
believe the end time to be imminent. In consequence, their
thought lacks the excruciating sense of urgency characteristic of
apocalyptic literature and displays in its stead a relaxed and often

playful attitude. The latter would have been abhorrent to those who believed themselves to stand at the turn of the aeon. They would have considered it frivolous.

It should also be noticed that in biblical, apocalyptic, and Rabbinic Judaism alike, the combat myth is only one component of an amorphous and highly variegated eschatological vision. In Talmud and midrash, the traditions about the sea monster are less important than in the Hebrew Bible and certainly less important than in postbiblical Jewish apocalyptic. This is, in part, because other ways of conceiving the eschatological foe, all of them likewise rooted in the Hebrew Bible, become more prominent and begin to eclipse the ancient combat myth. The war of Gog[37] is an example, as is the ancient archetypical enemy of Israel, Amalek. As early as Exodus 17:16, YHWH is seen as involved in a continuing war with this desert tribe, against whom he even enjoins Israel to commit genocide.[38] Indeed, one Amoraic midrash sees in the survival of the Amalekites a blemish upon the very nature and sovereignty of God:

Rabbi Levi said in the name of Rabbi Aḥa bar Ḥanina: As long as the descendants of Amalek are in the world, neither the name [i.e., YHWH] nor the throne is complete. When the descendants of Amalek will have perished, both the name and the throne will be complete. What is the reason? "The enemy is no more—/ruins everlasting," etc.[39] What is written thereafter? "But the LORD abides forever;/He has set up his throne for judgment."[40]

Here the darshan interprets the psalmist's celebration of a divine victory and the subsequent enthronement of YHWH as yet to be. In Rabbi Aḥa's mind, the psalmist did not commemorate; he prognosticated. Specifically, he predicted the eschatological annihilation of the Amalekites, although who precisely these were thought to be in third-century c.e. Palestine is unclear, the Roman Empire being our best guess. Underlying this curious exegesis is the unusual wording of Exodus 17:16:

He said, "It means, 'Hand upon the throne (kēs) of the LORD (Yāh)!' The LORD will be at war with Amalek throughout the ages."

If *kēs* means "throne," then it lacks the final letter of the ordinary word for "throne" *(kissē)*. Similarly, the name of YHWH here lacks the last two consonants that it usually (but not always) shows. Rabbi Aḥa interprets these apocopated terms as an indication of the unfinished quality of God's nature and his mastery over the world. So long as Israel's ancient and by now archetypical enemy endures, YHWH is not altogether YHWH, and his regal power is not yet fully actualized. Rather, he is the omnipotent cosmocrator only *in potentia*. His power and his majesty, not yet fully manifest, will become so when, acting in accordance with Psalm 9, he blasts his enemy from the world.

The typological identity of this Amalek-centered eschatology with the ancient combat myth as it appears in Jewish and early Christian apocalyptic is striking. To be sure, the enemy is not the sea beast, but a quasi-historical people. Yet the historicization of the myth, its application to a human foe in a discrete situation, is not unusual in any period. Consider, for example, Ezekiel's use of the tradition of God's catching Leviathan like a fish in oracles directed against the contemporary Pharaoh.[41] As we have seen, however, it is mistaken to interpret the combat myth as allegory, for Leviathan under whatever name or image survives the fall of historical enemies and comes as early as Isaiah 27:1 to be seen as the final obstacle to YHWH's claim of kingship. Amalek too ceases to be a marauding tribe on the southern fringe of Canaan and comes to represent any anti-Semite of murderous intent, even the prime minister of Persia in the days of Esther and Mordecai.[42] My point is that Leviathan, Amalek, Gog, and the like are symbols from different traditionary complexes for the same theological concept: the ancient and enduring opposition to the full realization of God's mastery, the opposition destined to be eliminated at the turn of the aeon. We must not forget that the optimistic element in this theology, which is the faith in God's ultimate triumph, is dialectically qualified by the pessimistic element, which is the tacit acknowledgment that God is not yet God. Our cup of salvation will indeed run over, but it is now only half full—and half empty.

Another of the multitude of beings to be eliminated in the

eschatological triumph according to the rabbis must not go unmentioned, for here we find a revealing indication of the relevance
of the eschatological drama to the daily life of the premillennial
Jew:

> The Holy One (blessed be he) said to Israel: "In this world you stray from
> the *mitsvot* on account of the Evil Impulse *(yēṣer hāra')*. In the coming age,
> I will uproot it from you, as the Bible says, 'I will remove the heart of
> stone from your body and give you a heart of flesh; and I will put My
> spirit into you. Thus I will cause you to follow My laws and faithfully
> to observe My rules,' etc."[43]

The notion of a recreation of humanity in which their better
impulses will no longer be dogged by their evil ones is to be found
not only in the passage from Ezekiel that the anonymous homilist
cites, but elsewhere in the same period. In texts such as Jeremiah's
prediction of a new covenant, the Torah will be made instinctual
and no longer in need of preaching and teaching. In the great
penitential Psalm 51, of uncertain date, the speaker calls upon God
to "Fashion a pure heart for me . . ./create in me a steadfast
spirit."[44] In all these texts, we detect the pessimistic assumption
that evil is not merely a characteristic of the deed, but also of the
will and the mind of the doer. What is needed is not still another
resolve of the same flawed heart, another act flowing from the
same misdirected spirit, but rather a new heart and a new spirit
that can embrace Torah and commandments without ambiva-
lence—in short, a new animal to replace *homo sapiens*. It is in this
stream of thought that we hear the Augustinian rather than the
Pelagian accents of ancient Judaism. It is a stream of thought that
surely refutes the shopworn cliché that Judaism, unlike Christianity, is optimistic and believes that we can be as good as we choose
to be, without the special action of God. The truth is that Judaism
is not optimistic but *redemptive,* and the creation of humanity without their powerful, innate and persistent will to evil is part of its
vision of redemption, not part of its description of present reality.

The good news is that alongside the Evil Impulse there stands,
according to the rabbis, its benign counterpoint, the "Good Im-

pulse" (*yēṣer haṭṭôb*),[45] not necessarily of equal potency, but real nonetheless and capable of pushing the inevitably ambivalent self toward obedience. In the Rabbinic concept that there is in the human heart a will to good, however battered and bruised, we hear a Jewish note of protest against the Augustinian notion of the radical depravity of human beings, in whom sin has effaced the image of God in which they were created. If Augustinian theologians would say that the rabbis underestimate the power of innate evil, the rabbis would rejoin that Augustine and other Christian thinkers in the same mold as he have underestimated the realism and the doability of the Torah, which was given to creatures of flesh and blood and, through the idea of repentance, takes account of the fragility and transiency of their good intentions. The Torah is not, in the words of Deuteronomy, "too baffling for you, nor is it beyond reach" in the empyrean or a distant land. "No, the thing is very close to you, in your mouth and in your heart, to observe it."[46] Life is a continual war against the Evil Impulse, a war that does not see a definitive victory in present reality, but in which battles can be won. The major weapon in that war is the Torah itself, for preoccupation with the Torah and observance of its *mitsvot* trains one's naturally unruly passions, civilizes the appetites, fortifies against temptation, helps identify failures, and directs the mind toward higher things. Victory in those battles is, once again, the fruit of conjoint grace and works, of humanity's inconstant will and God's perdurable revelation and indefeasible benevolence. A final victory, victory in the war itself, will come only when humanity's goodness becomes as constant and as reliable as God's, that is, when the prayers of prophets and psalmists for a new heart and a new spirit are at long last granted. Until then, evil too will be as near as one's mouth and one's heart, vigilance must be eternal, and penitence unending.

Those who are disposed to projectionist views of religion will be emboldened by the congruity of the psychology of the rabbis with their eschatology and philosophy of history. The survival and frequent triumph of the Evil Impulse corresponds to the survival and frequent triumph of Amalek, the demonic quasi-historical people who stands behind all the persecutions of the Jews and who is destined for annihilation at the end of days. The ultimate and definitive triumph of the Good Impulse corresponds to God's eschatological elimination of Amalek, but also to the defeat of Leviathan, *et al.* Leviathan is to creation as Amalek is to history and as the Evil Impulse is to the Good in Rabbinic psychology. Each is an ancient or even innate impediment to reality as God, the potentially omnipotent, wishes it to be. Each can be suppressed for the nonce, but will disappear only in the eschatological reversal. The suspicion arises that Rabbinic eschatology (and probably biblical eschatology as well) has projected the subjective experience of moral struggle onto the interpretation of history and the vision of the future. Indeed, in Rabbi Aḥa's midrash on Psalm 9:7, the projection goes as far as the inner being of God himself. The last two letters of the ineffable name do not (re)join the first two until Amalek has been destroyed. Like humanity's reigning impulse, God will not be truly one until the great victory. His oneness, like humanity's uninhibited goodness, is not real, but surely will be. Against the projectionist view, however, one may mention the possibility that this process is at least as well described as the internalization of history; the alternation of subjugation and sovereignty, of persecution and prosperity, which is the stuff of biblical history, has been appropriated into the inner life of the individual Jew. It has ceased to be a matter of antiquarian interest only and has been, like Scripture itself, reactualized in the spiritual dynamics of postbiblical Judaism. Whatever one chooses to call the process, it cannot be denied that there is a remarkable correspondence in Rabbinic theology between what happens in the individual self, in history, and even inside the one God.

The simultaneous existence of the great conflict on many levels is not an innovation of the rabbis. It is prominent in the documents found at Qumran, the Dead Sea Scrolls, literature mostly from the last two centuries of the Second Temple period. The Community Rule (IQS), for example, speaks of a heavenly conflict between "the prince of lights" and "the angel of darkness." These supernal beings correspond to the "Sons of Light" and the "Sons of Darkness," which are terms for the members of the apocalyptic sect itself and for their enemies, respectively. Yet the individual is not definitively and irreversibly assigned to one group or the other, for the conflict is also internal to the human self: "By the angel of darkness [comes] the aberration of all the sons of righteousness."[47] This is reminiscent of the much later midrashic statement that "In this world you stray from the *mitsvot* on account of the Evil Impulse."[48] Like the Evil Impulse in that midrash, deceit, which is characteristic of the Sons of Darkness and their angelic prince, is destined to be destroyed forever by God, and "then the truth of the earth will appear forever,"[49] the Sons of Darkness having been dispatched to everlasting perdition. Of this text, John J. Collins remarks:

The single dualism of Light and Darkness is found then on a series of distinct levels—the individual heart, the political and social order, and the cosmic level, embracing heaven and earth. The cosmic conflict of the two spirits may be used to express this dualism on any other level. The resolution of the conflict by the intervention of God to aid the Sons of Light may also indicate the anticipated resolution of the conflict at any level.[50]

The reverse, it seems to me, is also true: human goodness helps defeat the angel of darkness and his terrestrial subjects. It produces a unification toward goodness within the transcendent realm which is functionally equivalent to the completion of the divine name in Rabbi Aḥa's midrash on the destruction of Amalek. It is thus revealing that this instruction on the great duality (cols. 1–4) in the Community Rule serves as a preface to the specific laws of the conventicle (cols. 5–9). This is an eschatological adaptation of the old pattern that one finds in Deuteronomy, in which a paraenetic address on the significance of observance of *mitsvot* (chs. 4–11) serves as a preface to the law-code (chs. 12–26). The laws of the Community Rule are the weapons that defeat the malignant cosmic forces of deceit and injustice. Indeed, when one undertakes to observe them, he takes himself out of the dark domain and reinforces the Sons of Light and their celestial advocate. Although the anthropological dualism of the Community Rule is foreign to the world of most Rabbinic literature, the Rabbinic idea of the sacramental efficacy of observance of the *mitsvot* does have a forebear in the notion of a multilevel struggle and the possibility of human enlistment on the side of right. Just as Rabbi Berechiah some four centuries later was to see the observance of dietary laws as (partially) qualifying a Jew to dine at the eschatological banquet, so does this Qumran literature view the regimen of the sectarian community as enabling its members to participate in the eschatological victory, to immanentize it, to help it along.

The partial present availability of eschatological reality is, in various ways and degrees, a conviction characteristic of many communities in the spectrum of ancient Judaic culture—Qumranian, Rabbinic, early Christian, and perhaps others. In his valuable comparative study entitled *Paul and Palestinian Judaism,* E. P. Sanders argues for a dichotomy of "covenantal nomism" and "participationist eschatology,"[51] the former a rubric for all forms of postbiblical Palestinian Judaism and the latter a rubric for Paul's particular type of religion. This terminology is useful and heuristic, and one hesitates to cast doubt upon the work of a New Testament scholar who, breaking with the tradition of his profession, labors hard to describe Judaism fairly and does so with impressive success. Still, it is imperative to point out that this dichotomy would lead to misunderstanding if it were taken to mean that the observance of covenantal law was always thought to be devoid of eschatological significance. The mutual exclusion is, in fact, characteristic of Paul's theology, at least in its earlier phases, when the apostle exhorts his correspondents to choose between the Christ and the law (Galatians). But, as we have seen, in Qumranian Judaism consistently and in Rabbinic Judaism occasionally, observance of the law is held to have an eschatological dimension, and covenantal nomism and a participationist eschatology are not only compatible, but substantively and causally linked. It bears mention that Paul's is not the only way of thinking about these matters in the New Testament, and that other texts therein tie a tight connection between one's present practices and his destiny in the future age.[52] In whatever nuance, the theologies that make this connection continue the old covenantal thinking, which links observance of the stipulations of covenant with future beatitude. In the Torah, the future beatitude is conceived as serene and prosperous life in the Land of Israel. In these later literatures, although the Land is sometimes important, the blessed future is conceived as a new age or a new world.

The difference between a new land and a new age or world must not, however, be minimized. A key to the difference lies in the fact that in the apocalyptic scenario, the enemies cease to be merely earthly powers, like the petty kingdoms that attempt to prevent Israel from entering the Land,[53] and become, instead or in addition, cosmic forces of the utmost malignancy. Their evil reaches everywhere, even into the human heart, and their defeat requires nothing less than a cosmic transformation—a new cosmogony, a new creation. Apocalyptic eschatology can be fruitfully conceived as a process of purgation: reality sheds its negative aspects. In part, these doomed but still potent negative beings can be seen as hypostatizations of what earlier stages in the tradition had unselfconsciously considered the negative side of God himself. Such hypostatization can be seen already within the Hebrew Bible. An instructive example is the Chronicler's handling of David's catastrophic decision to take a census of Israel and Judah. Whereas 2 Samuel 24:1 says that "the anger of the LORD again flared up against Israel; and He incited David against them," 1 Chronicles 21:1 tells us that "Satan arose against Israel and incited David to number Israel." Satan has replaced YHWH in the morally questionable role of instigator of sin and cause of destruction. A more refined and sophisticated sensibility has proven less able to tolerate the idea that God can be a cause of evil. Indeed, the process can be seen in the very liturgy of the rabbis, which changes God's boast that he "makes peace and creates *evil*"[54] into the evasive affirmation that he "makes peace and creates *everything.*"[55] In both the biblical and the Rabbinic examples, the tendency is toward an exculpation of the deity. The reverse side of the coin should not, however, be overlooked: as God is exculpated, evil is divinized. A ragtag tribe like the Amalekites becomes an enduring principle of evil that interferes with God's very integrity. In Rabbinic thought Amalek is the hypostatization of God's authorship of a world in which Jewry suffers for being themselves and of his willingness to allow genocidal anti-Semites to survive to strike again. God becomes God, the good God realizes his goodness, only when he overcomes his negative pole. Until then, his unity is fragmented, and his name incomplete. This is a theology with absolute faith in God's *ultimate* goodness, but a rather qualified faith in his *proximate* goodness. God's goodness will be established. In the meantime, we have only earnests of it.

A similar process lies behind the evolution of the idea of the Evil Impulse (*yēṣer hāra'*), which I have argued is in some ways functionally analogous to Amalek. As the case of David's census demonstrates, earlier tradition could tolerate the notion that YHWH himself could be the source of a temptation to commit a sin. Yet the choice to sin is not always forced on the person. Sometimes it seems to be so, as when YHWH hardens Pharaoh's heart so as to ensure that his submission is ephemeral and his destruction inescapable,[56] but on other occasions, it would seem that the person remains free to resist God's malign tempting. But why does God present temptations? Why does humanity, created in God's image, find their will continually bombarded with temptations of the heart that they never chose to have? The earlier phases of tradition could see this too as God's work, as when "the spirit of the Lord had departed from Saul, and an evil spirit from the Lord began to terrify him,"[57] producing depression and a murderous paranoia. To be sure, Saul, like Pharaoh, is not an innocent man, and the "evil spirit" that YHWH inflicts on him is at least partially punishment for disobedience.[58] But the punishment is not external to the will—defeat, illness, impoverishment, the death of loved ones, or the like—but a pernicious infection of the will itself,[59] of the deepest part of his psyche, of his very ability to *perceive* his situation accurately and to conceive a plan of action that is moral. Here we confront the insidiousness of the Evil Impulse, its eerie ability to make persons of good intention "stray from the *mitsvot.*" The crucial difference is that in Rabbinic thought the Evil Impulse, although it too is a creation of God and not primordial (if innate), is distant from God's intentions and actions. Like Satan, it is an *adversary* of God's work. The midrash did not imagine God to say, in the manner of 1 Samuel 16:14, that "in this world you stray from the *mitsvot* on account of an Evil Impulse *from the* LORD," but rather on account of the Evil Impulse *as an autonomous aspect of the self,* which God vows to uproot in the future aeon. Here the Evil Impulse is the reification and personification of innate evil, the "prechoice" evil in the human heart, the element in humanness that frustrates obedience to God and casts a shadow of doubt upon the purity of God's benevolence in the act of creation. Why has he fashioned creatures whose hearts fool them into committing evil that they do not intend and that seems only good at the time?[60] God's rule will become complete only when the human heart, upon which it partly depends, will be enabled to embrace his commands with wholeness and integrity. The utterly benevolent God of creation will be himself only when humanity, male and female, created in his image, is able to be itself, without the interference of the malign forces. In this theology divine and human integrity are neither identical nor separable. Both are *ultimately* real, but *proximately* frustrated.

It is in moments of obedience to God's commandments that the ultimately real becomes available in the present order. It is in those elusive but ever available moments that the deeply flawed present is forced to yield to the perfect future. And it is in this idea of a multileveled act of unification—unification in God, in creation, and in the human self—that we find the deep root of the profound theology of the *mitsvah* as a theurgic act which flowers a millennium later in Spanish Qabbalah. It is the *mitsvah* that effects integrity throughout all tiers of reality and enables the life-enhancing divine energy to flow freely and without inhibition.

4. Conclusion: The Vitality of Evil and the Fragility of Creation

It is time to bring together the threads of our discussion and to draw some conclusions. I began by defining divine mastery as the critical element in the creation stories of the Hebrew Bible. What emerges in those stories is not the physical universe,[1] but an environment ordered for peaceful human habitation and secure against the onslaughts of chaos and anarchy. The concern of the creation theology is not *creatio ex nihilo*, but the establishment of a benevolent and life-sustaining order, founded upon the demonstrated authority of the God who is triumphant over all rivals. Their elimination, together with the joyful subordination to the divine victor of all that survive, is the tangible proof of his lordship and the enduring availability of a friendly world.

I went on to critique Yehezkel Kaufmann's influential idea that YHWH's mastery is the "basic idea of Israelite religion." In opposition to Kaufmann, I argued that the absolute sovereignty of the God of Israel is not a simple given in the Hebrew Bible; it lacks the solidity and fixity that Kaufmann tried to assign to it. Instead, YHWH's mastery is often fragile, in continual need of reactivation and reassertion, and at times, as in the laments, painfully distant from ordinary experience, a memory and a hope rather than a current reality. It is, in short, a confession of faith.

What makes this a confession of faith in YHWH's mastery rather than a shallow truism is the survival of those potent forces of chaos that were subjugated and domesticated at creation. Creation itself offers no ground for the optimistic belief that the malign powers will not deprive the human community of its friendly and supportive environment. In the story of Noah, the ground of security is not creation, which is undone in those days, but God's mysterious oath not to destroy his world. Only that oath, only that universal covenant sworn to Noah, and nothing more, keeps human life safe from total annihilation. In texts that (unlike Genesis) speak of an aquatic chaos-monster, the continuation of the hostile forces is sometimes articulated as the survival of Leviathan (under whatever name) in captivity. In a few places the battle with Leviathan is projected onto the decisive moment of the future, and we are left with the bittersweet impression that the travails of the present, indeed of all history, are owing to the fact that the present order of things stands *before* rather than *after* the triumph of God: Leviathan is still loose, and the absolute sovereignty of the absolutely just God lies ahead.

The eschatological combat myth, which is rare in the Hebrew Bible and absent altogether in the Pentateuch, survives and even grows in Jewish and early Christian apocalyptic literature and is found, with a phenomenal degree of continuity, in the *aggadah* of the Talmudic rabbis. In the case of the rabbis, Leviathan, Behemoth, and the like are some of several obstacles that YHWH must surmount in order to secure his reign. These include *inter alia* idolatrous worldly powers (Gog), anti-Semitic peoples (Amalek), and the very urge to do evil that lies deep in the ambivalent human heart (the *yēṣer hāra'*). Taking up an older theme, the rabbis tend to see the *mitsvot,* the divine commandments, as a means of contributing to the ultimate triumph of God, a means of immanentizing the unchallenged reign of the absolutely good and absolutely just God, whose will is so often frustrated in this premessianic world. On rare occasion the rabbis of the Talmudic period associate this future/present victory with a unification within God himself, and in this they anticipate the Qabbalistic system that would not flower until the thirteenth century C.E.

The survival and embellishment of the eschatological combat myth in postbiblical Jewish literature argues against the view that its presence in the Hebrew Bible is only vestigial. We have already seen that Kaufmann's belief that Israel recontextualized the cosmogonic myth as a mere rebellion is not generally borne out in the texts, which lack the rhetoric of revolt. The fact that the combat may take place after the origination of the physical universe would be decisive only if the point of creation in the Hebrew Bible were *creatio ex nihilo,* but this is not the point even in Genesis 1. In support of the conventional view that "the Hebrew myths dealing with the birth of the cosmos envision no struggle between the creator and any other beings," one scholar has recently noted that "with the most detail to be found anywhere, the poet in Job 40–41 can picture Behemoth and Leviathan as mere playthings in YHWH's hands."[2] This reinforces his assertion that "what is primordial is the goodness of this world and of humanity; what is radically intrusive is the evil which humanity does."[3] This statement is inadequate to capture even the theology of Genesis 1, which will occupy us in the next chapter. And, couched as a generalization about the Hebrew Bible, it is highly vulnerable. The truth is that Leviathan usually seems to be primordial. In fact, only Psalm 104:26 attributes his creation to YHWH. Whereas Job 40–41 explicitly states that Behemoth is a work of God,[4] no such statement is made of Leviathan in the much longer section devoted to him. Instead, we hear only of God's heroic capture and conquest of the great sea beast. The theology of the first chapter of the Bible surely relativized the old combat myth and *eventually* required that it be seen as a revolt—primordial, eschatological, or both—but the optimistic theology failed to uproot the older and more pessimistic combat myth altogether. The fuel that continued to drive the disturbing old myth for a thousand years and more after the promulgation of Genesis 1 was the harsh experience of Jewry in a world supposedly governed by the God who loves them more than anything else. Where evil is only of human origin, suffering is to be attributed only to sin, which intrudes into the pristine divine–human relationship: blame the victim. But in the Hebrew Bible, it is possible, as we have seen and shall see again, to fault God himself for the suffering and to dare him to act as the magisterial world-orderer that the old myth celebrates. This implies that more than just human repentance is necessary if life is to be just and

God is really to rule. It is the continuing, at times escalating, experience of evil that prevents Genesis 1 from turning the myth into "cut flowers," in Paul Ricoeur's term. What Ricoeur calls "the new system in which creation is good from the first" so that "neither Evil nor History can any longer be referred to some primordial disorder"[5] is but a gross overgeneralization from the conventional optimistic reading of Genesis 1. Even when the *Sitz im Leben* of the old myth in an enthronement ceremony vanished with the monarchy,[6] the myth endured, drawing new nourishment from that very experience of political heteronomy and national victimization. The central affirmation of apocalyptic is that the evil that occurs in history is symptomatic of a larger suprahistorical disequilibrium that requires, indeed invites, a suprahistorical correction. As evil did not originate with history, neither will it disappear altogether *in* history, but rather *beyond* it, at the inauguration of the coming world.

The God to whom this theology bears witness is not the one who continually acts in history, but one whose acts are clustered either in the primordial past or in the eschatological future, or both, that is, the God who will reactivate his mighty deeds and close the horrific parenthesis that is ordinary history. This is not the divine warrior of the classic theology of recital,[7] nor is it the *deus otiosus* whose prime is past and who has surrendered to younger, more virile members of the pantheon. Rather, YHWH in this theology is a deity who can still be aroused, who can still respond to the anguished cry of his cultic community to effect together a new victory. When this subtle, dialectical theology came into being is probably impossible to reconstruct. It is likely to have come to the fore whenever the disjunction of the old rhetoric of recital and the harshness of contemporary experience became too great to repress. In any event, by the time of the exile of the sixth century B.C.E., it was surely among the major components of the spiritual life of Israel, and it has been so ever since, even into the post-Holocaust era.

II. THE ALTERNATION OF CHAOS AND ORDER—GENESIS 1:1–2:3

The heavens are not guiltless in His sight. . . .

5. Creation Without Opposition: Psalm 104

In Part I, we examined critically the common observation that in the thinking of the Hebrew Bible, evil has no primordial existence, but results only from the choices human beings make in history. We found that this optimistic opinion fails to reckon with the combat myth of creation, in which the familiar, ordered world comes into being only after the primordial sea monster has been defeated. The assumption that the monstrous adversary of YHWH was not primordial, but had been created by him, so that the challenge was only an act of rebellion, derives ultimately from Genesis 1. Indeed, if the first chapter of the Bible is to be accorded the pride of place that the redactors have given it, then the common move of subordinating the combat myth to this more familiar theology is warranted. If, however, as I argued in Part I, such harmonization does violence to the plain sense of the text, then it is preferable to see Genesis 1 not as the magnetic pole from which all interpretations must take their bearings, but as the result of a long process of tradition that culminates in the Jewish, Christian, and Muslim philosophical doctrine of *creatio ex nihilo*. The chief objective of the following discussion is to explore the character of Genesis 1 as a point on the trajectory that runs from the ancient Near Eastern combat myth to the developed creation theology of the Abrahamic faiths.

In the conclusion to the preceding discussion, I pointed out that contrary to what one might expect, there is only one text in the Hebrew Bible in which Leviathan is said to have been created. In exultant praise of the skill of the creator God, Psalm 104 refers to the seas as containing innumerable creatures of YHWH as well as ships "and Leviathan that You formed to sport with."[1] Here the great aquatic beast is not merely captured and subjugated, as in Job 40:25–32, but actually fashioned by YHWH from the start and only for the purpose of his personal diversion and amusement. The terrifying monster of Job 40 has been emasculated into a toy that has always only delighted and never opposed its designer, maker, and owner. Leviathan in Psalm 104 is now just another of the myriad things whose existence prompts the psalmist to an ecstatic proclamation of the wisdom that God manifested when he filled the world with creatures of his own design.[2]

The stage beyond Psalm 104 in the demythologization of the sea monster is represented by Genesis 1. There Leviathan has been purged—almost, that is. For in v. 21, the description of the fifth day of creation, when God *('ĕlōhîm)* creates the swimming and flying things, the text pointedly tells us that he created "the great sea monsters" *(hattannînîm haggĕdōlîm)*. The term *tannîn* is elsewhere used to refer to Leviathan.[3] The special notice given the creation of these *tannînîm* in Genesis 1:21 is surely to be associated with the central role of Leviathan (under whatever name) in other creation stories, Gentile and Israelite alike. The author wishes us to know explicitly that these monsters are not primordial and neither free of God's rule nor an embarrassment to it. Indeed, whereas elsewhere in this chapter, God usually either calls entities into existence by his mere command or "makes" them *(wayya'aś)*, only in the case of the sea monster in this verse and of humanity in v. 27 is it said that he *created (wayyibrā')* a specific species. In light of known Mesopotamian myths in which the sea monster predates her slayer and in which it is not the victorious high god who creates humanity,[4] it is difficult to resist the suspicion that the special mention of the *tannînîm* in Genesis 1:21 is motivated by polemical intent.[5] The fact that more than one sea monster is created, and that only the generic name is mentioned, reinforces the suspicion. Leviathan is now only one member of a whole species of marine animals, a species that God not only creates, but pronounces good, blesses, and charges "to be fertile and increase."[6] All hint of opposition to God on the part of these animals has vanished. Indeed, only the similar charge to humanity in v. 28

surpasses that to the sea creatures and the birds: humanity is given the additional task of conquering the Earth and ruling all other creatures. They are thus placed higher in the plan of creation than the much-attenuated monster of the old mythology, but still below the God who has graciously and benevolently willed them and all other creatures into existence. The positive specialness of humanity has replaced the old negative specialness of the sea monster, as the sanguinary war for control has yielded to the uncontested sharing of sovereignty between God and his human stewards with which the great six-day cosmogony of Genesis 1 closes.[7]

That the great sea monsters of Genesis 1:21 are not created until the fifth day further underscores their subordination to God. Unlike him, they are not primordial, and far from playing an essential role in the emergence of the rest of nature, they in fact appear only toward the end of the primal week, one day before the stewards of God who are charged to rule in his name over the rest of creation. In this relative lateness of the mention of the monsters, Genesis 1 is again reminiscent of Psalm 104, in which Leviathan is mentioned only in v. 26 in a poem of thirty-five verses, of which only the first thirty-one are devoted to a survey of creation. In fact, the sequence of items in that survey generally betrays so high a degree of similarity to the sequence of creation in Genesis 1 that coincidence seems unlikely.[8] Just as God's first creative act in Genesis is the creation of light, so does Psalm 104 begin with an image of YHWH majestically donning his "robe of light."[9] As God in Genesis 1:6 next makes an expanse or firmament "in the midst of the water, that it may separate water from water," that is, the sky, which was thought to intervene between the supernal and the terrestrial waters, so does YHWH in Psalm 104:3-4 "set the rafters of His lofts in the waters" and use the clouds as his chariot, moving "on the wings of the wind." In Genesis God then proceeds to collect the waters in one spot, so that the dry land and the seas may appear. This corresponds to the psalmist's next point, that "he established the earth on its foundations" and forced the waters "to the place You established for them."[10] At this juncture

Genesis relates God's command to the Earth to "sprout vegetation: seed-bearing plants, fruit trees of every kind," whereas Psalm 104 speaks of springs that gush forth, providing water for beasts and birds (which, according to Genesis 1, have yet to be created). But this same section of the psalm does speak about the "foliage" in which the birds sing, the "earth which is sated from the fruit of Your work," the grass for the cattle and the herbage for man "that he may get food out of the earth," and the trees that YHWH plants and waters.[11] The correspondence of the two pieces of literature at this point is not exact, but it is real.

After this Genesis 1 relates the creation on the fourth day of the sun, moon, and stars.[12] (Presumably until now all light derived from God's initial command—"Let there be light,"[13] without any celestial intermediaries.) It is at this point that Psalm 104 tells of YHWH's making the moon and the sun and of the consequences for animals and humanity of sunrise and sunset.[14] In Genesis there then follow the events of the fifth day,[15] whose affinity to the psalmist's discussion of the sea and its contents we have already discussed. The creation of land animals and humanity on the sixth day of creation in Genesis 1:24–27 has no parallel in sequence in the psalm, wherein the creation of humanity is not mentioned. Yet it is interesting that the psalmist's survey of creation closes with a meditation upon the dependence of all life upon YHWH for food and indeed life itself, because Genesis 1 concludes the sixth and final day of its cosmogony with God's assignment of plants and fruits to humanity and beast for food.[16] It is also worthy of note that Genesis 1 and Psalm 104 have much diction in common, some of it rare. Because Paul Humbert tabulated these correspondences,[17] I need only illustrate them with one example, God's unusual charge to his animal and human creatures in Genesis 1:22, 28 (reiterated after the Flood in 9:1) to "fill" (mil'û) the sea and Earth. This recalls the psalmist's ecstatic exclamation:

> How many are the things You have made, O LORD;
> You have made them all with wisdom;
> the earth is full (māl'â) of Your creations. (Ps. 104:24)

Other passages speak of the Earth as full of violence, or of the glory or of the knowledge of God,[18] for example, and the nominal phrase the "fullness" (*mĕlō'*) of the Earth is fairly common. Yet only in these passages from Genesis 1 (and 9) and Psalm 104 do we find this verb form in association with creation.

We have now surveyed three factors that suggest a genetic connection between Genesis 1 and Psalm 104. The first was a point of theology: only in this psalm is Leviathan said to have been a creature of YHWH, a point that recalls the special mention in Genesis 1:21 of the creation *(wayyibrā')* of the great sea monsters on day five. The second and, in my judgment, most persuasive factor is the detailed order of creation in the two passages. The correspondences are not total, of course, but they are impressive and cast heavy doubt upon the possibility of coincidence. The last factor was the substantial overlap in vocabulary between Genesis 1 and Psalm 104, an overlap of the sort that one does not ordinarily find between Genesis 1 and other biblical cosmogonies.

The differences between these two related passages illumine the distinctive notes of each. Psalm 104 is not a depiction of the process of creation at all. It is a panorama of the natural world, conducted with a view to praising the creator for his superlative wisdom in conceiving and producing such an astonishing place. Although the order of items surveyed does indeed coincide roughly with the order of Genesis 1, Psalm 104 makes no claim to narrate a *sequence* of primal creation. Instead it shows nature in its present state—the clouds moving through the skies, the wild asses drinking from the *wadis,* the birds singing in the trees, man going out to work—in order to glorify YHWH for his authorship of a richly variegated, yet harmonious order of things. "Here," in A. van der Voort's words, "creation is not the chief thing, but rather material for illustration."[19] What it illustrates is the majesty, intelligence, and generosity of the God who authored and continually sustains this fascinating panorama of natural wonders. The created order is testimony to the wisdom of YHWH,[20] that is, his capacity to conceive and to craft marvelous things. Creation is the starting point for Psalm 104, but the end point is the God to whom it witnesses, the God encountered in the experience of wonder in the presence of nature. This experience might have led a philosopher to argue for the existence of God from the evident design of the world. It leads a psalmist to sing a magnificent hymn to the creator, upon whom all depend.

The only sour note in this exuberant psalm appears in its last verse:

> May sinners disappear from the earth,
> and the wicked be no more. (Ps. 104:35)

In a worldview in which even Leviathan was formed for benign purposes and continues to delight his creator, only humanity is capable of posing a challenge to God. The recognition of the possibility of human evil and its stubborn persistence suggests how humanity may participate in the grand cosmogonic drama. Humans do so by moral action, action in which the benevolent creator takes delight. The implication of this discordant last verse is that the bright and cheerful vision of the created order which has been the psalmist's subject is not fully in force so long as people resist the creator's will. The great struggle for the altogether good world has moved from cosmogonic myth into the human community and perhaps the human heart as well.

Genesis 1 also has a certain liturgical flavor, as we shall see, but its style is far from hymnic. Indeed, in vivid contrast with Psalm 104, the first chapter of the Torah exhibits an austere self-control: no burst of praise here, no expression of the author's feelings, no heartfelt petition, but only a highly regular and repetitive description of the *process* of creation, step by step, day by day, without sound or color. The tone is didactic; the chapter teaches a lesson about the organization and rulership of the world. Its concern is not praise, but order, and the lesson, as we shall soon see, is one that has practical implications.

Given the high degree of similarity of these two texts, different though they are in tone and purpose, the question arises as to which has priority. Although we are not given certainty in such matters, the likely answer is that Psalm 104 predates Genesis 1.[21]

In light of the roots of the Leviathan figure in Bronze Age ex-trabiblical texts, it would seem probable that a creation account in which he figures, however transformed, is older than one that has purged him by name altogether, speaking instead only of "great sea monsters." The demythologization that Psalm 104 represents has thus gone a step further in Genesis 1. Moreover, the six days of active creation in Genesis find no echo in the psalm, and the Sabbath, with which Genesis 2:1–3 crowns and consummates the activities of the previous chapter, is not mentioned. As we shall see in some detail, the heptadic principle pervades and structures Genesis 1:1–2:3. The absence of the number seven in Psalm 104[22] is difficult to explain if the psalm depends even indirectly upon the opening of Genesis. The Sabbath, infrequently mentioned in the Hebrew Bible, became increasingly important in the literature of the Exile and the Second Temple period.[23] It is exceedingly im-probable that a later text would delete the Sabbath where an earlier text featured it. The likelihood is that Genesis has struc-tured an old and traditional picture of creation around the sacred institution of the Sabbath. This is not to say that the author(s) of Genesis 1:1–2:3 at any stage in its composition deliberately fol-lowed Psalm 104 while writing the creation account. Rather, my point is that the two passages stand within the same stream of thought, with the Genesis text chronologically later, even as its present placement as the overture to the Torah renders it axiologi-cally prior.

If, on the one end, Psalm 104 influenced Genesis 1, on the other, it displays an extraordinary likeness to "The Hymn to the Aten," an Egyptian composition that can be dated with certainty to the reign of the Pharaoh Amunhotpe IV in the mid-fourteenth cen-tury B.C.E.[24] Because of his quasi-monotheistic reform, this Phar-aoh has attracted an extraordinary amount of attention, much of it admiring, almost from the dawn of modern Egyptology in the preceding century.[25] Briefly put, his reform consisted of a spirited campaign to suppress the god Amun, who had become amal-gamated with the ancient sun god Re, and to replace Amun-Re with the Aten, the solar disc understood as the manifestation of a universal creator god. In devotion to the Aten, Amunhotpe IV changed his own name to Akhenaten ("the effective spirit of Aten"), thus purging himself of his association with the traditional figure Amun (Amunhotpe means "Amun is satisfied"). He also took the more explosive step of founding a new capital city, Akhetaten, "Horizon of the Aten," in a deliberate slight to the splendid temple-city Thebes, with its associations with Amun and the old priestly establishment. Akhenaten had the names of Amun and other gods—even the plural word "gods" itself—effaced on existing monuments. For this he has been celebrated in modern times as the first monotheist (although whether his reform is correctly classed as monotheistic has been doubted[26]), and connections with the alleged "Mosaic Revolution" of biblical Israel have been suggested and debated. Among the more fanciful and historically implausible connections advanced is Sigmund Freud's belief that Moses grew up in Akhenaten's court and from him absorbed what became the doctrinal nucleus of Judaism.[27] In such speculations as these, we see the influence of the Romantic concept of the "great man" theory of history, with its passion for locating change, especially positive change, in the biographies of individuals rather than in larger patterns of social, political, and economic life. Writing in the same decade in which Freud's *Moses and Monotheism* was to appear, even the great Egyptologist James Henry Breasted went so far as to liken Akhenaten to Jesus and (giving away his Romantic bias) to Wordsworth and Millet as well.[28] Today scholars are more likely to note the elements of traditionalism in Akhenaten's reform, as well as its possible motivation in a desire to recapture for the monarchy the power and money that had been diverted into priestly hands.[29] In stressing these factors, the more recent scholarship conforms to the current tendency of most historians of all periods and cultures to place primacy upon the social roots and contextual limitations of historical change.

Even if one refrains from the Romantic idealization of Akhenaten and his reform and from the simplistic ascription of Israelite monotheism to this particular moment in Egyptian history, the fact remains that "The Hymn to the Aten" exhibits too many resemblances to Psalm 104 for this to be a matter of coincidence.[30] Indeed, one popular annotated translation of the "Hymn," which runs a page and a half, lists fully seven parallels to the psalm.[31] In several of these, even the wording of the two pieces is remarkably similar. The "Hymn" proclaims to the Aten that

> At daybreak, when you arise on the horizon
>
> All the world, they do their work.

The psalmist, although he celebrates not the solar disc but its divine maker, tells us of the lions that

> [22]When the sun rises, they come home
>   and crouch in their dens.
> [23]Man then goes out to his work,
>   to his labor until the evening. (Ps. 104:22–23)

Similarly, each poet interrupts his survey of creation with an exclamation of the marvelous character of the deity who is able to design it and bring it about. Again the language is similar:

> How manifold it is, what you have made!
> They are hidden from the face [of man].
> O sole god, like whom there is no other!
> You did create the world according to your desire
> When you were alone.
>
> How effective they are, your plans, O lord of eternity!
>
> How many are the things You have made, O LORD;
>   You have made them all with wisdom;
>   the earth is full of Your creations. (Ps. 104:24)

The deity's continuing sustenance of his creation also commands the attention of both authors. Akhenaten tells us that

> You set every man in his place,
> You supply their necessities:
> Everyone has his food, and his time of life is reckoned.

The psalmist likewise proclaims that

> [14]You make the grass grow for the cattle,
>   and herbage for man's labor
>   that he may get food out of the earth—
> [15]wine that cheers the hearts of men,
>   oil that makes the face shine,
>   and bread that sustains man's life. (Ps. 104:14–15)

In fact, the last verse of the "Hymn" quoted above is strikingly reminiscent of the psalmist's remark about the dependence of all life (or perhaps, in context, all sea creatures) upon YHWH for food:

> All of them look to You
>   to give them their food when it is due. (Ps. 104:27)

The last example of close verbal parallels between "The Hymn to the Aten" and Psalm 104 is the common picture of the waters cascading down the mountains. First the "Hymn":

> For you have set a Nile in heaven,
> That it may descend for them and make
>   waves upon the mountains.

Compare the preceding with these two verses in the psalm:

> [6]You made the deep cover the earth as a garment;
>   the waters stood above the mountains.

> [10]You made springs gush forth in torrents;
>   they make their way between the hills. (Ps. 104:6, 10)

In addition to these verbal correspondences, we should also note other, less precise, similarities between the two great compositions from antiquity. Each begins with an evocation of divine light, the "Hymn" with sunrise, the psalm with YHWH's wrapping himself "in a robe of light."[32] Each, in turn, includes a general evocation of night and therein a specific allusion to lions, which in the "Hymn" leave their dens at night and in the psalm "roar for prey," coming home at sunrise.[33] Each composition not only speaks generally of beasts and birds, trees and plants, but also makes special reference to the sea and both the living things and the ships on it.[34] Although one might find a few of these elements paralleled in other biblical literature, this degree of correspondence between an Israelite and a Gentile composition is almost unique,[35] and some of the specific images that the two poems share are, within the Bible, peculiar to Psalm 104. The evidence would seem conclusive that "The Hymn to the Aten" has influenced the psalm. Precisely how, we cannot and need not determine. Certainly the extreme view of Arthur Weigall earlier in this century that Akhenaten is the author of the psalm[36] is to be rejected. The case for connecting Moses with Akhenaten is weak enough; we need not indulge the groundless fantasy that this Pharaoh converted to YHWHism and therefore introduced a number of distinctive Syro-Palestinian features (such as Leviathan) into his religion. More reasonable is the hypothesis of a number of scholars that the "Hymn" influenced the psalm indirectly, after a long process of mediation through the West Semitic world.[37] The details of the process are presently unknown. They may remain so.

The larger theology of "The Hymn to the Aten" and Psalm 104 is one that celebrates, in Breasted's words, "the universal presence of God in nature" and the "mystic conviction of the recognition of that presence by all creatures."[38] If one may speak of the experience that gave rise to these two poems, which is, in turn, the experience they convey, it is what Abraham Joshua Heschel calls "radical amazement." "Awareness of the divine begins with wonder," Heschel writes, and "wonder or radical amazement, the state of maladjustment to words and notions, is therefore a prerequisite for an authentic awareness of that which is." In contradiction to the astonishment one experiences at this or that individual marvel, "radical amazement refers to all of reality."[39] The goal of these two poems is to evoke this experience by shocking us out of our familiarity with the natural order in which we find ourselves, by confronting us with the perpetual newness of nature and its humbling oddness. The reverence that follows from radical amazement, however, is not reverence for nature, perceived according to a rather pantheistic worldview. This is where Breasted's repeated references to modern "poets of nature" such as Wordsworth and to "a veritable gospel of the beauty of light," such as was preached by John Ruskin,[40] can be profoundly misleading. These two ancient hymns are too theocentric to be so quickly assimilated to the "natural supernaturalism" of the Romantic poets and painters and their heirs.[41] The recipient of the praise here is not nature, but the deity, and nature is but the all-encompassing evidence of his supernatural wisdom and the medium by which people come to suspect it. The point of the two poems is not contemplation. It is devotion.

For Yehezkel Kaufmann, convinced of the absolute uniqueness of Israelite religion, "The Hymn to the Aten" is not embarrassing, because it "regards the physical sun itself as a divine being" and conceives "the creative force of the sun . . . in wholly pagan terms of incorporation or generation."[42] The latter point is at least overstated, because the "Hymn" stresses that the Aten alone created the world, according to his desire, and that the world, in turn, is dependent upon him. The difference between this view and Psalm 104 is, if it exists at all, slight. Neither composition speaks of *creatio ex nihilo,* and the image of YHWH planting the cedars of Lebanon in Psalm 104:16, for example, does not imply any greater divine sovereignty over nature than the Aten manifests. In short, YHWH is more within nature, and the Aten more outside it, than Kaufmann's stark polarity of Israelite religion and "paganism" can accommodate.[43]

Kaufmann's other point, however, that "The Hymn to the Aten" "regards the physical sun itself as a divine being" has more validity. To be sure, the degree to which Akhenaten's deity was thought to be *limited* to the solar disc is not ascertainable. It is surely not the physical sun as we perceive it that he worshiped. On the other hand, it is telling that the "Hymn" never speaks of the creation of the sun: how can a god create himself? Psalm 104, in contrast, specifically mentions YHWH's creation of the solar body and ascribes to YHWH the onset of darkness.[44] Night is not, as in the Egyptian poem, the absence of the god, but something he causes. It is not a dangerous period of divine dormancy, but another manifestation of YHWH's creative sovereignty. Indeed, there is no evidence that the "robe of light" that the God of Israel dons at the beginning of the psalm emanates from the sun. The relegation of the creation of the heavenly bodies to a much later point in the survey of nature suggests that the primordial light is here differentiated from sunlight, an idea inconceivable to Akhenaten and his theologians. This demythologization of the sun proceeds a step further in Genesis 1, where, as we have seen, God creates light on the *first* day and the sun only on the *fourth.* In Psalm 104, light is not one of the things that YHWH *creates* at all. In sum, we are entitled to speak of a progressive growth of the sovereignty of the deity over nature from the "Hymn to the Aten" through Psalm 104 to Genesis 1 (both intermediate stages being presently irrecoverable)[45] so long as we do not slip into the reassuring but tendentious dichotomy of "monotheism" and "paganism."

All the exuberance and exultation that Psalm 104 exhibits and evokes must not permit us to forget the dark side of the picture. Though the combat myth has faded to the point that Leviathan seems never to have posed a threat to YHWH, it is also true that YHWH is not here portrayed as the creator of the waters that Leviathan once personified. A close examination of vv. 6–9 shows instead that God only established the boundaries that the primordial waters dare not cross, "so that they never again cover the earth." Similarly, though vv. 19–23 make it clear that darkness is at God's beck, it too is not his creature; in the new order, darkness must yield daily to the sun, which "knows when to set." Order is now a matter of *the maintenance of boundaries,* and even when the forces of chaos pose no threat to the creator, they still persist, and their persistence qualifies—and defines—his world mastery. In this too Psalm 104 adumbrates the great cosmogony of Genesis 1:1–2:3.

6. Creation in Seven Days

The formal feature that most strikingly sets Genesis 1:1–2:3[1] off from its Egyptian, Mesopotamian, and Israelite antecedents and parallels is its heptadic structure. In none of the other literature that we have examined so far do we find anything reminiscent of the schema of seven days of creation that dominates the overture to the Bible. There is, to be sure, no dearth of scholars who argue that even here the seven days is a late imposition upon a text that originally exhibited no arithmetic principle of structure. These scholars are not without evidence. Already in the Mishnah it was observed that "the world was created with ten utterances,"[2] a statement that is countered in the Gemara with the position that there were actually only nine.[3] The lower figure, which expresses the occurrences of the clause "God said," is then disputed on the ground that the first word of the Torah *(bĕrē'šît)* must be included in the tabulation: does not the psalmist tell us that "By the *word* of the LORD the heavens were made"?[4] More recently, scholars have observed that two acts of creation characterize both the third and the sixth day, so that the total number of creative acts reaches eight, and it has been pointed out that the creation of the sky as we know it "cuts across the second and third day."[5] To give one last example of many that might be cited, scholars have often detected a contradiction between God's creation through a verbal command alone and his creation through more vivid, anthropomorphic images—separating, making, and setting.[6] All of this suggests an unevenness in Genesis 1:1–2:3 which belies our first impression of an exceedingly schematic creation story with nothing out of place. The unevenness has occasionally emboldened biblical critics to reconstruct the *Urtext* with a freedom and a zeal that would have shamed Bowdler.[7]

Against the claims of those who see the heptadic structure of

Genesis 1:1–2:3 as a late imposition, one can cite the remarkable discoveries of Umberto Cassuto.[8] Cassuto found that the heptadic principle extends far deeper into the text than had been thought. Hardly limited to the seven days in which the action takes place, groups or multiples of seven appear throughout the passage. The first verse, for example, consists of seven words; the second, of fourteen. Of the three dominant terms of v. 1—"God," "heaven," and "earth"—the first occurs thirty-five times in Genesis 1:1–2:3, and the third twenty-one times.[9] (If one follows the scholarly consensus that ends the first creation account after 2:4a, this last heptad disappears.)[10] In the description of the first day, "light" is mentioned five times and "day" (which 1:5 defines as its synonym), twice: the total is again seven. The expression $k\hat{i}\ \underline{t}\hat{o}b$ ("that it was good") appears seven times; mysteriously omitted on the second day,[11] it occurs twice on the third and the sixth, the last time with extra force ("very good").[12] The paragraph devoted to the seventh day consists of thirty-five words, twenty-one of which form three sentences of seven words,[13] each of which includes the expression "the seventh day." Building on Cassuto's observation, Aryeh Toeg notes that the first sentence of the paragraph[14] includes five words, that is, two fewer than we expect, but that the last sentence, which follows the three heptads,[15] consists of nine words and thus compensates for the deficiency of the incipit, leaving us with five sentences that average seven words apiece for a total of thirty-five.[16]

Some of Cassuto's examples are less convincing than these. For example, he claims that seven terms for light ($\hat{o}r$) appear in the paragraph devoted to the fourth day, but this requires us to count only the nouns of this root ($\hat{o}r$ and $m\bar{a}\hat{o}r$) and to neglect the two occurrences of the denominative verb $h\bar{e}\hat{i}r$, "to shine." He correctly observes that the word $mayim$ ("water") appears altogether seven times in the descriptions of the second and third days, but why count these together and discount the other occurrences in the descriptions of the first day or, for that matter, of the fifth?[17] Nonetheless, even if one demurs on these points, Cassuto is surely right to conclude his discussion of the significance of seven in

Genesis 1:1–2:3 with the remark that "it is impossible to think that all this is nothing but coincidence."[18]

The question, rather, is what the heptadic structure proves. For Cassuto, it proves the compositional homogeneity of the passage: no text with so many heptads subtly threaded in from beginning to end could possibly have been stitched together from preexistent documents. This is a point that scholars would be well advised to concede to Cassuto, although many have not done so. Our discussion, in any event, will treat Genesis 1:1–2:3 as entirely the work of the Priestly source (P) of the Pentateuch,[19] and will prescind from the highly conjectural enterprise of reconstructing a more "consistent" text. The futility of that enterprise is nicely demonstrated by the fact that so many eminent exegetes over the centuries have missed the extent of the heptadic structure that Cassuto developed. My treating the text as a homogeneous composition of P does not imply, however, that the Priestly tradent created it *ex nihilo.* On the contrary, my discussion of Psalm 104 sought to demonstrate that Genesis 1:1–2:3 stands toward the end of a long chain of tradition whose beginnings lie outside Israel altogether. This Priestly author did not stitch together anyone else's documents, but neither did he make up out of whole cloth the world picture that his composition projects, nor did he work in the absence of traditional lore about the sequence of creation. It was this traditional lore that served as the raw material for his impressive authorial labors. There is no evidence that the raw material had featured creation in seven days.

The absence of the idea of creation in seven days elsewhere in the ancient Near East must not be taken to mean that Genesis 1:1–2:3 is radically discontinuous with its cultural background. We shall discuss at length the fact that it stands in considerable continuity with some Egyptian, Mesopotamian, and Canaanite literature, and not merely with Psalm 104 and its Egyptian antecedents. In one case especially, the case of the Babylonian *akītu* festival, scholars have long been encouraged to believe they have found an extrabiblical antecedent to creation over a period of several days. The *akītu* was a New Year's festival that occupied the

first eleven days of the vernal month Nisan.[20] On the fourth day
the creation epic, the *Enuma elish*, was read, in all likelihood in
reactualization of the primordial events that the great poem narrates. If so, then the New Year's festival must be seen not simply
as a celebration of a calendrical milestone, but as an actual renewal
or re-creation of the ordered world. Here it is essential to recall the
caveat in Part I[21] that creation in the ancient Near East was not a
matter of cosmogony as a modern westerner would conceive it, but
rather a decisive instance of the victory of the forces of order
(which are necessarily social and political) over potent opposition:
what emerges from creation is a secure and ordered community
whose center of authority is unchallenged, effective, and just. If
we keep this in mind, then the combination in the *Enuma elish* of
the defeat of Tiamat, the acclamation of Marduk as king, and the
construction of his capital (Babylon) and his royal palace (the
temple Esagila) will not strike us as incongruent, nor shall we be
inclined to see the *akītu* festival "neither in terms of repetition of
the past nor in terms of future fulfillment, but rather in terms of
a difficult and incongruous present" in need of "rectification."[22] In
this worldview the present is *always* incongruous and in need of
rectification because social, political, and natural chaos (which
were not distinguished) are never far away, and the efficacious
recitation of primordial events works for the fulfillment of hopes
for the newborn year. The recital of the creation epic on the fourth
of Nisan[23] is not to be conceived as the center or the essence of
the New Year's festival, and the sequence of the festival cannot
be associated one-to-one with the order of events in the epic. It
can be said, however, that the renewal of cosmic order is a central
theme and function of the *akītu* and that this cannot be irrelevant
to the recitation of a creation text during the eleven days of this
ritual in Babylon.

As conjectural as any reconstruction of the *akītu* and its meaning
must be, its relevance to biblical Israel is even murkier. On the one
hand, one could claim that the cultic calendars of the Hebrew Bible
provide for no New Year at all. The term *rō̆š haššānâ*, which later
became the name of the New Year's Day, occurs only once in the

Hebrew Bible, at the onset of Ezekiel's vision of the new temple,[24] and there it appears to designate "the beginning of the year," as a literal translation of the Hebrew would suggest. The precise day within this unspecified period is the tenth of an equally unspecified month, but scholars have long been inclined to make a connection with the tenth of Tishri, which in the Priestly Code is the Day of Atonement.[25] The rites of this autumnal holy day parallel those of the fifth of Nisan in the *akītu,* when the Babylonian priest would purify the temple with the head of a decapitated ram in a ritual called *kuppuru* ("to purge," "to expiate" in Akkadian).[26] Tishri 10 is the most probable date for Ezekiel's vision, but it bears mention that the tenth of Nisan is also important in Priestly thought. On that date the Israelite household was to select its paschal lamb,[27] and in the significant variant of the Priestly calendar that appears in Ezekiel, the priest purifies the temple with a slaughtered bull on the *first* of Nisan and possibly on the first of Tishri as well.[28] The oddity is that in spite of all the close parallels with Babylonian practice, none of the *biblical* texts clearly designates any single day as New Year's.

In the liturgical calendars of the Pentateuch, the first day of the seventh month (that is, Tishri) appears only twice, once as a day of "complete rest, a sacred occasion commemorated by loud blasts" and once as "a sacred occasion . . . a day when the horn is sounded."[29] Because the acclamation of a king was one of the several instances in which the horn was blown in ancient Israel,[30] scholars have suspected that Tishri 1 served as a celebration of YHWH's enthronement, as the analogy of the Babylonian *akītu* festival, with its recitation of the *Enuma elish,* would suggest. This suspicion draws added strength from the fact that at least by early Tannaitic times, this date appears as one of four New Year's Days in the Jewish liturgical calendar.[31] Indeed, the other three soon became only a matter of scholarly lore, and it has long been the case that the first of Tishri has been known simply as *rō'š haššānâ,* "New Year"—a name it never has in the Bible. The liturgy for the Rabbinic New Year features both the blowing of the horn *(šôpār)* and the acclamation of YHWH's kingship. The position of some scholars that this particular set of connections is late and its parallel with Babylonian practice, presumably coincidental[32] strains the imagination.

The fact that the first day of the seventh month, whatever its character, is mentioned only twice in the Hebrew Bible has long raised a suspicion in the minds of critical scholars that it is a holy day of late origin. Indeed, not only is it missing in the cultic calendar of Ezekiel, but it is without mention even in most Pentateuchal calendars. The Deuteronomic Code knows of no such sacred occasion nor of any explicit commemoration of the change of years.[33] In the two brief calendars in Exodus, it is the fall "Feast of Ingathering" (which the other calendars call the "Feast of Booths") that is described as occurring "at the end of the year" or "at the turn of the year."[34] The great Norwegian scholar Sigmund Mowinckel argued that originally New Year's Day, the Day of Atonement, and Booths were not distinguished.[35] In the postexilic era, the unity of the original fall festival of enthronement, purgation, and fertility was shattered, with the result that the Jewish calendar has ever since fixed three festivals within the first three weeks of Tishri. When, under the pressure of the Babylonian example, the vernal month Nisan came to be fixed as the first of the year,[36] there developed the anomaly of a New Year's Day in the seventh month. The Mishnah mitigates the oddness of this by counting both Nisan 1 and Tishri 1 as New Year's Days, only for different purposes, somewhat like our calendrical, fiscal, and academic years.[37] It cannot be assumed, however, that the Mishnaic system of New Year's Days represents only a late, learned attempt to account for the fact that the New Year's of the Torah comes half a year after the first month. Some biblical scholars have, in fact, posited two New Year's festivals in early Israel, one in the fall and one in the spring, perhaps at different shrines.[38] In spite of the clear Babylonian practice of a spring *akītu,* there is Mesopotamian evidence to support this supposition. In origin, the *akītu* was a fall festival, and in Ur it was celebrated twice yearly, in the spring and the fall, until the neo-Babylonian period.[39] The practice of Ur is a striking anticipation of the Mishnaic law and a strong indication that the Mishnah is conservative here rather than innovative.

On the basis of the two old calendars in Exodus, one cannot say how long the fall festival lasted, although they agree that the vernal festival of Passover is to last seven days. Indeed, this is the position of all the biblical codes. The Deuteronomic and the Priestly (P) materials do, however, define the autumnal Festival of Booths too as a seven-day feast.[40] Now if we put together the various threads that we have been spinning, we can formulate a plausible speculation (although nothing more than that) about the origins of P's seven-day creation scheme in Genesis 1:1–2:3. If in early Israel there was a seven-day festival in the fall and again (although with differences) in the spring and if this festival in either form or both was at least in part a celebration of the New Year, with the reactualization of cosmogony and enthronement, as was the case in some places and times in Mesopotamia, then it would be natural to think of the creation of the world as occurring within a seven-day period. When New Year's Day split off from Booths or Passover (or both) to become fixed on Tishri 1 or Nisan 1 (or both), as is the case in some P material, the old seven-day festivals would have lost their cosmogonic character, and creation would have come increasingly to be associated with the New Year, as was the case in Babylon. Again, we are reduced to hypothesis, because no biblical text explicitly associates any New Year's Day with creation. On the other hand, early in the Rabbinic period, one finds a debate between Rabbi Eliezer and Rabbi Joshua (both of whom did their most important teaching about 80–120 C.E.) which has striking connections to the material that we have been discussing:

Rabbi Eliezer says, From what text do we know that it was in Tishri that the world was created? Because the Bible says, "And God said, 'Let the earth sprout vegetation: seed-bearing plants, fruit trees. . . .'" In what month does the earth put forth vegetation and the trees are full of fruit? You have to say that this is Tishri, and that period was the rainy season, so that the rains fell and caused vegetation to sprout, as the Bible says, "a flow would well up from the ground."[41]

Rabbi Joshua says, From what text do we know that it was in Nisan that the world was created? Because the Bible says "The earth brought forth vegetation: seed-bearing plants . . . and trees of every kind." In what month is the earth full of vegetation and trees are bringing out fruit? You have to say that this is Nisan, and that period was the season when cattle and game and birds mate, as the Bible says, "The meadows are clothed with flocks, [the valleys mantled with grain]."[42]

The assumption common to both Tannaitic debaters here is that the creation text of Genesis refers to the month in which New Year's Day falls, that is, either Tishri or Nisan. The other two minor New Year's Days of Rabbinic law, Ellul 1 and Shevat 1 (or 15), are not considered, nor are any of the (other) months contiguous with Nisan and Tishri. One is tempted to say that these two months vie for the honor because in them alone we see both a New Year's Day and an older seven-day festival, but this would be to go beyond the evidence and imply Rabbinic memory of the changeover from a seven-day to a one-day New Year, which is unlikely. In any event, the method of Rabbi Eliezer and Rabbi Joshua is to cite verses from Genesis 1–2 that suggest an autumnal or a vernal setting, respectively. In a sense it was Rabbi Eliezer whose position was to win out, because it is in the Rabbinic liturgy for Rosh Hashanah (that is, Tishri 1) that Jews recite the words, "This is the day on which you began your acts of creation—the anniversary of the first day."[43]

The absence of an explicit biblical association of New Year's Day with creation must not be taken to exclude implicit associations. We have, for example, already observed that the story of Noah and his survival of the great deluge is a reiteration of primordial creation. In the end the lethal watery chaos yields to habitable land, and upon Noah, whose very name symbolizes relief from the curse of Adam,[44] is reenjoined the primal charge to "be fertile and increase, and fill the earth" and take charge of it.[45] In light of this, it is of great import that according to Genesis 8:13 (P), it is on Nisan 1 that "the waters began to dry from the earth" and Noah saw dry land for the first time in a year. It is appropriate that this should have happened in the spring, that is, at the conclusion of the rainy season. We must not, however, miss the fact that it is precisely on the spring New Year's Day that the habitable world (re)emerges from the chaotic waters. It cannot be coincidence that this occurs on the very day that the Babylonians commenced their *akītu.* In both examples, the biblical and the Babylonian, the occasion of the vernal New Year is associated with the subsidence of the lethal waters, the emergence of dry land, and the establishment of cosmic and civil order.[46]

If the date of the subsidence of the great deluge in Genesis 8:13 recalls Babylonian parallels, the image of creation as dry land emerging from the waters is equally suggestive of some Egyptian material. In Egypt it was often thought that life originated on a hillock that emerged from the primordial waters. In the "Book of the Dead," for example, the onset of the rule of the god Re is identified with the appearance of the primeval hillock:

Re began to appear as king, as one who existed before (the air-god) Shu had (even) lifted (heaven from earth), when he (Re) was on the primeval hillock which was in Hermopolis.[47]

In the Bible this idea can be detected in Ezekiel's oracles against the king of the island-state Tyre, who says, in his arrogance, "I am a god: I sit enthroned like a god in the heart of the seas." Elsewhere in the same chapter, the origin of the king of Tyre is called "Eden, the garden of God," "his holy mountain."[48] Here Eden is identified with Zion, God's mountain and seat of the Temple, and it is this primal paradise/sacred mountain that Ezekiel associates with the island on which Tyre stood. The grandeur of the Tyrean king and his special divine protection—until his own hubris fells him—recall God's reiteration to Noah of the Adamic charge to "be fertile and increase, and fill the earth," for "the fear and the dread of you shall be upon . . . everything with which the earth is astir."[49]

In Egypt "ultimately every temple which had a high place for its god probably considered that high place to be the place of creation. The pyramids themselves borrow this idea of a rising hill as a promise to the deceased Egyptian buried within the pyramid that he will emerge again into new being."[50] In light of this it is striking that apart from the emergence of land in Genesis 8:13, the other Pentateuchal event that occurs in Nisan is the erection of the Tabernacle, or portable Temple, meticulously constructed in the wilderness at the instruction of God through Moses.[51] If the vernal New Year's Day was thought to be the day creation began or was consummated, then it would be fitting for the original temple to have gone up on that day. This is to be expected on the basis of both Babylonian evidence (the construction of Esagila for the newly victorious creator god Marduk at the end of the *Enuma elish*) and Egyptian parallels (the Hermopolitan and other temples as the primeval hillock). In fact, we see here a general ancient Near Eastern mythos that identifies the temple with the world viewed *sub specie creationis*. In Joseph Blenkinsopp's words, "For P the deluge served not just as a paradigm of judgment but also as the Israelite version of the cosmogonic victory of the deity resulting in the building of a sanctuary for him."[52]

If Rosh Hashanah (Tishri 1) originally broke off from the seven-day festival of Tabernacles, then it is equally plausible that the spring New Year's Day (Nisan 1), of which we have been speaking, broke off from the seven-day festival Passover. J. B. Segal advances detailed arguments in support of his hypothesis that the Hebrew Passover is best seen as a New Year's festival.[53] To his points I would add that the story of the exodus from Egypt, which serves as a charter myth for Passover, manifests the same pattern of a cosmogonic victory over lethal waters, the salvific appearance of dry land, and the construction of the sanctuary. The pattern is most vivid in the great hymn that Moses and Israel sing after their successful passage through the Sea of Reeds.[54] In it we hear of YHWH's ferocious combat against the Pharaonic army at the violent waters, combat that eventuates in his bringing his redeemed to his temple. In this poetic version of the crossing of the sea, dry land is not mentioned, and it has been argued that the original picture of the event was one of "a storm-tossed sea that is directed against the Egyptians by the breath of the Deity":[55] Israel survives the hostile waters; the Egyptian army does not. In the preceding prose account, however, which is almost certainly a later composition, "the waters were split, and the Israelites went into the sea on dry ground," whereas "the waters turned back and covered the chariots and the horsemen—Pharaoh's entire army."[56] Here again God's redemptive benevolence manifests itself in the appearance of dry land out of the death-dealing flood. After an assertion of YHWH's incomparable status within the pantheon, the hymn concludes with an acclamation of his kingship within his temple:

> [17]You brought them and planted[57] them in Your mountain,
> The place You made to dwell in, O Lord,
> The sanctuary, O Lord, which Your hands established.
> [18]The Lord will reign for ever and ever! (Exod. 15:17–18)

This pattern of combat at the sea, the miraculous appearance of dry land, the construction of the temple, and the enthronement of the deity recalls both the *Enuma elish* (and its Canaanite congeners) and, more distantly, the Egyptian notion of the primeval hillock. The principal difference is that the charter myth for Passover claims to relate not primordial creation, but rather the decisive instance of historical redemption. The enemy is not the sea (which is totally under YHWH's control), but Pharaoh. In short, if, as I think certain, a cosmogonic combat myth underlies the story of Israel's crossing the Sea of Reeds, that myth has been historicized. The historicization, however, has only relativized the cosmogonic myth; it has not replaced it. If Noah reiterates Adam, he also anticipates Moses.

To conclude: we have seen that if creation is understood in the ancient Near Eastern context, then the Priestly scheme of seven days of creation has its precedents in the autumn and spring New Year's festivals of early Israel. To be sure, this theory explains the origins of neither the week nor the Sabbath.[58] The fact that Tabernacles and Passover were seven-day festivals in the earlier calendars suggests that this unit of time was already known before the P calendar came into being. What P has done is to play down the New Year, so much so that it designates no day as *rōʾš haššānâ* (in spite of, or perhaps because of, the existence and prominence of the Akkadian *rēš šatti*) and leaves us in doubt as to the nature of the "sacred occasion commemorated with loud blasts"[59] on Tishri 1 and the relationship of this day to Nisan 1 half a year earlier. The positive side of P's downplaying of New Year's Day is the assignment of cosmogonic significance to the Sabbath. It is now the Sabbath and not New Year's on which creation is completed, consummated, and mimetically reenacted by the worshiping community, the people of Israel. Although the Rabbinic Rosh Hashanah demonstrates that P's reassignment of cosmogonic themes from New Year's to Sabbath was either not total or not totally successful, the fact remains that P has routinized the profound experiences associated with the old enthronement festivals. The annual renewal of the world has become a weekly event.

7. Cosmos and Microcosm

The erection of the Tabernacle in Exodus 40:2, 17 on the vernal New Year's Day and the appearance of dry land to Noah on the same date are not the only connections of temple and creation in the Hebrew Bible. As we have seen, the old combat myth in its Mesopotamian form also joined cosmogony with temple building. In fact, the rites of Temple dedication in the Bible indicate that the connection of these great themes was not severed even in ancient Israel. 1 Kings 8, which narrates Solomon's dedication of his temple, is at pains to tell us that this took place in the seventh month, indeed during Tabernacles, the seven-day feast in the seventh month.[1] The parallel text in Chronicles depicts the dedication of the First Temple in two sets of seven-day festivals, the first for the altar and the second for the Feast of Tabernacles,[2] which apparently served as the general temple-dedication festival. The speech that Solomon makes on that occasion is structured in seven specific petitions.[3] Indeed, the construction of that Temple is said to have taken seven years,[4] and this too betrays a more general Near Eastern mythos, one that may well have relevance to the question of the origins and meaning of the Israelite Sabbath. Gudea, king of the Sumerian city Lagash toward the end of the twenty-second century B.C.E., held a seven-day festival of dedication for one of the temples that he built.[5] Closer in time and space to ancient Israel is a Ugaritic text that tells of the seven days that it took to build Baal's temple:

> They set fire to the house,
>   they inflamed the palace.
> One day passed, then two:
>   the fire ate the house,
>   the flames consumed the palace.
> Three days passed, then four:

the fire ate the house,
the flames consumed the palace.
Five days passed, then six:
the fire ate the house,
the flames consumed the palace.
Then, on the seventh day,
the fire died down in the house,
the flames died down in the palace;
the silver had turned into blocks,
the gold had become bricks.
Baal the Conqueror was glad:
"I have built my house of silver,
my palace of gold."[6]

The extinction of the flames on the seventh day of casting Baal's temple is strangely reminiscent of the biblical prohibitions against kindling a fire, baking, or boiling on the Sabbath.[7] It is possible, but far from demonstrable, that this Ugaritic passage witnesses to a Sabbath of sorts among the Canaanite antecedents of Israel. If so, then the fact that it should have taken exactly a week to cast Baal's temple may suggest a connection of the week or Sabbath with cosmogony/temple building which is far older than P and its seven-day creation scheme. In Loren Fisher's words, "If these temples were constructed in terms of 'seven,' it is really no wonder that the creation poem of Gen. i is inserted in a seven-day framework. One must speak of ordering the cosmos in terms of seven even as the construction of the microcosm must be according to the sacred number."[8] In any event, Solomon's dedication of his temple during the seven-day Festival of Tabernacles was hardly idiosyncratic. Jeroboam dedicated his temples during Tabernacles, although for reasons that remain unclear, he is said to have celebrated this feast a month later than what we expect.[9] Later, with the return of exiles from Babylonia at the end of the sixth century, Tabernacles alone is mentioned in connection with the reconstruction of the raised altar in Jerusalem.[10] In sum, whatever the origin, there was in Israel a clear association between temple building and the seven-day celebration of Tabernacles, just as there was an association, less clear but still likely, between that holiday and cosmogony. Given the more general involvement of temple building and creation in the ancient Near East, this is as we should expect.

In rabbinic Judaism, the festival that commemorates a Temple dedication is not Tabernacles *(sukkôt),* but Chanukkah, whose very name means "dedication" *(ḥănukkâ).* This holiday celebrates neither the dedication of Solomon's Temple nor that of its postexilic successor, but rather the rededication of the latter by the Maccabees in the winter of 165 B.C.E., exactly three years after it had been desecrated by the Seleucids.[11] The rabbis explained the eight days of Chanukkah by reference to a miracle involving the candelabra in the Temple:

When the Greeks entered the Temple, they desecrated all the oils in it, and when the Hasmonean dynasty defeated them, they searched, but could find only one flask of oil, which had been put away with the seal of the high priest. In it there was enough to burn for only one day. A miracle was performed, and from it they lit the lights for eight days.[12]

This etiology of the eight-day celebration is as suspect as it is famous. For one thing, in the time of the original Maccabees there was as yet no "Hasmonean dynasty"; Judah Maccabee was never declared king. This suggests considerable distance from the event. More serious is the fact that the episode of the single flask is first mentioned only in the anonymous passage in the Gemara, which is most unlikely to have been composed earlier than two hundred years after the event. In fact, even the insert into the special Rabbinic liturgy for Chanukkah *(ʿal hannissîm)* makes no mention of this miracle. This omission it shares with the books of the Apocrypha and the works of Josephus that describe the wars of the Hasmoneans and without which we would know precious little about the historical background of the festival. Second Maccabees terms the festival the "Feast of Tabernacles in the month of Kislev"[13] and describes its original celebration in a way that leaves no doubt that it was Tabernacles that was being celebrated, albeit more than two months late. Unfortunately, we are not told the precise reason for this manner of celebration. Some scholars believe that the Maccabees were simply making up the last holiday that they should have celebrated, but could not because of the occupied and defiled Temple. In support of this, one can cite the precedent of Hezekiah's observance of Passover a month late because of a similar impediment.[14] Indeed, the congregation's resolution to keep a second set of seven days thereafter as "seven more days of rejoicing" might well have suggested the idea of a second Tabernacles. If this was the Maccabees' motivation, they were indeed fortunate that the last holiday that had gone unobserved in the Temple had been Tabernacles, for, as we have seen, this was the festival most closely and explicitly associated with the dedication of temples in Israel. It has been plausibly proposed that there had long been an annual feast of the rededication of the Temple which was celebrated in connection with the observance of Tabernacles, so that the accounts of dedication that we have examined are more than historical notices: they reflect a continuing cultic reality.[15] If this is so, then the Maccabees were more traditional and Chanukkah less innovative than might otherwise be thought. Given the secure historical associations of Tabernacles with temple dedication in biblical Israel, it is surely an error to say, as does one contemporary scholar, that Judah Maccabee's "proclamation of the feast of Hanukkah had Hellenic, not Biblical precedents."[16]

The eight days of Chanukkah reflect the Priestly calendar, which has appended an eighth day of celebration to the seven days of Tabernacles.[17] This notion of eight days of temple dedication can also be detected in narrative texts of a Priestly cast. Moses' erection of the portable temple of the wilderness period on Nisan 1, that is, the vernal rather than the autumnal New Year's Day, begins an eight-day period that closes with the consumption of the sacrifices by the heavenly flames and the people's joyful recognition that their cultus has indeed found favor with their God.[18] This is undoubtedly related to the calendar in Ezekiel, which prescribes that the Temple be cleansed on the first and the seventh of Nisan.[19] The Maccabees, of course, would have followed the Pentateuchal rather than the Ezekielian norms and celebrated eight rather than seven days of Temple renewal. As Jews continue to celebrate the renewal of the world through the Sabbath, so they continue to celebrate the renewal of the long-vanished Temple through Chanukkah.

In chapter 6 I argued that Tabernacles and Passover displayed strong cosmogonic features, that they once served, in fact, as New Year's celebrations, and that celebration of these two festivals in seven days may be connected with the prehistory of P's seven-day creation scheme. Now we see that both festivals were also associated with the dedication or renewal of temples and that in the case of Tabernacles, this association endured at least into the second century B.C.E. In light of the nearly universal connection of temples and cosmogony,[20] this is to be expected. One recalls here the fact that on the fifth day of the *akītu,* the Babylonian priest would cleanse the temple of Marduk of ritual contamination with the severed head of a ram; this followed the recitation of the great cosmogonic poem, *Enuma elish,* on the fourth day. There is no reason to think that the historical character of the religion of Israel, its emphasis upon the exodus and the conquest of the Land, altogether replaced these older, all-pervasive myths and rituals of cosmogony. My investigation leads me to reject Roland de Vaux's opinion that the key to the Israelite Temple lay "not in myths nor in cosmology, but in Israel's history, for the religion of Israel is not a religion of myths nor a nature religion, but a historical one."[21] This propounds a false dichotomy. To give only one example, Israel comfortably accepted both a cosmological and a historical etiology of the Sabbath: the latter is *both* a mimetic reenactment of the creator God's primordial rest *and* an enduring memorial to Israel's relief from slavery after the exodus.[22] There is no indication of a tension between cosmology and history in this instance. The two could coexist nicely, for they reinforce each other: history concretizes cosmology, and cosmology lifts history above the level of the mundane.

In light of the homology of temple and created world, we expect to encounter in the reports of each building project reminiscences of the other, and in this expectation we are not disappointed. Peter

Kearney observes that P's instructions about the Tabernacle in Exodus 25–31 occur in seven distinct speechs of YHWH to Moses.[23] Alone, this observation is inadequate to demonstrate a connection between P's temple-building project in the wilderness and P's world-building project in Genesis 1:1–2:3. Not every heptad suggests creation; most do not. But Kearney goes on to point out that the sole subject of the seventh address is the high importance of sabbatical observance. Indeed, the conclusion of this last speech is an explicit reference to the sort of etiology of the Sabbath that we find in Genesis 1:1–2:3, and in language that is more similar than coincidence will allow:

For in six days the LORD made heaven and earth, and on the seventh day he ceased from work and was refreshed. (Exod. 31:17)

On the other hand, Kearney's efforts to connect the instructions in each of the first six addresses in Exodus 25–31 with the acts of creation in the six days of Genesis 1:1–2:3 are implausible.[24] We may take as our example his claim that the mention of Aaron's setting out lamps to burn from evening to morning in the first speech is to correspond with God's bringing light into darkness on the first day of creation.[25] The problem with this is that Aaron's lamps are mentioned in only 4 verses of the 197 that make up this speech and their position within it is neither first nor otherwise prominent. In point of fact, Aaron's lamps are simply one of dozens of items discussed in this mammoth first address, and the other five addresses show no more correspondence with their respective days in the hexaemeron than the first, or even less.

More ambiguous is the passage that summarizes the actual erection of the Tabernacle after all the instructions have been delivered and then executed. The passage begins with the identification of the date of this momentous event with the spring New Year's Day, Nisan 1.[26] This alone, for reasons we have already explored, raises the suspicion of cosmogonic events in the making. The narrative that this date formula introduces includes seven instances of the expression "just as the LORD had commanded Moses."[27] The effect of this is similar to the sevenfold appearance of the words "And God saw that it was good" (in slight variations) in Genesis 1.[28] In formal terms, each refrain serves as a structuring feature, although in a muted or secondary way. The theological substance of the two similar refrains is a pointed insistence upon the correspondence of the object constructed with the intentions of God. The temple and the world both result from the perfect realization of divine commandments, and nothing that God has commanded falls short of his expectations. In the case of the Tabernacle, the exactitude of the correspondence of construction with divine commandment is underscored powerfully by the notice that the master craftsman Bezalel has been endowed with the spirit of God *(rûaḥ 'ĕlōhîm)* for the purpose of this work. This is the same term that in P describes reality just before the great cosmogony: "a wind from God *(rûaḥ 'ĕlōhîm)* sweeping over the water" in the dark chaos.[29] Whether we are to understand this "wind from God" as the divine spirit stirring into activity after an eternity of lassitude is unclear. The term may mean nothing more than "a great wind," and the scene may be that of a gigantic oceanic vortex, or perhaps a storm at sea that raged from all eternity until dawn on the first day. In light of the other correspondences between the P texts about creation and those about the Tabernacle, the likelihood lies with the more positive and theological interpretation of *rûaḥ 'ĕlōhîm.*[30] In any event, the absence of the term anywhere between the two texts suggests the homology of world building and temple building, which is the burden of my argument here. That the homology is not explicit deprives us of the certainty we should like, but it is still the case that the cumulative effect of all these correspondences places the burden of proof upon those who would deny the point.

In a brilliant study entitled "The Structure of P," Joseph Blenkinsopp finds correspondences between the two building projects which elude Kearney. He too points to the fact that the execution formula ("X did according to all that YHWH God commanded him"), a classic indication of P, tends to appear in three episodes— the creation, the construction of the Tabernacle, and the establishment of the Tabernacle in the land of Israel and the allocation of that land among the tribes.[31] Blenkinsopp's list of the instances of the execution formula, however, does not bear out this claim of a triadic structure. Instead it suggests that the execution formula appears in most P narratives, including even Abraham's observ- ance of the commandment of circumcision and Israel's observance of the paschal sacrifice.[32] More supportive of Blenkinsopp's claim of a triadic structure is his identification of a "conclusion formula," which serves as a notice that significant work has been completed. Unlike the execution formula, this item does tend to cluster in three episodes—the etiology for the Sabbath, the construction of the Tabernacle, and the division of the land in Joshua.[33] For our purposes it is safe to ignore the last of these, except to note that the homology of created order/temple with the Land of Israel goes a long way toward explaining the origin of the idea of the sanctity of the land, which is of capital importance in Priestly theology.[34] The verbal parallels of the other two items in the triad are too striking, for coincidence:[35]

Creation	Temple
1. And God saw all that He made, and found it very good. (Gen. 1:31)	[13]And when Moses saw that they had performed all the tasks—as the LORD had com- manded, so they had done— Moses blessed them. (Exod. 39:43)
2. The heaven and the earth were finished, and all their array. (Gen. 2:1)	[32]Thus was completed all the work of the Tabernacle of the Tent of Meeting. (Exod. 39:- 32)
3. On the seventh day God finished the work which He had been doing, and He ceased on the seventh day from all the work which He had done. (Gen. 2:2)	[33]When Moses had finished the work, [34]the cloud covered the Tent of Meeting, and the Presence of the LORD filled the Tabernacle. (Exod. 40:33b–34)

4. And God blessed the seventh day and declared it holy, because on it God ceased from all the work of creation which He had done. (Gen. 2:3)

Exodus 39:43 (no. 1)

5. Gen 2:3 (no. 4)

[9]You shall take the anointing oil and anoint the Tabernacle and all that is in it to consecrate it and all its furnishings, so that it shall be holy. [10]Then anoint the altar of burnt offering and all its utensils to consecrate the altar, so that the altar shall be most holy. [11]And anoint the laver and its stand to consecrate it. (Exod. 40:9–11)

Collectively, the function of these correspondences is to underscore the depiction of the sanctuary as a world, that is, an ordered, supportive, and obedient environment, and the depiction of the world as a sanctuary, that is, a place in which the reign of God is visible and unchallenged, and his holiness is palpable, unthreatened, and pervasive. Our examination of the two sets of Priestly texts, one at the beginning of Genesis and the other at the end of Exodus, has developed powerful evidence that, as in many cultures, the Temple was conceived as a microcosm, a miniature world. But it is equally the case that in Israel (and probably also in the other cultures), the world—or, as I should say, the ideal or protological world, the world viewed *sub specie creationis*—was conceived, at least in Priestly circles, as a macro-temple, the palace of God in which all are obedient to his commands.

The double directionality of the homology of Temple and world must not be overlooked. One vector of the homology accounts for instances in which the Temple is depicted in cosmic terms, indeed in terms that recall the language of creation:

> He built His Sanctuary like the heavens,
>   like the earth that He established forever. (Ps. 78:69)

The placement of this verse after the election of Judah and Mount Zion makes it clear that the sanctuary in question is the great Temple of Jerusalem. Because *rāmîm* is not a common word for "heavens," scholars have often wanted to emend the text, but the existence of the expression *šmm rmm* ("high heavens") in Ugaritic and Phoenician[36] warns against this and, more important, suggests that the phraseology of Psalm 78:69 may not be so distant from that of Genesis 1:1 ("heaven [*šāmayim*] and earth") after all. The connection between the substance of the two verses (no genetic relationship or direct influence is here alleged) grows when one considers that the subject of "built" in the psalm is unquestionably YHWH and not, as is usually the case,[37] Solomon. The statement that God has built his Temple like the heavens and the earth may be a hyperbole of the order of another psalmist's claim that the low hill called Zion is actually "fair-crested, joy of all the earth."[38] It may be nothing more than an indication of the grandness of the Temple in the minds of those who worship there. On the other hand, the simile with "the earth that He established [*yĕsādāh*] forever" argues that the psalmist wishes to evoke the aura of cosmogony by associating the Temple with the belief that God "founded [*yĕsādāh*] the earth upon the ocean/set it on the netherstreams."[39] In fact, one manuscript reads *mē'ôlām* ("from eternity") instead of *lĕ'ôlām* ("forever") as the last word of Psalm 78:69,[40] and a plausible case has been made that *lĕ'ôlām* itself can mean "from eternity."[41] If this is how we are to interpret the word, then the claim for a cosmogonic or miscrocosmic conception of the Temple in this verse rests upon more than merely its evocation of creation language and its assignment of temple building directly to God. The foundation of the Temple is as unshakable as the Earth itself because the same agent established them both through an act of the same sort.

If the double directionality of the homology of temple and world sometimes yields texts such as Psalm 78:69, in which the Temple is described as a world, it also yields texts in which the world is described as a temple:

> ¹Thus said the LORD:
> The heaven is My throne
> And the earth is My footstool:
> Where could you build a house for Me,
> What place could serve as My abode?
> ²All this was made by My hand,
> And thus it all came into being
>
> —declares the LORD.
>
> Yet to such a one I look:
> To the poor and broken-hearted,
> Who is concerned about My word. (Isa. 66:1–2)

To de Vaux, who rejects the idea of a cosmic conception of the Temple; these verses could only mean that "YHWH has no need of any Temple."⁴² *Any* Temple? The point seems rather to be that the Temple presently under construction (the Second) is superfluous because *YHWH already has his Temple,* "the heaven and the earth"—creation. It is creation that serves as the palace of the divine king, the site of his throne and footstool. Like any good ancient Near Eastern monarch, YHWH shows special solicitude for the poor and destitute, and for these people his enthronement is a dramatic instance of redemption. The target of the prophetic oracle in Isaiah 66:1–2 is those who, bringing coals to Newcastle, build a *temple* in the *world,* all the while neglecting the ethical implications of the creator God's cosmic sovereignty. If I may bring an analogy from the Psalms, these people are like those who imagine that their sacrifices feed God, whereas, in fact, as he admonishes:

> Were I hungry, I would not tell you,
> for Mine is the world and all it holds. (Ps. 50:12)

It is God's authorship *of* the world that establishes his sovereign independence *from* the world and demythologizes all human efforts to enthrone him *within* the world. In Isaiah 66:1–2, the homology of Temple and world cease to function as a charter myth for the earthly Temple. The cosmic archetype, now broken loose from its earthly antitype, has been set against the antitype with potent effect: the Temple within the world is absurd because the world is itself a temple.

The homology of temple and world also accounts for the prominence of the idea of a new creation in texts that date from the period when the new Temple, the Second, was under construction in Jerusalem at the end of the sixth century B.C.E. In fact, the reconstruction of the temple-city is explicitly called an act of creation in a text whose similarity to Genesis 1:1 is probably no coincidence:

> [17]For behold! I am creating
> A new heaven and a new earth;
> The former things shall not be remembered,
> They shall never come to mind.
> [18]Be glad, then, and rejoice forever
> In what I am creating.
> For I shall create Jerusalem as a joy,
> And her people as a delight. (Isa. 65:17–18)

Were Jerusalem, the city of YHWH's enthronement, other than a microcosm, these verses would manifest the anomaly that some have sensed in them: is God creating a new world—heaven and earth—or only a new Jerusalem?[43] Is this renewal universal, as v. 17 would indicate, or only Jewish, as v. 18 would have it? In truth, in the minds of Jews for whom the bond of archetype and antitype had not been severed, the dichotomy would have seemed simplistic. The re-creation of the temple-city could only have been conceived as a reenthronement of YHWH after a long period in which his palace lay in ruins, and his faithful subjects seemed abandoned and helpless. The reconstruction of the temple-city was not only a recovery of national honor, but also a renewal of the cosmos, of which the Temple was a miniature. It is for this reason that YHWH is here said not to *build* Jerusalem, but to *create* it (*bōrē,'* v. 18), just as he creates (*bōrē,'* v. 17) the new heaven and the new earth. In Part 1 we saw that the combat myth of creation came to be projected onto the eschatological future: in the days to come, YHWH will slay Leviathan.[44] In Isaiah 65:17–18, we see that the somewhat different image of creation in Genesis 1—God creating heaven and earth without resistance—has also been eschatologized. The theological point is the same: the world order that creation denotes is not the present one in which evil is triumphant, obedience is unrewarded, and faith seems discredited, but the future one dawning just now, in which God will vanquish his foes, repair and mount his long dilapidated throne, and reward his band of faithful and obedient servants. As in those texts about the eschatological victory, so here the projection of creation onto the future is a profound, though indirect, acknowledgment of the inadequacy of the present world order, of "the former things [that] shall not be remembered."[45] The creation that is an unanswerable justification of God lies ahead.

THE TEMPLE AS MICROCOSM

The association of the Temple in Jerusalem with "heaven and earth" is not without Near Eastern antecedents, nor is it limited in the Hebrew Bible to texts whose subject is creation. At Nippur and elsewhere in ancient Sumer, the temple held the name Duranki, "bond of heaven and earth," and we hear of a shrine in Babylon called Etemenanki, "the house where the foundation of heaven and earth is."[46] These parallels raise the tantalizing possibility that "heaven and earth" *(šāmayim wā'āreṣ)* in the Hebrew Bible may, on occasion, be an appellation of Jerusalem or its Temple. It is curious that the first time we hear the deity called "creator of heaven and earth" *(qōnēh šāmayim wā'āreṣ)* is in the blessing bestowed upon Abram by Melchizedek, king of Salem.[47] Salem, as Psalm 76:3 demonstrates, is another name for Zion, the Temple Mount in Jerusalem. The suspicion cannot but arise that a liturgical formula

associated with the Jerusalem cultus has been retrojected into the
blessing of a pre-Israelite ruler of the same site. A psalm reinforces
the suspicion:

> [1] A song of ascents.
>
> Now bless the LORD,
>   all you servants of the LORD
>   who stand nightly
>   in the house of the LORD.
> [2] Lift up your hands toward the sanctuary
>   and bless the LORD.
> [3] May the LORD,
>   maker of heaven and earth,
>   bless you from Zion. (Ps. 134:1–3)

The original setting of this little liturgy is self-evidently the Jerusalem Temple. The night shift of that sanctuary, who are going
either on or off duty, are being invited to bless the God in whose
house they serve. The appellation of YHWH, "maker of heaven
and earth" (*'ōśēh šāmayim wā'āreṣ*), is most reminiscent of Melchizedek's beatification of Abram. But in the psalm, the connection
with Zion and its Temple is direct, and one is led to wonder
whether it is not the case that just as "maker" (*'ōśēh*) seconds or
re-presents "LORD," so does "heaven and earth" second or represent "Zion." If so, then we have further evidence that Zion was
thought in some sense to be "heaven and earth," that is, creation,
and the association of the new creation with the new Jerusalem in
Isaiah 65 is all the more readily understood. I claim neither that
YHWH as creator could be understood *only* in relation to the
Temple nor that cosmology exhausts the significance of the Temple. My point is that the idea of creation in the Hebrew Bible often
has a more specific life setting than a disembodied, ahistorical
theological analysis would lead us to believe. Cosmogony is not
fully grasped until it has been related to the microcosm and to the
rites that took place there and were thought to allow human
participation in the divine ordering of the world.

Complementing these literary indications of a conception of the Jerusalem Temple as microcosm are a series of observations made in our century by archaeologists who have related the description of the Temple to ancient Near Eastern cosmologies. The dean of American biblical archaeologists, William Foxwell Albright, suggests, for example, that Boaz and Jachin, the two mysterious pillars standing free in the Temple courtyard, "may have been regarded as the reflection of the columns between which the sun rose each morning." More certain is the case of the copper "Sea" (yām), which also stood in the courtyard, atop twelve cast bulls. According to Albright, this object "cannot be separated from the Mesopotamian apsû, employed both as the name of the subterranean fresh-water ocean . . . and as the name of a basin of holy water erected in the Temple." Yām is, as we have had occasion to see,[48] the name of one of the challengers both of Ugaritic Baal and of YHWH, God of Israel, and, at least in the Israelite case, his defeat is the pivotal point in YHWH's enthronement and creation of the world. It would make sense for the Temple, which bears witness to both enthronement and creation, to have featured a metallic representation of the vanquished adversary, now reduced to no more than an item of decoration in the precincts of his victor's royal palace.[49] The arrangement of the twelve bulls upon which the Sea rested into groups of three served, in Albright's thinking, as a representation of the four seasons of the year.[50] This is possible, but one should not exclude a connection with the idea of the world as divided into four quadrants. One thinks of the Akkadian expression kibrāt arba'i (and its alloforms), which literally means "the four shores," but was used as a designation of the whole known world.

Albright thinks that the term ḥēq hā'āreṣ, which appears in the description of the altar in Ezekiel 43:13–17, recalled similar terminology (irat erṣtti/kigalle) in Akkadian inscriptions, where the term is to be translated "bosom of the earth" and to be understood as having cosmological connotations.[51] Again, Albright may be right; the Akkadian parallel is indeed suggestive. On the other hand, caution is advisable, for the appearance of ḥēq apart from hā'āreṣ in

vv. 13 and 17 suggests that the term may mean simply "trench," so that the item that Albright renders with the highly cosmological locution "bosom of the earth" may be nothing more than a "trench in the ground," as the NJV renders it.[52] Even so, it is possible, but far from established, that the trench suggested cosmic realities to the ancient Israelite adepts who formulated the Temple-building program at the end of Ezekiel. The term *har'ēl* in the same passage,[53] which means "altar hearth," reinforces a bit Albright's view of the altar as the representation of a cosmic entity. He connects *har'ēl* with *arallû,* an Akkadian term for "the netherworld," or in the words of the *Chicago Assyrian Dictionary,* a "cosmic locality opposite of heaven."[54] Albright notes that the ancient Israelites, ignorant of Akkadian, may have understood the term as "the mountain of God" (*har'ēl*).[55] If they did so, this reinforces from another direction his point about the cosmic symbolism of the Temple. Note, for example, that Ezekiel can refer to the same locality as "Eden," "God's holy mountain" *(har qōdeš 'ĕlōhîm),* and "the mountain of God" *(har 'ĕlōhîm),* all of them simply variant names for the original home of the primordial man (the *Urmensch*), "seal of perfection/Full of wisdom and flawless in beauty."[56] Thus, even if it is understood in its Hebrew rather than its Akkadian etymology, as would seem the likelier case, the mysterious term *har'ēl* strongly suggests the connection of creation with Temple through the idea of the sacred mountain, which the two complexes of ideas share. The likely connection with the equally mysterious term *'ărî'ēl* in Isaiah 29:1–8 (which some would also derive from *arallû*[57]) reinforces the suggestion. For, whatever its scientific or folk etymology, *'ărî'ēl* there denotes the "city where David camped," that is, Jerusalem, and "Mount Zion," seat of the Temple. None of this is to deny that *har'ēl* in Ezekiel 43:15 designates the hearth of the altar, but given the precedent of *'ărî'ēl* in Isaiah 29:1–8, it would seem that this term for the altar hearth was one with a long line of tradition behind it, tradition that involved the notion of a sacred and inviolable temple-city with cosmogonic associations. Ultimately, that line of tradition may go back to the

Akkadian term *arallû,* with the sense of a "cosmic locality," although this is less certain.

In 2 Chronicles 6:13, in a section describing Solomon's speech upon the dedication of the Temple which is not paralleled in 1 Kings 8, the king is said to have stood upon a "bronze platform" *(kiyôr)* five cubits squared by three cubits high. Albright connects this *kiyôr* with the Akkadian *kiūru,* a term that can denote either a "metal cauldron" or the "earth" or a "[sacred] place" according to the *Chicago Assyrian Dictionary.* [58] With the definition of "metal cauldron," *kiyôr* is familiar as the designation of the laver associated with the cult both at the old Tabernacle and at the great Temple of Jerusalem.[59] With the meaning of "bronze platform," the term is unique to 2 Chronicles 6:13, and it is Albright's position that the origin of the word ultimately is in the second, or cosmic, sense of the Akkadian *kiūru.* [60] If he is right, then we have here another instance of cosmic symbolism in the Temple precincts. The most plausible alternative is to see this *kiyôr* as a "metal cauldron" on a grand scale and to interpret it as a congener of the "Sea" *(yām).* In this case too cosmic imagery would obtain. Although the brief description of the item in 2 Chronicles 6:13 gives no impression of internal depth or capacity, and the image of King Solomon standing in a huge tub as he gives his address may seem strange to us, Albright points to Syrian and Egyptian stelae in which a worshiper is depicted standing on such an object, apparently in the act of prayer.[61]

Our last instance of possible cosmic symbolism in the Temple involves the golden lampstands *(měnōrâ),* of which one stood in the Tabernacle but ten in Solomon's Temple.[62] On the basis of the rich arboreal imagery used in the description of the *měnōrâ,* Carol L. Meyers convincingly argues that the lampstand was the representation of "a cosmic tree," "a symbol that contributed to the assurance of divine accessibility . . . and participated in the cosmic paradigm."[63]

In all the instances in which cosmic symbolism of the Temple appurtenances has been alleged, a fair measure of uncertainty remains. This is because all we have are descriptions of the items

themselves, sometimes with elaborate detail, but never with interpretative comment. We usually know what the item looked like,
but what it meant, why it was chosen, why it looked this way and
not some other way, remain unknown. Usually in Hebraic thought
the visual side of perception is downplayed to the advantage of the
auditory: we are told what Moses said, but we haven't a clue as
to how he looked, whether he was tall or short, light or dark, bald
or with a full head of hair. It is the oracles, the conversation, the
dialogue, the word, which, in the main, occupies our authors. But
in the instance of the Temple, the reverse is the case, and the text
presents us with only mute description and itemization. This
muteness, this refusal to relate meanings, may be another example
of the demythologizing current in biblical thought. By keeping a
tight control upon the cosmogonic significance of the Temple appurtenances, the text stresses in austere fashion their subordination to the free and sovereign will of YHWH, the creator who
majestically refuses to accord *intrinsic* meaning to his creation.

In spite of the inevitable uncertainty in individual instances, the
cumulative weight of the cases of alleged cosmic symbolism, com-
bined with the literary correspondences that I have already developed, argues potently in favor of the hypothesis that the Temple
in Jerusalem was indeed conceived as a microcosm. The authors of
our texts may have sought to downplay this explosive side of the
Temple theology a bit, but if so, they have not eradicated it, and
we have no basis to assume that the Israelites who participated in
the Temple cultus over the centuries shared this austere theology.
Rather, the likelihood is that for them the Temple meant, among
other things, a rich and powerful re-presentation of creation. The
fact that we know anything at all about the appearance of the
Temple is itself an indication of the spiritual power of their experiences.

The arguments of modern archaeologists for cosmic symbolism
in the Tabernacle or Temple, although they have no explicit basis
in the biblical text, do revive an ancient interpretation of the
Temple. Hellenistic Jewish writers were especially inclined toward

an allegorical understanding of items in the ancient shrines. Josephus, for example, writing of the veil over the door to the Tabernacle, remarks

Nor was this mixture of materials without its mystic meaning: it typified the universe. For the scarlet seemed emblematical of fire, the fine linen of the earth, the blue of the air, and the purple of the sea. . . . On this tapestry was portrayed a panorama of the heavens.

Similarly, the twelve loaves of the "bread of display"[64] represent, in Josephus' system, the months of the year, and the Holy of Holies, the sacrosanct *cella* of the Tabernacle, symbolizes heaven, where God alone reigns in majesty. "In fact," Josephus writes, "every one of these objects is intended to recall and represent the universe."[65] The shrine is an *eikōn,* an image of the world, a microcosm.

The affinity of Josephus' method of interpreting the Temple with Hellenistic allegory, Jewish and Gentile, and ultimately with Platonic philosophy, is unmistakable. This granted, however, it would be an error to see this allegory as the aberration of a Jew writing in Greek largely for the benefit of a mixed Hellenistic intelligentsia. For this sort of allegorical reading of the Tabernacle/Temple is also abundant in Rabbinic literature, written in Hebrew for a Jewish readership. Most noteworthy is the *Midrash Tadshe,* a work of uncertain date whose entire second chapter is devoted to illustrating its thematic sentence: "The Tabernacle was made in correspondence to the creation of the world." In some cases the illustrations are identical to the old Hellenistic allegory: "The Holy of Holies was made in correspondence to the highest heavens," we are told, and the bread of display "corresponds to the months of summer and winter."[66]

Elsewhere in Rabbinic literature we see attempts to argue for the homology of world and shrine that are not so dependent upon the one-to-one correspondence of allegory. In one such case we hear an ancient analogue to the critical arguments of Peter Kearney, Joseph Blenkinsopp, and Moshe Weinfeld, which we examined earlier:

Rabbi Jacob ben Assi said: Why does it say, "O LORD, I love Your temple abode / the dwelling-place of Your glory"?[67] Because it is parallel to the creation of the world. How so?

On the first day it is written: "In the beginning God created heaven and earth," and it is written, "You spread the heavens like a tent cloth," and of the Tabernacle what is written? "You shall then make cloths of goat hair."[68]

On the second day: "Let there be an expanse," and it speaks of a separation, as it says: "that it may separate [mabdil] water from water." And of the Tabernacle it is written: "so that the curtain shall serve you as a partition [hibdilâ]."[69]

On the third day water is discussed, as it says: "Let the water . . . be gathered." And of the Tabernacle it is written: "Make a laver [kiyôr] of copper and a stand of copper for it. . . . Put water in it."[70]

On the fourth day he created lights, as it is written: "Let there be lights in the expanse of the sky." And of the Tabernacle it is written: "You shall make a lampstand of pure gold."[71]

On the fifth day he created birds, as it says: "Let the waters bring forth swarms of living creatures, and birds that fly." In the Tabernacle, sacrifices of lambs and birds correspond to them. [Variant text: In the Tabernacle, "The cherubim shall have their wings spread out above."][72]

On the sixth day man was created, as it says: "And God created man in his image"—in the glory of his creator.[73] And in the Tabernacle, a man is [also] mentioned, for he is the high priest who is anointed for service in the presence of the Lord.

On the seventh day: "The heaven and the earth were finished [way-kullû]." And of the Tabernacle, it is written: "Thus was completed [wattē-kel] all the work of the Tabernacle."[74] And of the creation of the world, it is written: "And God blessed." Of the Tabernacle, it is written: "Moses blessed them."[75] Of the creation of the world, it is written: "God finished." And of the Tabernacle it is written: "On the day Moses finished."[76] Of the creation of the world, it is written: "[And God] declared it [i.e., the Sabbath] holy." And of the Tabernacle, it is written: "he anointed and consecrated it."[77]

The method of this elaborate midrash must be distinguished from the arbitrary correlation of items in the Tabernacle with elements of the created order, the method of Josephus and the *Midrash Tadshe.* Like our modern exegetes, the Rabbinic darshan seeks out verbal correspondences between the account of the creation of the world in Genesis 1:1–2:3 and the instructions for the construction of the Tabernacle in Exodus 25–30. This, of course, requires him to omit many items in the latter passage, and even those he mentions do not occur in the order of their correlatives in the great cosmogony that is the overture to the Bible. Nonetheless, the midrash does suffice to show that the insight underlying Albright's interpretation of the Temple as exemplifying cosmic symbols is neither unique to him nor of modern origin; it is the unwitting restatement of an ancient concept in new terminology and with some new data (such as the connection of the Sea with *apsû*). The arguments in support of the concept vary among the Hellenistic allegorists, the Rabbinic darshanim, the contemporary critical exegetes, and the archaeologically informed historians. The concept of the Temple as microcosm endures, however, because it is a notion inherent in the biblical text, an ancient notion of pre-Israelite origin, which, though muted and transformed, continued to find expression in the spirituality of the Temple and the theology of creation in both biblical and later forms of Judaism.

There remains to be examined a remarkable midrash that presents temple-building not merely as homologous or parallel to creation, but as its completion, the consummation of the primordial cosmogony:

"All the work [that King Solomon had done in the House of the LORD] was completed." "The work" is not written here, but *"all* the work"—the work of the six days of creation: "God ceased from *all* the work of creation which He had undertaken to do."[78] "Had done" is not written here, but "to do": there remains another work. When Solomon came and built the Temple, the Holy One (blessed be He) said, "Now the work of heaven and earth has been completed"—"all the work . . . was completed." For this reason he was called Solomon [*šělōmōh*], for the Holy One (blessed be He) completed [*hišlim*] the work of the six days of creation through his handiwork.[79]

The connection of creation and Temple is here effected through the appearance of the expression "all the work" (in variant constructions) at the end of the great cosmogony of Genesis 1:1–2:3 and at the end of the detailed account of Solomon's Temple-building project in 1 Kings 6–7. In effect, this midrash extends to the Jerusalem Temple the theology that the midrash of Rabbi Jacob ben Assi, just examined, concentrates upon the Tabernacle: 1 Kings 7:51 replaces Exodus 39:32 as the affirmation of "completion" that is to be correlated with the theology of the seventh day in Genesis 1:1–2:3. The difference is that here the Temple has been assimilated phenomenologically to cosmogony or, to state the converse of the same point, cosmogony has become the prelude to temple building: the world, "heaven and earth," are not complete until the Jerusalem Temple has gone up. Though the medium of expression of this idea is Rabbinic midrash, the idea itself is essentially the same as in the *Enuma elish:* Marduk's cosmogony culminates only with the construction of Esagila, his temple in Babylon. And, indeed, in several Rabbinic legends, the Jerusalem Temple is depicted as the cosmic capstone that prevents the great abyss (*těhômā'*) from rising again to inundate the world and undo the work of creation.[80] In this current of Rabbinic thought, as in the older temple mythos of the Hebrew Bible and its Near Eastern antecedents, the point is not simply that the two projects, world building and temple building, are parallel. Rather, they implicate each other, and neither is complete alone. The microcosm is the idealized cosmos, the world contemplated *sub specie creationis,* the world as it was meant to be, a powerful piece of testimony to God the creator, a palace for the victorious king. To view creation within the precincts of the Temple is to summon up an *ideal world* that is far from the mundane reality of profane life and its persistent evil. It is that ideal world which is the result of God's creative labors.

8. Rest and Re-Creation

We have established that the distinctive aspect of the great cosmogony of Genesis 1:1–2:3 is its heptadic structure. Groups and multiples of seven are to be detected through the unit (and, in turn, help define 2:3 as its inner boundary); they are not limited to the obvious feature of the seven primordial days, the hexaemeron plus the first Sabbath.[1] The heptadic principle is so thoroughly woven into the fabric of the P account of creation that it is bootless to attempt to reconstruct a form of this text that was not so organized.

Although the heptadic structure of Genesis 1:1–2:3 is not limited to the seven days of creation, the latter seems to be its source. For whenever the occurrence of the Sabbath is specified in the Hebrew Bible, whether in P or elsewhere, it is defined as the seventh day, whereas the other accounts of creation in the same body of literature, which do not mention the Sabbath, have no such involvement in the specialness of the number seven. The most reasonable conclusion is that P reflects its momentous decision to organize its creation story around the Sabbath in the several other less obvious heptads that appear in the text. As a result, both overtly and covertly, the text of Genesis 1:1–2:3 points to the seventh day as the clue to the meaning of creation. The Priestly theology of creation is inextricably associated with the observance of the Sabbath. And inasmuch as it is the P creation story which now serves as the overture to the entire Bible, dramatically relativizing the other cosmogonies, it is fair to say that the text of the Hebrew Bible in the last analysis forbids us to speak of the theology of creation without sustained attention to the sabbatical institution.

The present location of the P cosmogony can obscure the fact that many references to the Sabbath in the Hebrew Bible fail to

suggest a connection with creation. One such text, the Deuteronomic Decalogue,[2] has already been mentioned. There the seventh
day is presented as a humanitarian easement for the benefit of
servants and farm animals, in extension of the easement YHWH
granted Israel in the exodus from the house of bondage. This
etiology is to be contrasted with the parallel text in Exodus, which
presents the Sabbath as a memorial to YHWH's primordial rest
and does not mention the exodus.[3] If, as most scholars think, the
Decalogue in Exodus predates P, then the association of creation
and Sabbath, although hardly universal in the Hebrew Bible, has
deep roots. It was not the innovation of the Priestly school, which,
nonetheless, developed it into the classic statement with which the
Bible now opens.

It would be convenient at this point to conclude that the Hebrew Bible reflects two broad interpretations of the Sabbath. The
first—anthropocentric, rationalistic, humanistic, and utilitarian—
sees the Sabbath as an implication of Israel's distinctive experience
of liberation from slavery. The second—highly theocentric, cultic,
sacral, and perhaps magical—sees in the seventh day a mimetic
reenactment of the primordial divine repose. In short, the first
interpretation speaks of rest, the second of re-creation. The principal deficiency of this dichotomy is that in driving a wedge between
the two themes, it fails to reckon with the prominence of *rest* in
ancient Near Eastern *creation* stories. It is the attainment of rest
which marks the completion of the act of creation in many of these
stories; in others, it is the gods' need for rest which initiates the
creative process.[4]

In the *Enuma elish,* for example, Marduk proposes the creation of
humanity so that upon them "shall the services of the gods be
imposed that they may be at rest." Ea, Marduk's father, persuades
him to allow the creation of humanity out of the blood of Tiamat's
general Kingu, in order to impose "the services of the gods [upon
them] and set the gods free." The lesser gods, acclaiming Marduk
as the one "who has established our freedom from compulsory
service," demonstrate this gratitude by building him a temple,
Esagila, and a royal city, Babylon. Esagila, they say, "shall be for

our rest at night; come, let us repose therein."[5] Here we see not only the familiar dyad of cosmogony and temple building, but also, as part of the same complex of ideas, a third element, liberation from drudgery, a liberation that results not in autonomy for the gods, but in their willing and joyful subordination to their liberating savior. His creative word enables them to rest; their rest memorializes his act of creation.

A similar note is sounded at the onset of the *Atra-Ḥasis* poem, the Babylonian flood story. The action begins with a violent work stoppage by the subgroup of gods known as the Igigi against the great god Enlil. In order to provide relief for these gods, Enlil authorizes the creation of a new species: "and let man bear the toil of the gods." When the birth goddess Mami has produced this new creature, she proudly proclaims, "I have loosed the yoke, I have established freedom."[6] The term here translated "to establish freedom," *andurāra šakānu,* is well known from the world of Mesopotamian law and statecraft, where it signifies a royal decree that results in some combination of the following easements: emancipation of slaves, cancellation of debts, amnesty for prisoners, repatriation of captives, exemption from taxes, restoration of real estate to the clans that originally owned them, and distribution of lands to the needy.[7] As in the *Enuma elish,* so here we see a connection between the liberation provided by social reforms and the act of creation, if not in the sense of cosmogony, at least in the sense of the genesis of the human race. Creation results in the gods' being free at last to rest. And lest we draw too sharp a distinction between the cosmogony of Genesis 1:1–2:3 and the exodus from Egypt, we should note that the latter reflects several of these same elements of progressive Near Eastern social policy: newly freed slaves reclaim the lands to which they once held legal title and redistribute those lands among themselves, making provisions for the needy.[8] In fact, the substance and language of Mesopotamian social reform pervades the Pentateuch, ensuring that the origins of the people of Israel in an experience of liberation are kept forever in mind, forever fresh. "You shall not oppress a stranger," warns the Book of the Covenant, "for you know the feelings of the stranger, having yourselves been strangers in the land of Egypt." The following verses then specify the Sabbath and the sabbatical year as institutions mandated for the benefit of the needy, the slave, and the alien.[9] In this way the historical event of the exodus from Egypt provides the human community the same experience of rest and relief that the creation of humanity provides the lesser gods in the *Enuma elish* and *Atra-Ḥasis*. One might put the transformation this way: in this Israelite literature humanity has assumed the position of the lesser gods of Babylonia, so that creation now works not against the human interest, but for it. The Sabbath, the sabbatical year, and the Sabbath of sabbatical years, that is, the Jubilee, recollect God's primordial rest in a form that human beings do not dread, but instead can share. Israel participates, through the very forms of her collective existence, in the divine rest that consummated creation. In this transformation no group takes the menial place that humanity vacated when it was assigned prerogatives formerly reserved for the gods. It must not be overlooked, however, that the various law codes within the Pentateuch are at pains to point out that liberation after six years or in the Jubilee applies only to Israelite slaves, not to Gentile slaves.[10] The chosenness of Israel acts as a limitation upon the democratization of divine perogatives that Israel's own experience so vividly exhibits. The philanthropic attitude of biblical law is not presented as a timeless, universal principle. This law exists within the unique covenantal relationship of YHWH and Israel, his "treasured possession among all the peoples,"[11] and often reflects the specialness and differentness of the covenantal nation, as indeed it does here. Still, the historical evidence does not suggest the existence of great masses of foreign slaves providing opportunities for leisure for their Israelite masters,[12] and for most of biblical history it was the Israelites themselves who were more likely to be on the wrong side of the slave trade transaction.

Despite the differences between the Babylonian and the Israelite images of primordial divine rest that we have been examining, the fact remains that in both cases a social reform has been retrojected into creation itself. Moshe Weinfeld convincingly argues that the

concept of the creation of the world as an act of divine philanthropy extends far beyond the theology of the Sabbath on which
our discussion has so far concentrated. Weinfeld demonstrates
that the Akkadian expression *andurāram šakānum* and its frequent
variant, *mīšaram šakānum* (both mean "to establish freedom") have
as one ancient Hebrew equivalent *la'ăśôt şĕdāqâ ûmišpāṭ*, usually
rendered into English as "to do justice and righteousness," or the
like.[13] This translation is misleading, however, in that it suggests
a juridical denotation, whereas, in fact, the idiom is often employed to denote acts of societal benevolence that are not located
exclusively or even primarily in the courtroom. Jeremiah, for example, itemizes deeds that together suggest a much broader meaning of the hendiadys than the juridical language of the conventional translation would indicate:

Thus said the LORD: Do what is just and right [*'ăśû mišpāṭ ûşĕdāqâ*]; rescue
from the defrauder him who is robbed; do not wrong the stranger, the
fatherless, and the widow; commit no lawless act, and do not shed the
blood of the innocent in this place. (Jer. 22:3)

With the philanthropic denotations of the idiom in mind, we will
not be surprised that a text can juxtapose "justice" and "compassion" (to give the traditional renderings) without a hint of tension,
as in this oracle in Zechariah:

[9]Thus said the LORD of Hosts: Execute true justice [*mišpaṭ 'ĕmet šĕpōṭû*]; deal
loyally and compassionately [*wĕḥesed wĕraḥămim 'ăśû*] with one another.
[10]Do not defraud the widow, the orphan, the stranger, and the poor; and
do not plot evil against one another. (Zech. 7:9–10)

It would be a mistake to see in these words a call to justice *tempered*
by compassion, or to a compassion that *goes beyond* justice, as David
Kimhi suggests in his medieval commentary. Rather, justice here
is *constituted* by compassion, by special solicitude for the powerless
and disadvantaged, a determination that they not be victimized.
That determination is not peculiar to courts of law. The Hebrew
Bible expects it of everyone.

Weinfeld points out examples in which the author of this *şĕdāqâ-*

ûmišpāṭ is divine and its particular manifestation is the creation of the world,[14] as in Psalm 33:

> [4]For the word of the Lord is right;
>   His every deed is faithful.
> [5]He loves what is right and just [*ṣĕdāqâ ûmišpāṭ*];
>   the earth is full of the Lord's faithful care [*ḥesed*].
> [6]By the word of the Lord the heavens were made,
>   by the breath of His mouth, all their host.
> [7]He heaps up the ocean waters like a mound [*nēd*],
>   stores the deep in vaults. (Ps. 33:4–7)

These verses recall the conclusion of the combat myth, as the divine victor, having achieved indisputable mastery over the waters of chaos, proceeds with the creation of the familiar world. Here that act of creation is presented as an instance of liberation, just as the creation of humanity in *Atra-Ḥasis* and the *Enuma elish* represents an *andurāru* for the lesser gods. In Psalm 33 cosmogony is a manifestation of God's love and mercy, his faithfulness toward the underlings who have no hope but him.[15] The use of the rare term *nēd* in v. 7, translated here as "mound," recalls the Song of the Sea in Exodus 15, in which "the floods stood straight like a wall [*nēd*],"[16] and thus further underscores the essential unity of creation and exodus, two great acts of deliverance wrought by the gracious God on behalf of his powerless allies. This is another instance in which cosmogony and redemption or, if you wish, myth and history, or creation and revelation, work in tandem and not independently of one another. The very endurance of the world offers testimony to the boundless benevolence of its author, his indefectible resolve that the dark forces of chaos not triumph.

A more explicit association of creation after combat with the aquatic monster, on the one hand, and YHWH's *ṣedeq ûmišpāṭ*, on the other, appears in Psalm 89:

> [10]You rule the swelling of the sea (*yām*);
>   when its waves surge, You still them.
> [11]You crushed Rahab; he was like a corpse;
>   with Your powerful arm You scattered Your enemies.

¹²The heaven is Yours,
   the earth too;
   the world and all it holds—
   You established them.

¹³North and south—
   You created them;
   Tabor and Hermon sing forth Your name.
¹⁴Yours is an arm endowed with might;
   Your hand is strong;
   Your right hand, exalted.
¹⁵Righteousness and justice [*ṣedeq ûmišpāṭ*] are the base of Your throne;
   steadfast love and faithfulness [*ḥesed weʾĕmet*] stand before
   You. (Ps. 89:10–15)

Earlier I noted that the coincidence in this hymn of the slaying of Rahab and his confederates with the creation of the world belies the position that denies cosmogonic significance to the combat myth in Israel.¹⁷ Indeed, it is over the dead body of the great sea monster that YHWH stakes his claim to kingship and authors the world as we know it. His throne symbolizes and manifests a cosmic order that is indistinguishable from the unshakable establishment of generosity and good will. Creation is a victory and an act of liberation—YHWH's defeat of the angry, roiling waters of chaos and his redemption of the lowly from their grasp. If we bear this in mind, we shall not miss the appropriateness of the profound theological statement that Priestly and other circles made when they retrojected the humanitarian institution of the Sabbath (and, by implication, the Sabbatical and Jubilee years) into creation itself. As creation is a continuing cipher for divine philanthropy, so is the Sabbath a regular and unending implementation of the philanthropic attitude within the domain of ordinary human affairs.

We have now seen that the prominence of rest on the seventh day in the creation story of Genesis 1:1–2:3 reflects a much more widespread theology in which creation is a paradigm of God's gracious and perdurable will to save the defenseless. In more specific fashion, the description of the deity's sabbatical repose in

Genesis 2:1–3 parallels the relief from toil granted to the gods
through the creation of humanity in some Mesopotamian creation
stories. This particular parallel, however, does not shed much light
on the specific assertion of Genesis 2:1–3 itself that there was not
simply rest in heaven directly after the creation of humanity, but
that cosmogony came to its conclusion with the cessation from
activity of the creator God himself. Such respose is, nonetheless,
to be glimpsed now and then in other Near Eastern literature. In
the *Enuma elish,* for example, Ea, after killing his primordial ancestor Apsu, god of the fresh waters, and building himself a temple
named after his later enemy, "peacefully rested in his abode."[18]
Still earlier, in the Egyptian text known as the *Memphite Theology,*
we read this of the god Ptah, "he who made all and brought the
gods into being" simply by pronouncing "the name of everything":

Thus it was discovered and understood that his strength is greater than
(that of the other) gods. And so Ptah rested, after he had made everything.[19]

The idea that a deity finds rest in his temple is, as several scholars
have recently pointed out,[20] one that is in evidence in the Hebrew
Bible as well. In Psalm 132:14 God avers to David that Zion, the
Temple mount and seat of the divine throne, "is my resting-place
[*měnûḥātî*] for all time."[21] In Isaiah 66, YHWH points to his cosmic
temple, the world, in order to belittle the Jews' efforts to build him
an earthly one. "Where could you build a temple for Me," he asks
rhetorically, "/ And where is the place for Me to rest [*měnûḥātî*]."[22]
In Psalm 95:11, YHWH's "resting-place" *(měnûḥātî)* seems to denote not the Temple, but the Holy Land itself, which, as we have
seen, is sometimes conceived as a vast sanctuary.[23] It is probably
pertinent to this that David first got the idea to build YHWH a
temple "when the king sat enthroned in his palace and the LORD
had granted him rest [*hēniaḥ-lô*] from all his enemies around
him."[24] Now if we recall the homology of temple and world,
temple building and world building, which was the argument of
chapter 7, we shall readily understand how it is that YHWH, like

Ptah, finds rest in his newly created world, just as he does in the Temple in which he is enthroned.

Weinfeld cites the order of recitation of Psalms 92 and 93 in the Second Temple as evidence for an early association of Sabbath and enthronement, the two paradigmatic instances of divine "rest." According to the Mishnah, when the Temple stood, the Levites recited these poems in the reverse of the order in which they now appear in the Psalter, that is, Psalm 93 on Friday and Psalm 92 on Saturday, the Sabbath.[25] Psalm 93 is an exquisite evocation of YHWH as he dons his royal robes in his Temple, having overcome the angry waters and established the world unshakably. In a baraita ascribed to Rabbi Aqiva, the reason given for the recital of this psalm on Friday, that is, the sixth day of the sabbatical week, is that "he [God] then finished his work and reigned over them as king."[26] This is apparently prompted by the psalmist's observation that "The world stands firm; / it cannot be shaken."[27] In an anonymous parallel to this baraita in the *Abot de-Rabbi Nathan,* it is said that Psalm 93 is appropriate for Friday because on that day in the primordial week God "finished all his works and ascended to sit enthroned in the celestial regions of the universe."[28] Presumably, then, the first full day on which he could sit enthroned in regal repose, without work altogether, was the next, the Sabbath. Weinfeld argues that the rabbis, and perhaps their Second Temple forerunners as well, here associate the Sabbath with the rest that is associated with enthronement elsewhere in the ancient Near East. His argument would be stronger were it not that the same baraita also says of Monday, when Psalm 48 is recited, that God "reigned over them as king" or, in the striking words of the *Abot de-Rabbi Nathan,* "he was made king over his universe" that day. Still, it was well-nigh inevitable that the two biblical instances of divine repose, the primordial Sabbath and the enthronement in the Temple, would be explicitly identified in Rabbinic midrash. My claim is that this identification only makes explicit what had been implicit in the deep structure of the theology of the Sabbath all along, and even in the ancient Near Eastern cosmogonies, wherein lie the roots of that theology.

The repose of the enthroned creator is only one explanation for God's cessation from work on the seventh day in Genesis 2:1–3. Another is the well-known fact that these verses serve as an etiology of the Sabbath. The text simply depicts the deity as himself observing the commandments to cease from labor on the seventh day and to make it sacred.[29] This invests the Sabbath with what Mircea Eliade calls "the prestige of origins,"[30] reinforcing its suprahuman authority and transcendent character and making its observance a matter of *imitatio Dei*. All this is true, but to treat the inactivity of God in these verses as solely etiological misses a few important details. For one, the text never uses the term "Sabbath" (*šabbāt*); the closest it comes is in the two forms of the cognate verb *šābat*, which appear in vv. 2–3. These, however, must be translated "to cease," as they lack the cognate object and are followed instead by the phrase "from all the work." Moreover, one hears in these verses neither a charge to humanity to observe the Sabbath nor an etiological notice that the divine cessation from labor is the origin of the weekly festival, this in pointed contrast to the Fourth Commandment as it appears in Exodus 20:8–11. And although Genesis 2:1–3 employs the expression "the seventh day" three times, it does not leave us with the impression that this refers to the same chronological unit that defines the other six days of the original week. For, in contrast to them, the primordial Sabbath is never said to end. Our passage lacks the expected conclusion: "And there was evening and there was morning, the seventh day." If we read these three verses as referring to God's observance of the familiar Israelite Sabbath, then our assumption is that his inactivity did indeed come to an end, and on the first day of the second week of the universe, he went back into action. But the text does not say that. Instead, it leaves us with an impression of the deity in a state of mellow euphoria, benignly fading out of the world that he has finished and pronounced to be "very good."[31] In sum, God's inactivity on the seventh day of the Priestly cosmogony exhibits features that cannot be *exhaustively* explained by reference to the Sabbath.

In part, this overplus can be ascribed to the ancient Near Eastern motif of the enthroned god satisfied and at rest after success in cosmogony, as we have seen. This motif, however, extends far beyond the confines of the ancient Near East, characterizing numerous creation myths throughout the world. Raffaele Pettazzoni, who studied the motif of the otiosity of creator gods, states its meaning as follows:

It may . . . be the case that the *otiositas* itself belongs to the essential nature of creative Beings, and is in a way the complement of their creative activity. The world made and the cosmic established, the Creator's work is as good as done. Any further intervention on his part would be not only superfluous but possibly dangerous, since any change in the cosmos might allow it to fall back into chaos. Once the world is made, the existential function of the Creator could be nothing but prolonging its duration and ensuring its unaltered and unalterable stability.[32]

Whether the truth of Pettazzoni's observations matches their generality is not at issue here; the fact is that his point does apply nicely to the striking inactivity of God in Genesis 2:1–3. What remained for the creator to do after he had surveyed "all that He had made and found it very good"[33] at the end of his creative labors on the sixth day? Indeed, the emphatic term *"very good,"* which appears only here in this text, underscores the perfection of the new order of things and prepares the reader for the transition within God from magisterial activity to lordly inactivity on the seventh day, when he makes nothing, but only blesses and consecrates the day itself.

If, as we have seen, the motif of divine otiosity after the labors of creation is older and more widespread than the particularly Israelite idea of the Sabbath, then Nils-Erik A. Andreasen is probably correct that Genesis 2:1–3 is intended to give a certain interpretation to that motif. The real meaning of this inactivity is not "a divine retirement from engagement into the affairs of the world," but rather the special form of repose which is the biblical Sabbath.[34] This is not the inactivity of the *deus otiosus* of which Pettazzoni wrote, impotent and remote, but rather an inactivity that is limited in its duration and positive in its effect: the Sabbath represents a regularly recurring occasion of sanctity within the profane time that is the ordinary week. This is the ultimate consequence of the idea of creation without opposition: even the moments in which God is inactive are harmless, in fact positive in their own special way, and the order that he brings into existence through creation is so secure and self-sustaining that it can survive a day without his maintenance. Compared with the stories of creation after combat in which the vanquished foe survives in confinement or subjugation, Genesis 1:1–2:3 exhibits a high order of optimism. This is undoubtedly related to the more philanthropic and anthropocentric theology of the Priestly school. Note again that the sabbatical rest of God is not obtained at the expense of humanity, but is, or at Sinai will come to be, something in which human beings may participate. By reinterpreting the divine otiosity as sabbatical in nature, the Priestly account of creation accentuates the possibility of human access to the inner rhythm of creation itself. Israel can rest the rest of God.

THE DYARCHY OF GOD AND HUMANITY

Traditionally, this high view of humanity and its rights and potentials within the created order has been related to the statement in Genesis 1:27 that "God created man in His image, in the image of God He created him; male and female He created them." As the last clause makes clear, "man" *(hā'ādām)* here denotes the species, not the gender: men and women alike are created in God's own image.[35] What precisely that means has been a debated question throughout the history of interpretation.[36] Some of the older commentaries were quite able to tolerate a mildly anthropomorphic interpretation, while steering clear of the grosser implication that people have a physical resemblance to God. Rashi (1040–1105 C.E.), for example, thought "image" *(ṣelem)* here refers to a mold or stamp, although he quickly glossed its synonym *dĕmût* as a reference to cognitive and intellectual capacities.[37] Modern critical commentators are more thoroughly resistant to anthropomorphic interpretations, and this has resulted in all kinds of exceedingly rarefied and highly theological proposals. In Claus Westermann's opinion, for example, the point is that 'humanity as a whole . . . is created as the counterpart of God" so as "to render possible a happening between creator and creature . . . the holy event in which history reaches its goal."[38]

There is, fortunately, an alternative to both the pedestrian anthropomorphic interpretation and the vague, abstract theological reading represented by Westermann. Already a millennium ago the philosopher and commentator Saadya (882–942 C.E.) associated the image of God in Genesis 1:26–27 with humanity's God-like rule over creation.[39] This association fits nicely with the charge to newly created humanity to "fill the earth and master it [*kibšúhû*]; and rule [*rĕdú*] the fish of the sea, the birds of the sky, and all the living things that creep on earth."[40] Elsewhere in the Hebrew Bible, it is primarily in divine commissions to Judean kings that we hear the charge to conquer, although without the particular military term *kābaš*. Consider this decree of YHWH to his royal vicegerent and son, enthroned upon Mount Zion:

> [8]"Ask it of Me,
> and I will make the nations your domain;
> your estate, the limits of the earth,
> [9]You can smash them with an iron mace,
> shatter them like potter's ware." (Ps.2:8–9)

In a similar poem the use of the verb *rādâ*, "to rule, hold sway," suggests a connection with the creation of humanity and the charge to them in Genesis 1:26–28:

> The LORD will stretch forth from Zion your
> mighty scepter;
> hold sway [*rĕdēh*] over your enemies! (Ps. 110:2)

Indeed, *rādâ* would seem to be an important element in the stock language by which YHWH conveys the universal *imperium* to his royal vicar on Earth.[41] One thinks here of this plea of the psalmist on behalf of the Davidic monarch:

⁸Let him rule [*yērd*] from sea to sea,
   from the river to the ends of the earth.
⁹Let desert-dwellers kneel before him,
   and his enemies lick the dust.
¹⁰Let kings of Tarshish and the islands pay tribute,
   kings of Sheba and Seba offer gifts.
¹¹Let all kings bow to him,
   and all nations serve him. (Ps. 72:8–11)

Psalm 8 presents us with a variant meditation on the creation of humanity, one that is not necessarily dependent upon Genesis 1:26–28, but illumines it nonetheless:

⁴When I behold Your heavens, the work of Your fingers,
   the moon and stars that You set in place,
      ⁵what is man that You have been mindful of him,
      mortal man that You have taken note of him,
         ⁶that You have made him little less than divine [*'ĕlōhim*]
         and adorned him [*tĕ'attĕrēhû*] with glory and majesty
[*kābôd wĕhādār*];
            ⁷You have made him master [*tamšīlēhû*] over Your handiwork,
            laying the world at his feet,
               ⁸sheep and oxen, all of them,
               and wild beast, too;
                  ⁹the birds of the heavens, the fish of the sea,
                  whatever travels the paths of the seas. (Ps. 8:4–9)

Here the status of humanity as a species just a bit less than a god is realized in their sovereignty over the rest of creation, which is described in language reminiscent of Genesis 1: "the birds of the heavens, the fish of the sea." The idiom of this godlike sovereignty is the idiom of kingship. God has "adorned" humanity or, more accurately, "crowned" (*tĕ'attĕrēhû*) them, "with glory and majesty" *(kābôd wĕhādār),* two more stock terms of the royal theology. In fact, the psalmist praises YHWH for having set humanity up as the ruler *(tamšīlēhû)* over creation. Here again, the language is that used elsewhere for God's own mastery over the world,⁴² and the assumption is that he has appointed humanity to be his viceroy, the highest ranking commoner, as it were, ruling with the authority of the king.[43] The human race is YHWH's plenipotentiary, his stand-in.

The link between the creation of humanity "in the image of God" in Genesis 1 and their status as royalty can be clearly seen in ancient Near Eastern inscriptions in which it is the king who is described as the "image" of the deity. Hans Wildberger assembled a rich and convincing collection of such passages from both Egypt and Mesopotamia, of which a sample will suffice for purposes of illustration here.[44] In the Rosetta Stone, to begin with a late example, the Hellenistic Pharaoh Ptolemy V Epiphanes is called *eikōn zōsa tou Dios*, "the living image of Zeus." About twelve hundred years earlier, Amunhotpe III was described as the god Amun's "beloved son," his "living image." Another Pharaoh, perhaps his successor Thutmosis IV, is called "the image of Re, son of Amun, who tramples down foreigners." Wildberger noted the similarity of this epithet to the use of *rādâ* in Genesis 1 and Psalm 110, but he might have drawn attention as well to the statement in Psalm 8:7 that God has laid "the world at his feet," made not of the individual, but of humanity in their regal role within the created order. Of Wildberger's Mesopotamian examples, the most striking is an Assyrian letter from the seventh century B.C.E. in which the priest and court astrologer Adad-šum-uṣur terms the king "the image [ṣalam]" of the god Bel, using the Akkadian cognate of the Hebrew *ṣelem*, the term for "image" in Genesis 1:26–27.[45] On the basis of these examples, and apparently without knowledge of Saadya's precedent, Wildberger makes a persuasive case for seeing the creation of humanity "in the image of God" as a statement of the sovereignty of the human race over the rest of creation. The entire race collectively stands vis-à-vis God in the same relationship of chosenness and protection that characterizes the god–king relationship in the more ancient civilizations of the Near East. "The image of God" is his chosen viceroy.

To Wildberger's interpretation Westermann objects that humanity, being a species rather than an individual, cannot take God's place as the king does.[46] In this he overlooks the tendency toward democratization of offices in evidence in the ancient Near

East, especially Israel. Wildberger had already drawn attention to an extraordinary passage in *The Instruction for King Meri-Ka-Re,* an Egyptian composition of the late twenty-second century B.C.E.:

Well directed are men, the cattle of the god. He made heaven and earth according to their desire, and he repelled the water-monster. He made the breath of life [for] their nostrils. They who have issued from his body are his images. He arises in heaven according to their desire. He made for them plants, animals, fowl, and fish to feed them.[47]

In this text it is not merely the king, but all humanity who stand in the relationship of children to the god, his "images." Wildberger connects this democratization of the royal epithets with the tendency in Egypt for nobles and even commoners to become eligible for apotheosis and the rites that went with it, once the prerogatives of kings alone.[48] He and Westermann might have noted a similar ambiguity in the Hebrew Bible, where it is sometimes the Davidic king and sometimes all Israel who are called YHWH's "son" or his "first-born son."[49] In Isaiah 55:3–5, the "everlasting covenant / The enduring loyalty promised to David" is extended to the whole nation.[50] A parallel tendency toward democratization can be traced for the office of priest *(kōhēn)*. In some biblical texts, for example, the prohibition on eating carrion or meat from an animal that has been killed by other beasts is enjoined upon the priesthood alone, whereas in others, it is incumbent upon all Israel.[51] Indeed, the very obligation to be holy is sometimes an obligation of the priesthood, and sometimes again of all Israel—a whole "kingdom of priests and a holy nation."[52] The extension of the language of kingship and of priesthood to the entire nation is a good parallel to the extension of the royal status of the image of God to all humanity, whether in Egypt or in Israel. This does not imply that the school of thought that produced the Priestly creation story had ceased to believe in the chosenness of Israel. The democratization of kingship and priesthood stood side by side with the continuation of those offices as special sacral institutions. In short, if "democratization" implies the abolition of the office through infinite extension, then it is the wrong word. Whatever one calls the process, the fact remains that Genesis 1:26–27 does exactly what Westermann says is impossible: it appoints the entire human race as God's royal stand-in.

The association of cosmogony with the appointment of a viceroy for the deity is not unique to the Priestly source. To see another instance of it, one that puts Genesis 1 in perspective, we must return to Psalm 89. Many scholars have thought this psalm to be a clumsy combination of three distinct poems, a cosmogonic hymn reminiscent of the psalms of enthronement, a royal oracle establishing the House of David and unconditionally guaranteeing its continuance, and a lament about a national defeat that has brought dishonor to the ruling Davidide and cast doubt upon the perdurability of God's good will.[53] To be sure, there is a certain unevenness at the onset of the psalm, when vv. 4–5 interrupt the smooth transition between vv. 3 and 6 and begin the Davidic theme, which is cut off abruptly and not resumed until v. 20. James M. Ward, however, argues against the assumption of clumsy redaction by pointing out that vv. 1–5 serve as an *incipit* that announces "the two aspects of the kingship of God which will be expounded more fully in the body of the poem, namely the eternal, cosmic foundation of God's covenant love and fidelity (vss. 2 f) and the divine choice of David as his earthly vicegerent (vss. 4 f)."[54] In a detailed study of the language of the psalm, Ward finds that "twenty-six significant terms are common to both the hymn and the oracle, and many of them appear more than once in either or both."[55] One particular instance of this common vocabulary must not go unmentioned: this is the fact that both thrones, YHWH's and David's, rest upon "steadfast love and faithfulness" *(ḥesed weʾĕmet/ʾĕmûnâ).* [56] The two great manifestations of these are God's cosmogonic victory over the sea monster,[57] which immediately preceded his establishment and ordering of the world, and his exaltation of David, with its irrevocable oath that divine grace shall always follow his unshakable dynasty. These two manifestations of "steadfast love and faithfulness" are not unrelated, for in v. 26, YHWH commits to David the containment of enemies vanquished in cosmogonic combat:

> I will set this hand upon the sea *(yām),*
> his right hand upon the rivers *(nĕhārôt).* (Ps. 89:26)

The theology of Psalm 89 is thus one that sees the governance of the world as lying in the hands of a dyarchy of God and king, a dyarchy that, as vv. 27–28 make clear, is one of father and son. The human correlative of this arrangement was most probably the coregency of the king and his heir designate, such as occurred in David's own reign, when Solomon was anointed king before his father had died, or in the time of Jotham, who governed the kingdom when his father, Uzziah, was stricken with leprosy.[58] Of course, in Psalm 89, YHWH's commitment of the governance of the world to his son and human counterpart David is not the result of his own incapacitation, but the extent of his transfer of power is striking nonetheless. If, as I have argued, the creation of humanity "in the image of God" in Genesis 1:26–27 represents a democratizing adaptation of the royal theology, then the role of humanity there is properly compared to the role of the House of David in Psalm 89. In both cases, creation ends, as it were, with the commission of human agents to rule the world in the name of the creator God.[59]

The coregency of God and humanity in Genesis 1:1–2:3 goes a long way in explanation of why divine rest is not obtained in this text at the expense of human rest, as in *Atra-Ḥasis* and the *Enuma elish,* but is, rather, something human beings can share through observance of the Sabbath. Not only is the antinomy between the divine and human realms overcome, as is also the case in *Meri-ka-re,* but here God and humanity rule the world jointly (though not equally). The priority of God and the lateness of the creation of human beings make the term "cocreator" or "partner in creation" inaccurate. In fact, the verb translated in Genesis 1:1 as "create" *(bārā')* occurs nowhere in the Hebrew Bible with a subject other than God. It is, however, still appropriate to speak of a certain subordinate role that humanity is to play in the cosmogonic process. One form of this we have already examined at length, the

mimetic reenactment of the primordial divine repose of Genesis
2:1–3 in the ongoing Israelite institution of the Sabbath. Another
is to be found in the dietary laws, especially as these are given in
Leviticus 11. Here, as always in the Hebrew Bible, the rationale
for the laws is something other than hygiene or sensitivity to life
or the other explanations that apologists—ancient, medieval, and
modern—have tried to offer for them. Rather, the rationale is
holiness: "You shall sanctify yourselves and be holy, for I am
holy."[60] Holiness in this case seems to be a matter of the scrupu-
lous observance of the boundaries that define the categories of
creation:

> [24b]I the LORD am your God who has set you apart [*hibdalti*] from other
> peoples. [25]So shall you set apart [*wĕhibdaltem*] the clean beast from the
> unclean, the unclean bird from the clean. You shall not draw abomination
> upon yourselves through beast or bird or anything with which the ground
> is alive, which I have set apart [*hibdalti*] for you to treat as unclean. [26]You
> shall be holy to Me, for I the LORD am holy, and I have set you apart
> [*wā'abdil*] from other peoples to be Mine. (Lev. 20:24b–26)

The fourfold occurrence here of the verb *hibdîl*, "to set apart,
separate," recalls its repeated occurrences in Genesis 1.[61] In fact,
these two passages account for well over a third of the attestations
of the *hiphil* of *bdl*. If, as seems likely, this is not coincidence, the
point would appear to be that the distinction of Israel from the
nations is as fundamental to cosmic order as the separations
through which God first brought order out of chaos. This is a
natural implication, given that the primordial institution of the
Sabbath has been made known and commanded to Israel alone.
More telling is the fact that the passage just quoted views Israel's
own separation of fit from unfit foods as a continuation of the
process of her own separation from the Gentiles so that even so
humble an activity as eating replicates the ordering that is fundamental to God's good world.

Mary Douglas has gone further, arguing that even the detailed
laws about which animals are permissible and which are not reflect
the categories in which creation took place. "Holiness," she main-

tains, "requires that different classes of things shall not be confused,"[62] so that a sea animal that lacks either fins or scales, for
example, is unfit,[63] because it straddles the boundary between sea
and land. This fits nicely with the Priestly creation story, which
has sea animals and land animals appearing on different days,[64]
but it does not explain why land animals must both chew the cud
and have a cloven hoof.[65] Were not the cow and the camel both
created on the fifth day? In sum, it would seem that the dietary
laws do have some connection with the boundaries and categories
of creation, though the connection is not so tight as Douglas
suggests. The self-conscious formulation of the text itself suggests
a connection not with the substantive *content* of creation, but with
the *process of distinction making* as an imitation of the holy creator God
incumbent upon his people, the House of Israel: "You shall be
holy, for I am holy."[66] Israel's obligation to hallow the Sabbath
day is another instance of this Priestly theology of *imitatio Dei*.

We see, then, that Genesis 1:1–2:3, the priestly cosmogony,
presents creation as an event ordered toward the rest of God, with
which it closes, a rest that signifies an act of redemption and social
reform and an opportunity for human participation in the sublime
quietude of the unopposed creator God. The prominence of the
Sabbath in this passage is hardly unique within biblical materials
that may be broadly designated Priestly. On the contrary, in this
school of thought, the Sabbath has assumed the cosmogonic role
that the New Year held in some other ancient Near Eastern cultures and probably in Israel as well. In chapter 6 of our study, we
saw that although hints of the significance of Nisan 1, the spring
New Year's Day, remain in Priestly narrative, neither that day nor
even Tishri 1, the fall New Year's Day of the Rabbinic calendar,
is ever designated as *rōš haššānâ* ("New Year's Day"), and Nisan 1
is not even mentioned in the great Priestly calendar of Leviticus
23.[67] "These are My fixed times, the fixed times of the LORD,"
begins that calendar, "which you shall proclaim as sacred occasions." And which is the first such occasion? The Sabbath, and
from there the text jumps to the fourteenth of Nisan and the
passover sacrifice.[68] The vernal New Year has dropped out alto-

gether, and in its place stands something new in ancient Near Eastern religion, a *weekly* celebration of the creation of the world, the uncontestable enthronement of its creator, and the portentous commission of humanity to be the obedient stewards of creation. If Genesis 1:1–2:3 has democratized kingship, it has also routinized the New Year.

The power of this routine is shown by the fact that in all of Jewish history, there has never been a generation bereft of Jews committed to the regimen of rest and re-creation which is the Priestly Sabbath.

9. Conclusion: Chaos Neutralized in Cult

We have had occasion to observe that, properly understood, the overture to the Bible, Genesis 1:1–2:3, cannot be invoked in support of the developed Jewish, Christian, and Muslim doctrine of *creatio ex nihilo.* The traditional translation of v. 1—"In the beginning God created the heaven and the earth"—fails to reckon with the fact that these were created on different days—the heaven on the second day, the earth on the third.[1] Rather, as scholars from Rashi to Speiser have argued, it is best to take the verse as a temporal clause: "When God began to create the heaven and the earth—." As Speiser points out, this fits nicely with the opening words of the *Enuma elish,* from which the name of the poem has been drawn.[2]

> When above [*enuma eliš*] the heaven had not [yet] been named,
> [and] below the earth had not [yet] been called by a name . . .[3]

Genesis 1:2 thus describes the "world," if we may call it that, just before the cosmogony began: "unformed and void, with darkness over the surface of the deep [*tĕhôm*] and a wind from God sweeping over the water." Here again, a parallel with the *Enuma elish* readily offers itself. Marduk, having utilized the winds to overcome Tiamat, "rested, examining her dead body" just before he split her in half to form the sky and the Earth.[4] In Genesis 1, God acts similarly, creating the sky as a "divider" *(mabdîl)* that will separate the supernal and the terrestrial waters, until now one undifferentiated mass, and then commanding the terrestrial waters to "be gathered into one area, that the dry land may appear."[5]

In spite of some variations, it should now be clear that Genesis 1:1–2:3 is quite close to the *Enuma elish.* The essential differences are twofold. First, in Genesis there is no active opposition to God's creative labor. He works on inert matter. In fact, rather than *creatio ex nihilo,* "creation without opposition", is the more accurate nutshell statement of the theology underlying our passage. The second essential difference from the *Enuma elish* is that Genesis 1:1–2:3 *begins* near the point when the Babylonian poem *ends* its action, with the primordial waters neutralized and the victorious and unchallengeable deity about to undertake the work of cosmogony. This has at times led some scholars to the belief that in an earlier form of the traditions that have crystallized as Genesis 1, there had also been a battle.[6] Perhaps so, but, as I have already noted, speculation about the prehistory of this text is futile and, more important, if a theomachy did once precede the overture to the Bible, the fact that it was dropped and the text begins when it does is a matter of high theological import that must not be obscured by tradition-historical conjecturing. Elsewhere in the Bible, Tiamat (in various forms and under various names) was indeed alive and well, challenging order and casting doubt upon YHWH's mastery over the world. But in Genesis 1:1–2:3 she has disappeared, and all that remains, apart from God and his "wind" or spirit, is dark, inert chaos upon which form and order are about to be imposed.

One thing that this primordial chaos shares with Tiamat is that it does not *disappear,* but rather is *transformed* during the act of creation. In Genesis 1 the primordial waters come to be confined to two places, the space above the sky and the seas on Earth. This confinement of the waters is a common theme in the Hebrew Bible, appearing even in cosmogonies that betray no acquaintance with Genesis 1:1–2:3.[7] In these other examples, however, the waters retain more of their mythic vitality, as in Job 38:8–11, which speaks of God's closing and bolting a door on the newborn sea (or Yamm) and telling it (or him), "You may come so far and no farther; / Here your surging waves will stop." In Genesis 1, the waters have been not only neutralized but demythologized and even depersonalized. They have not, however, been eliminated. Instead, the process of setting up boundaries and making separations that we have come to call creation forces them to alternate with other elements—the sky (perceived as a kind of sheet of metal stretched out as a vault over the Earth),[8] the atmosphere, the dry land. God has not annihilated the primordial chaos. He has only limited it.

The same holds for the other uncreated reality, darkness. Light, which is God's first creation,[9] does not banish darkness. Rather, it alternates with it: "there was evening and there was morning" in each of the six days of creation.[10] The mention of evening first recalls the Priestly law that a holy day begins the evening before, at least in the case of the Day of Atonement, which is called a sabbath, and perhaps in the case of the other holy days and even ordinary days.[11] But the priority of "evening" over "day" reminds us of which is primordial and recalls again that chaos in the form of darkness has not been eliminated, but only confined to its place through alternation with light. The function of the heavenly luminaries, created on the fourth day, is to announce the boundary between these realities, to "serve as signs for the set times . . . to separate [lĕhabdîl] light from darkness."[12] It is noteworthy that in Genesis 2:1–3, the Sabbath, the only day blessed and sanctified by God, is also the only day without an evening, a day's period without night, as it were. It is conceivable that this is an oversight of the author or redactor, but it may also be the intention to declare that the sanctity of the Sabbath excludes the malign powers that Israelite tradition very often associated with darkness:[13] on only one day out of every seven is that horrific primordial chaos banished rather than neutralized by confinement. If so, then it is no wonder that the Mishnah can call the eschatological future "a day that is entirely Sabbath and rest for eternal life" and designate Psalm 92, the song "for the Sabbath day,"[14] as the special hymn for that aeon.[15] The reality that the Sabbath represents—God's unchallenged and uncompromised mastery, blessing, and hallowing—is consistently and irreversibly available only in the world-to-come. Until then, it is known only in the tantalizing experience of the Sabbath.

If Genesis 1:1–2:3 is not a witness to the developed creation theology of the Abrahamic religions, neither is it the typological last stage in biblical thinking on the subject. Whereas in this passage God is the creator only of what is good or, to state the converse, God pronounces everything that he creates to be good, in the great anonymous prophecies from the end of the Exile (ca. 540 B.C.E.) we hear a bold proclamation that God is the author of everything, even of evil:

> [5]I am the LORD and there is none else;
> Beside Me, there is no god.
> I engird you, though you have not known Me,
> [6]So that they may know, from east to west,
> That there is none but Me.
> I am the LORD, and there is none else,
> [7]I form light and create darkness,
> I make weal [šālôm] and create woe [rā']
> I the LORD do all these things. (Isa. 45:5-7)

No longer is darkness primordial and merely accommodated through creation into a new order of things. Now darkness too, no less than light, is a creation of the God of Israel. And no longer is God responsible only for the good that there is. Now he is the creator of evil [ra'] as well, and no more is the existence of evil a blemish on his claim to absolute mastery over all that is. The message of the prophet here is that the God who created evil and alone is responsible for it is also about to annihilate it, to break the back of Israel's oppressors and to restore Israel to her former and promised glory. Chaos is now not simply passive before God, but dependent upon him, and he is not able simply to use it, but even to "de-create" it.

Moshe Weinfeld believes that a number of affirmations in the anonymous collection now called Second Isaiah were intended as critiques of the Priestly creation story.[16] Thus when the prophet asks, "To whom, then, can you liken [tĕdammĕyûn] God, / What form compare to Him?",[17] Weinfeld interprets this as a statement of opposition to the idea that humanity is "the image" or "likeness" (dĕmût) of God, as asserted in Genesis 1:26-27. Similarly, when the prophet asks rhetorically, "Whom did He consult, and

who taught Him?" and answers that YHWH "unaided spread out
the earth," this is, according to Weinfeld, in opposition to God's
apparent consultation with the lesser deities in Genesis 1: "Let *us*
make man in *our* image, after *our* likeness."[18] The stirring announcement in Isaiah 40:28 that the "Creator of the earth from
end to end / . . . never grows faint or weary" can be seen as a
counterpoint to the Priestly image of God ceasing from his work,
resting and being refreshed on the seventh day.[19]

From an even later collection in the same book, known now as
Third Isaiah, we hear a prediction of the transformation of reality
which further points up the inadequacy of creation as it is known
from Genesis 1:

> [19]No longer shall you need the sun
> For light by day,
> Nor the shining of the moon
> For radiance by night[20]:
> For the LORD shall be your light everlasting,
> Your God shall be your glory.
> [20]Your sun shall set no more,
> Your moon no more withdraw;
> For the LORD shall be a light to you forever,
> And your days of mourning shall be ended. (Isa. 60:19–20)[21]

In this oracle the alternation of night and day, which serves as a
refrain throughout Genesis 1, is to be brought to an end, as YHWH
will ceaselessly enlighten the world. The light of the first three
days of the hexaemeron, which derived from God without celestial mediation, will return. Only now it will not alternate with the
primal darkness, as it did in Genesis 1, but will shine forth con-
tinuously upon a world comforted and healed. This is the character of the new creation, "a new heaven and a new earth" that the
same collection announces, a creation that so surpasses the other
that "the former things shall not be remembered."[22]

The claim that passages such as these were composed in con-
scious opposition to the Priestly cosmogony that has become the
overture to the Bible is doubtful. The instances of common vocab-

ulary are few, and even here the possibility of coincidence is high. In short, nothing in Second or Third Isaiah betrays awareness of the seven-day creation scheme of Genesis 1:1–2:3. In fact, given the importance of both creation and Sabbath observance in Third Isaiah, where the latter even defines Gentile admissibility to the cultic community,[23] the absence in that anthology of any reference to seven days of creation is remarkable. If direct influence is unlikely, we can, however, still speak of a certain typological opposition, one that presupposes the acquaintance of these late prophets not with Genesis 1:1–2:3 as it stands, but with some of the theological currents that went into it. Weinfeld is right to speak of Second Isaiah's polemical attitude toward the kind of anthropomorphic language that appears in P, but the essence of the critique is deeper than this. Second Isaiah objects to the notion that God is somehow limited and thus not altogether free, even though he is omnipotent. A God who exists in a pantheon (even if he is supreme within it), a God who consults his colleagues (even if their response is only affirmative), a God who creates only light and only what is good, leaving darkness and evil free (though harmless to him), a God who is humanly imaginable—this is not the God who, against all odds, will overturn the Babylonian juggernaut and restore the pathetic band of Israelite exiles to their land, their royal eminence, and their cosmic centrality. Viewed against Genesis 1:1–2:3, Second and Third Isaiah take a decisive step in the direction of YHWH's transcendence. To be sure, their theologies are subtle and complex, and some older themes, such as the combat myth, remain alive,[24] as they will be for hundreds of years, even after *creatio ex nihilo* has become axiomatic. The God who "never grows faint or weary"[25] was more a hope and a promise than a static reality after two generations of ostensible divine dormancy during the Exile. And even when YHWH's unaided authorship of the whole world—even evil—is affirmed, we are not permitted to conclude that we have at last come upon creation without preexistent chaos. Second and Third Isaiah do, however, approximate Kaufmann's "basic idea of Israelite religion," that "there is no realm above or beside YHWH to limit his absolute sovereignty."[26] This is, as I have had occasion to remark, a confession of faith rather than an unexceptionable description of self-evident reality. It is, nonetheless, a confession that moves dramatically toward the doctrine of *creatio ex nihilo*.

To conclude: Gen 1:1–2:3, the Priestly creation story, is not about the banishment of evil, but about its control. It describes a process of separation and distinction making in which the dark, ungodly forces are effortlessly overcome by placement in a structure in which they are bounded by new realities created by divine speech alone. This new structure is essentially cultic in character. Its construction is highly reminiscent of the rites of temple building, and even the seven-day sequence shows a probable affinity with the old autumnal and vernal New Year's festivals. More important, in building the new structure that is creation, God functions like an Israelite priest, making distinctions, assigning things to their proper category and assessing their fitness, and hallowing the Sabbath.[27] Priestly tradition has adapted to its own sacral *regimen* the picture of creation without opposition as evidenced in Psalm 104. As a result, the creative ordering of the world has become something that humanity can not only witness and celebrate, but something in which it can also take part. Among the many messages of Genesis 1:1–2:3 is this: it is through the cult that we are enabled to cope with evil, for it is the cult that builds and maintains order, transforms chaos into creation, ennobles humanity, and realizes the kingship of the God who has ordained the cult and commanded that it be guarded and practiced. It is through obedience to the directives of the divine master that his good world comes into existence.

III. CREATION AND COVENANT: THE DYNAMICS OF LORDSHIP AND SUBMISSION

What then of one loathsome and foul,
Man, who drinks wrongdoing like water!

10. The Two Idioms of Biblical Monotheism

In the subordination of the other gods to Marduk in the *Enuma elish,* we see the emergence of a pattern that can, with appropriate qualification, be termed monotheism. Marduk, it will be recalled, demanded as the terms for his taking on Tiamat that his father Ea "convene the assembly and proclaim my lot supreme" so that he, instead of them, might "determine the destinies" and whatever he creates "shall remain unaltered."[1] Anxious to avert the lethal threat, the gods hold court and, in an atmosphere of bibulous festivity, carefree and exalted at last, they proclaim him their lord and erect him a royal dais.[2] The keynote of the homage that they then pay him is his incomparability: "You are [the most] important among the great gods" and "none among the gods shall infringe upon your prerogative." "To you," they announce, "we have given kingship over the totality of the whole universe."[3] This preliminary exaltation of Marduk at the expense of the other gods is ratified and established in perpetuity when he wins his victory and receives his temple and temple-city. In building these, the gods demonstrate their gratitude to Marduk for having beaten back the threat of chaos and for having liberated them from drudgery through the creation of humanity.[4] His acts of prowess, together with the gods' formal acknowledgment of the legal implications of them, thus become the basis of both cosmic and political order. They are the foundation of Babylon's very existence and the ground of her claim to world dominance.

As it appears in the *Enuma elish,* the creation of the world involves a movement from plurality to unity, from the fragile and cumbersome system of "primitive democracy" among the gods to the tougher and more efficient monarchy of the divine military hero, Marduk.[5] Consensus is not, however, abolished. Rather, the endless and tiresome process of deliberation is reduced to the formulation of only one resolution—whether to accept Marduk's offer, whether to make him king. On this alone is consensus necessary and, it must be noted, easy to reach in light of the certain defeat that lies ahead without his leadership. In short, their choice for him is not much of a choice at all, the alternative being death. This is underscored by the imprisonment of those who confederated with Tiamat and the obvious absence of neutrality as an option. It is, nonetheless, remarkable that even the emergence of monarchy is here presented as having required a vote, as it were, and the supremacy of Marduk is not seen as primordial, self-evident, and self-sufficient, but as dependent upon the consent of the other gods.[6] In practice his elevation ends their autonomy, but in theory it does not nullify it. In full autonomy, they choose to subordinate themselves forever in order to live and be free. The paradox of world order is, to adapt Paul Ricoeur's characterization of Pharisaism, that it rests on "voluntary heteronomy."[7] It is the gods' glad willingness to *choose heteronomy* that allows order, safety, and even liberty to appear.

The periodic public recitation of the *Enuma elish,* especially during the New Year's festival, indicates that this choice of heteronomy, the willing acceptance of Marduk's lordship, was never so final as a superficial reading of the great creation poem might suggest. Tzvi Abusch has recently opposed the conventional view that the *Enuma elish* is simply a reflection of the ascent of Babylon to hegemony, preferring instead to date it to "some time during the early first millennium in a period of political *weakness* of the city Babylon."[8] This fits nicely with my argument that in Israel the combat myth of creation increasingly tended to appear in moments in which YHWH and his promises to the nation seemed discredited.[9] In both cases the myth and its ritual reiteration would have had a compensatory or restorative role, serving to counter the persistence of the dark forces identified with the chaos monster. By reciting the *Enuma elish,* the cultic community overtly casts its lot with the gods acclaiming Marduk and differentiates themselves from the army of Tiamat, destined for perdition. Covertly, they acknowledge the incompleteness of Marduk's supremacy and the persistence and resilience of the evil whose destruction *in illo tempore* they celebrate. The recitation of the *Enuma elish* is, in part, a reestablishment of social consensus, which readily dissolves when the community evades their task of self-subordination. Only the inextinguishable urge to do so accounts for the continuing pertinence of the poem.

In spite of the commonplace that Israel was monotheistic and thus radically distinct from the rest of the ancient world, clear echoes of this subordination of the pantheon to its king are to be heard in the Hebrew Bible as well:

> [1]Ascribe to the Lord, O divine beings,
> ascribe to the Lord glory and strength.
> [2]Ascribe to the Lord the glory of His name,
> bow down to the Lord when He appears
> in holiness.

> [10]The Lord sat enthroned at the Flood;
> the Lord sits enthroned, king forever. (Ps. 29:1–2, 10)[10]

That Psalm 29 is a YHWHistic adaptation of Baal hymns has long been recognized.[11] This, together with the context, makes it all the more certain that the "Flood" in v. 10 is not the great deluge of Noah's time, but rather the assault of chaos upon order in the form of the sea monster's bellicose challenge to the pantheon. It is possible that this allusion hints at a time when YHWH had not yet attained to supremacy, becoming, like Marduk, king only upon his victory. Even if this be so, the emphasis in the hymn is not upon the old and presumably failed arrangement of "democracy" in the pantheon, but upon the awesomeness of YHWH's mastery and the corollary obligation of the lesser gods to render him homage. Were those gods nonexistent or that homage never in doubt, Psalm 29 would have no point.

In Exodus 15, the Song of the Sea, we again read the hymnic affirmation of YHWH's incomparability:

Who is like You, O Lord, among the gods;
Who is like You, majestic among the holy ones,
Awesome in splendor, working wonders? (Exod. 15:11)[12]

The difference is that here YHWH's band of loyal confederates is not divine, but human, the people he acquired through manumission and settled on his mountain, the site of the sanctuary in which his everlasting kingship is proclaimed. Similarly, the confederates of the vanquished enemy are also human—Philistia, Edom, Moab, and Canaan, all of them panicked and aghast at the sight of YHWH's deliverance of Israel at the sea.[13] Israel's indomitability follows from her identification with the cause of YHWH, just as the defeat of her neighbors follows from their failure to submit to him and their choice of other gods. This too becomes explicit in the Psalter:

> [7]All who worship images,
>   who vaunt their idols,
>   are dismayed;
>   all gods bow down to Him.
> [8]Zion, hearing it, rejoices,
>   The towns of Judah exult,
>   because of Your judgments, O Lord,
> [9]For You, Lord, are supreme over all the earth;
>   You are exalted high above all gods. (Ps. 97:7–9)[14]

The other gods and their worshipers are forced into submission, even as Judah and its Temple Mount, Zion, rejoice at the decrees *(mišpāṭîm)* of YHWH, great king and greatest God.

If we bear in mind this partial replacement of the other gods with the people Israel, then we shall see that in its broadest outlines, the Exodus–Sinai narrative conforms to the same pattern as that of the *Enuma elish.* An enslaved people calls out to YHWH to rescue them, and he responds in a wondrous way, saving them at the sea and drowning the picked troops of the god incarnate of Egypt. Israel acclaims YHWH as incomparable, their king forever, and he, having brought them to Sinai, offers them a covenant, by which they may become his "treasured possession among all the peoples . . . a kingdom of priests and a holy nation." Unanimously they accept: "All that the LORD has spoken we will do."[15] The entire revelation at Sinai is a specification of what that commitment entails. First and foremost is the demand that no other god infringe upon the claim of him who redeemed Israel from the house of bondage.

In spite of some demurrals, there is today wide agreement among scholars that the theology of the Pentateuch is deeply imbued with the idiom of the Near Eastern suzerainty treaty: YHWH, acting in the role of an emperor, cites the record of his benefactions to his needy vassal Israel and elicits from her a sworn commitment to observe the stipulations he imposes, to the benefit of both so long as she keeps faith.[16] As persuasive as the treaty analogy is, it should be noted that much the same pattern can be detected in mythic literature, such as the *Enuma elish* and its Canaanite and Israelite parallels: the gods willingly and gladly accept the kingship of their heroic savior, grant him the right to determine the destinies, and redefine themselves as his servitors. It is this act of voluntary heteronomy that, by establishing his kingship and ensuring their survival, works to the benefit of both lord and liege. There is, of course, a vast formal difference between the covenant and the combat myth. The first originates in the world of diplomacy, the second in cult. But when the language of diplomacy is transposed into theology, YHWH replacing the emperor, and the language of cult is substantially historicized, people (largely) replacing gods, the convergence is remarkable. In the Hebrew Bible, covenant and combat myth are two variant idioms for one ideal—the exclusive enthronement of YHWH and the radical and uncompromising commitment of the House of Israel to carrying out his commands. If "monotheism" refers to anything in the conceptual universe of biblical Israel, it refers to that ideal.

The great threat to monotheism, so understood, is defection. In the mythic idiom defection takes the form of a challenge to YHWH's supremacy among the gods. The allusions to YHWH's composure in the face of the angry, roiling sea reflect such a challenge, although in a rather demythologized way.[17] More pertinent are the instances in which YHWH pronounces a verdict upon other gods, as in Psalm 82, in which the failure of the others to practice justice (in the classic form of special protection for the poor and the orphan) results in a death sentence. In a few other passages, mostly in the prophets, we find allusions to a lost myth in which, having failed to make good on his claim of sovereignty, a god is ejected from the pantheon.[18] Later this story of the excommunicated deity will fuse with the biblical figure Satan, the heavenly attorney general, to produce the myth of Lucifer, the fallen angel who rules hell in Christian demonology. But in the Hebrew Bible, the fusion has not taken place, and the myth of the primordial theomachy or the revolt in heaven (*which* of them is unclear and must be determined in each case) is barely recoverable. That snippets of it are indeed to be found evidences profound insecurity about YHWH's kingship even within the world of Israelite myth. The absence of the full-blown myth has been taken by Kaufmann and others as proof of the radical demythologized character of Israelite religion.[19] To me it seems more consistent and more reasonable to conclude the opposite: it is precisely what is most dangerous and most alluring that must be repressed. That the myth of theomachy or rebellion has been repressed rather than destroyed accounts for the fact that we now have snippets, and only snippets.

In the other idiom of monotheism, the idiom of covenant, defection takes the form of Israel's worship of other gods, either in place of YHWH or alongside him. This aspect of biblical monotheism derives from the demand of ancient Near Eastern covenant lords (suzerains) that the vassal forswear allegiance to rival suzerains, taking special precautions to avoid the appearance of obeisance to any but his own lord in covenant. "Do not turn your eyes to anyone else," Mursilis, Hittite emperor of the fourteenth century B.C.E., warned his vassal, Duppi-Tessub of Amurru.[20] One of the great breakthroughs in the study of covenant occurred when William L. Moran identified "love" as one of the central items in the vocabulary of this idea of exclusive allegiance.[21] In an Assyrian treaty of the seventh century B.C.E., King Esarhaddon, anxious that

his vassals may break faith with his designated successor, Assurbanipal, stipulates that "You will love Assurbanipal as yourselves." Elsewhere, the vassals swear that "the king of Assyria, our
lord, we will love."[22] It is this covenantal use of "love" that makes
the transition between the first two verses of the great Jewish
affirmation, the *Shema'*, smooth and natural:

> [4]Hear, O Israel! The LORD is our God, the LORD alone. [5]You shall
> love the LORD your God with all your heart and with all your soul
> and with all your might. (Deut. 6:4–5)

The threat to covenant love is the allure of the other gods. By
and large, the texts in the Hebrew Bible that show the most affinities with the suzerainty treaties also regard the other gods as
extant, real, and potent:

> [2]If there appears among you a prophet or a dream-diviner and he gives
> you a sign or a portent, [3]saying, "Let us follow and worship another
> god"—whom you have not experienced—even if the sign or portent that
> he named to you comes true, [4]do not heed the words of that prophet or
> that dream-diviner. For the LORD your God is testing you to see whether
> you really love the LORD your God with all your heart and soul. [5]Follow
> none but the LORD your God, and revere none but Him; observe His
> commandments alone, and heed only His orders; worship none but Him;
> and hold fast to Him. [6]As for that prophet or dream-diviner, he shall be
> put to death; for he urged disloyalty to the LORD your God—who freed
> you from the house of bondage. (Deut. 13:2–6)

In this text, a false prophet is defined by his allegiance to a god
other than YHWH, and that allegiance, in turn, is defined by
disregard for YHWH's directives or obedience to the other deity.
Had that god been only a lifeless, storyless fetish in the Israelite
mind, as Kaufmann thinks, then the temptation to abandon
YHWH for him would have been slim, and the centuries of hard-
fought competition between YHWH and his rivals for the heart,
soul, and mind of Israel would never have been. In fact, however,
texts such as this one are struggling to neutralize the *power* in Israel
of deities other than YHWH by providing a YHWHistic explanation of their appeal. The supernatural gifts of their prophets and

diviners testify not to the power of those gods (unlike the supernatural gifts of exclusively YHWHistic prophets and diviners), but
to the desire of YHWH to test Israel's exclusive allegiance to him:
will Israel abandon him and his *mitsvot* for the other gods and their
cults, or will they cleave devotedly to him even in the face of the
dramatic and persistent inducements to do otherwise?

The fact that the urge to serve the other gods continues and is,
to all appearances, validated by compelling empirical evidence, is
itself proof that Israel's consent to serve YHWH alone was never
so final and unshakable as a reading of the passages about revelation at Sinai would suggest. Instead, YHWH's kingship in Israel,
like his kingship in the pantheon and his mastery over creation,
remained vulnerable and in continual need of reaffirmation, rera-
tification, reacclamation. The re-presentation of the Sinaitic moment on the plains of Moab, which is the burden of Deuteronomy,
is born of a profound awareness of the waywardness of Israel, on
the one hand, and her indispensability to the suzerainty of
YHWH, on the other. The covenant of Sinai has not the fixity and
irrevocability of a royal decree; demanding human participation,
it is fully realized only with the glad consent of the cultic community of Israel, a consent that is often denied—such is the risk that
the consensual basis of the covenant entails—yet never destroyed.
Texts like the one in Deuteronomy 13, previously cited, are at-
tempting to make the consent to obey YHWH alone the prime and
irreducible element in Israel's collective and individual life. Obedience is not to be predicated upon YHWH's ability to work
miracles and predict the future; the prophets of the other deities
can do these as well, and when they do, this empirical evidence
on behalf of those deities is to be disregarded in the name of an
increasingly nonempirical faithfulness, a faithfulness founded
upon YHWH's acquisition of Israel through the nonrepeating
foundational event of the exodus. The failure of the present to
match the glories of the past, in which YHWH did his work in a
pyrotechnic spectacular, is no grounds for defection or faithless-
ness. The very existence of the non-YHWHistic Israelites is to be
seen as treasonous[23]; they and their gods are classified in Deuter-

onomy as intolerable and unassimilable foreigners. Only the fragility of YHWH's covenantal lordship can account for this nervousness and defensiveness with the presence of an alternative to him and his cult. The theology of the fragile lordship of YHWH is, in turn, partly a reflection of the fragility of religious consensus within Israelite society in biblical times.

A long process of development lies between this theology and the mature Rabbinic thought of the Talmud. One difference is that the latter is more rigorously monotheistic, treating the other gods as unreal and nonexistent. This, however, makes it all the more remarkable that the ideas of the fragility of God's reign in Israel and the continual necessity of Israel's active consent to it remain central to Rabbinic Judaism. The recitation of the *Shema'*, already the watchword of the faith, became early on in Rabbinic law an obligation incumbent upon the Jew every morning and every evening. Its covenantal acclamation of the uniqueness of YHWH and his exclusive claim upon Israel, a claim honored by observance of his *mitsvot*, became known as the "acceptance of the yoke of the kingdom of heaven." The Jew begins and ends his day with a miniature covenant renewal ceremony.[24]

More striking still is this late midrash:

"So you are My witnesses
              —declares the LORD—
And I am God." That is, if you are My witnesses, I am
God, and if you are not My witnesses, I am, as it were, not God.[25]

Here the consensual basis of the divinity of the God of Israel and the fragility of his reality in the world appear with shocking clarity. God depends, "as it were," upon the witness of Israel: without it, his divinity is not realized. The actualization of the full potential of God requires the testimony of his special people. Like Marduk in the *Enuma elish* or YHWH himself at Sinai, the elevation of the God of Israel is partly a function of those who elevate him. In the covenantal idiom of monotheism, Israel is the functional equivalent of the pantheon,[26] wisely and joyfully acclaiming their lord and deliverer.

11. The Dialectic of Covenantal Theonomy

The need for a *continual* surrender of autonomy, which is prominent in biblical thought and results in a crucial daily obligation in Rabbinic practice, testifies to the incompleteness of all such acts of surrender in the past. One can never achieve heteronomy of the will by an act of will alone; the will cannot effect is own extinction. In this sense, Ricoeur's term "voluntary heteronomy" can be seriously misleading. The Jewish theology at point is actually one that centers spiritual life upon a hard-won, indeed precious notion of *service*, hard-won because the will continually must work in part against itself, precious because it is precisely the enormous difficulty of this task that renders its achievement worthy. Here too, Hegel's "master–slave dialectic," to which reference was made earlier,[1] aids in clarifying the nature of this ever-recurring moment in the religious life of the faithful Jew. In Michael Wyschogrod's words,

Hegel's understanding [is] that mastery is real only if the slave is a human consciousness whose conquest is worthwhile. A slave who is totally enslaved is an inanimate object, the control of which does not bestow mastery. God's lordship therefore requires the humanity of man rather than the collapse of man before God.[2]

The obedience YHWH requires of Israel is not the conformity of an automaton with its computer programmed by God, but the obedience of an ancient Near Eastern vassal, that is, a king loyal to a greater king. The covenant that specifies this obedience must not be confused with the bill of sale of a slave or a statement of unconditional surrender on the part of the vassal. Indeed, the very choice of the covenant document as the metaphor by which to render this delicate relationship evidences the free will with which Israel enters into the new arrangement. The bilateral character of the suzerainty treaty underscores the freedom and dignity of the lesser partner even within the new relationship of fealty to his lord. That this vassal is himself a king makes the same point. Through covenant the people Israel steps into a position that is fundamentally royal in nature. Her obligation to serve does not compromise her majesty; indeed, it defines it. It is obedience in covenant that confers upon Israel the status of God's "treasured possession among all the peoples . . . a kingdom of priests and a holy nation."[3] Or, in the words of a covenant renewal address:

[16]The LORD your God commands you this day to observe these laws and rules; observe them faithfully with all your heart and soul. [17]You have affirmed this day that the LORD is your God, that you will walk in His ways, that you will observe His laws and commandments and rules, and that you will obey Him. [18]And the LORD has affirmed this day that you are, as He promised you, His treasured people which shall observe all His commandments, [19]and that He will set you, in fame and renown and glory, high above all the nations that He has made; and that you shall be, as He promised, a holy people to the LORD your God. (Deut. 26:16–19)

The recollection of the moment in which Israel affirmed that YHWH would be her God remains as a sign of the freedom in which she chooses to serve him. The re-presentation of that moment of choice keeps alive the element of human autonomy in the dialectic of divine suzerainty. This is the element that distinguishes covenantal theonomy from theocratic tyranny.

The other element in the dialectic is the heteronomy involved in service to God. This is seen in the simple fact that, for all the language of choice that characterizes covenant texts, the Hebrew Bible never regards the choice to decline covenant as legitimate. The fact that a choice is given does not make the alternative good or even acceptable, as a proponent of a purely contractual ethic might wish. In fact, the wrong choice results in nothing short of death:

[19]I call heaven and earth to witness against you this day: I have put before you life and death, blessing and curse. Choose life—if you and your offspring would live—[20]by loving the LORD your God, heeding His commands, and holding fast to Him. For thereby you shall have life and shall long endure upon the soil that the LORD your God swore to Abraham, Isaac, and Jacob to give them. (Deut. 30:19–20)

The qualification upon the free will and dignity of Israel as she confronts the choice of whether to obey is that her would-be suzerain has already stacked the deck, as it were: Israel will live only if she freely makes the *right* choice. Covenant is an offer that the vassal cannot refuse, especially if the suzerain is omnipotent.

It might be argued that this lack of an unqualified choice results from the fact that Moses is here reiterating on the plains of Moab a covenant already made nearly forty years earlier at Sinai/Horeb, so that the choice not to obey is a violation of an existing pact rather than a declination of an initial offer of covenant. The retort to the argument, however, is convincing: even when YHWH appears to be offering Israel a covenant for the first time, as in Exodus 19, he does so on the basis of a prior claim upon her, a claim that she was never allowed to refuse—"You have seen what I did to the Egyptians, how I bore you on eagles' wings and brought you to Me."[4] The redemption from bondage in Egypt, in turn, is based not on God's opposition to slavery (neither the Hebrew Bible nor the New Testament is opposed to slavery), but upon his prior covenant with Abraham, Isaac, and Jacob.[5] In the exodus, God fulfills his pledge to make the family of Abraham into a great nation with a land of its own and a byword of blessing.[6] When the pledge is formulated as a covenant, God identifies himself thus: "I am the LORD who brought you out from Ur of the Chaldeans to give you this land as a possession," in an obvious adumbration of the Sinaitic announcement that "I the LORD am your God who brought you out of the land of Egypt, the house of bondage."[7] The difference is that Abraham is never offered the choice of covenant, as Israel is in Exodus 19. In biblical thought (unlike Rabbinic), the covenant with Abraham is a matter of prevenient grace: it results from a mysterious and unmotivated decision of God, without regard to the merits or sins of Abraham and, more important, without negotiations between him and God. This is why that covenant can serve as a basis for reconciliation with God even after Israel has violated and desecrated the covenant of Sinai.[8] Because the Abrahamic Covenant is the basis and motivation for the redemption from Egypt, and because the redemption from Egypt is the basis of the Sinaitic Covenant, Israel at Sinai is no position to decline. The language of free choice notwithstanding, to decline at this point would be an unpardonable act of ingratitude.

This curious dialectic of autonomy and heteronomy, each qualifying the other, can be clarified if we recall again the Near Eastern suzerainty treaty, which is our closest analogue to the Sinai Covenant. As we have observed, the weaker party, the vassal, enters the treaty of his own free will. He retains his throne, and his entrance into the new arrangement has the force of an act of state. The vassal, in short, is not an agent of his suzerain; hence the *autonomy* of Israel in covenant. On the other hand, a treaty, especially of the suzerainty kind, that is, one between unequals, does not emerge out of thin air. Behind every treaty lies a threat, usually a threat of violence. Without the threat there would be no impetus for a negotiated settlement; negotiation is war carried on by other means. In the case of the suzerainty treaty, the weaker signatory freely chooses to obviate the potential for destruction that lies in the disparity between his power and that of his liege lord. Without the treaty, the disparity will remain and, the lord's offer having been rebuffed, grow more menacing; hence the *heteronomy* of Israel in covenant, her lack of a real alternative to YHWH's suzerainty. If, on the other hand, the treaty is ratified, then both parties stand to gain. The suzerain wins a measure of control over the vassal's domain, and the vassal wins an alliance with a great power, thus converting potential calamity into reassuring amity. The fearsome disparity in power remains, but whereas it might have proven crushing, it is now rendered harmless, in fact positive.

Because the potential vassal is not yet under the control of the aspiring suzerain and, if war is to be avoided, must *choose* to accept the latter's yoke, then the suzerain must *woo* his vassal. This element of courtship can be observed in the historical prologue of some ancient Near Eastern treaties, wherein the great king rehearses the prior history of the parties, emphasizing the unmerited benefactions that he has performed for the subordinate partner in covenant.[9] In the Sinai Covenant, at least in its Deuteronomic formulation, this element is in plentiful evidence:

[20]When, in time to come, your son asks you, "What mean the exhortations, laws, and rules which the LORD our God has enjoined upon you?" [21]You shall say to your son, "We were slaves to Pharaoh in Egypt and the LORD freed us from Egypt with a mighty hand. (Deut. 6:20–21)

Or in YHWH's words quoted by Joshua during the covenant-making ceremony at Shechem:

[13]"I have given you land for which you did not labor and towns which you did not build, and you have settled in them; you are enjoying vineyards and olive groves which you did not plant.

[14]"Now, therefore, revere the LORD and serve him with undivided loyalty." (Josh. 24:13–14)

This element of courtship mediates between autonomy and heteronomy. Because Israel is not God and never had the possibility of rejecting his benefactions, the ethic that characterizes her relationship to him is not autonomous. Because his commandments are grounded in the history of redemption, they are not the imposition of an alien force, but rather the revelation of a familiar, benevolent, and loving God, and the ethic is not one of pure heteronomy. At Sinai/Horeb and at Shechem, YHWH reminds Israel that he is not altogether "other," not utterly alien to her identity, but involved with her from the beginning. This continuous and beneficial involvement of YHWH in Israel's life makes the convenient dichotomy of autonomy and heteronomy grossly inadequate for understanding the dynamics of obedience in covenant. Only when the opposition of dichotomy yields to the subtlety of dialectic can we begin to grasp the Jewish dynamics of lordship and submission.

In the Talmud the same issue is discussed in a different idiom. There the question is whether Israel's acceptance of the Torah at Sinai was owing to duress:

"And they took their places at the foot of the mountain."[10] Rabbi Avdimi bar Ḥama bar Ḥasa said: This teaches that the Holy One (blessed be he) turned the mountain over on them like a tub and said to them: "If you accept the Torah—well and good, but if you do not, there will your grave be." Rabbi Aḥa bar Jacob said: From this one can derive a great objection to the Torah. Said Rava: Nonetheless, they did accept it later, in the days of Ahasuerus, as it is written, "The Jews confirmed and accepted"[11]—they confirmed what they had already accepted.[12]

The expression bĕtaḥtît hāhār in Exodus 19:17 means "at the foot of the mountain." But if one reads it with etymological literalism, translating the first word as if it were its cognate taḥat ("under"), then one can, with Rabbi Avdimi, conjure up the scene of God's uprooting Mount Sinai and holding it over Israel's heads until they consent to accept his Torah. The point of this midrash is a theology that sees obligation by Torah as heteronomous: Israel never had a choice. David Novak points out the affinity of this theology with a number of Rabbinic statements to the effect that the laws of the Torah are in the nature of an unimpugnable royal decree (gĕzērâ) and not examples of some generally understood and respected value, such as mercy.[13] For example, the law in Deuteronomy 22:6–7, which forbids taking the mother bird along with her chicks or eggs, is not to be ascribed to God's compassion, as a more anthropocentric and anthropopathic theology would have it. Rather, the laws of the Torah "are nothing but decrees (gĕzērôt)" and must be practiced whether we deem them humane or not.[14] The authority behind them is not the values they may be construed to manifest, but the sovereign and inscrutable will of God.

The second speaker in this debate of Babylonian masters of the fourth century C.E., Rabbi Aḥa bar Jacob, objects that if at Sinai God threatened Israel's life, then the latter's acceptance of his Torah is impaired because it was obtained under duress. This Amora thus counterposes a theology of autonomy, daring to suggest the impropriety of obligation without consent even when imposed by the deity himself. Finally, the great authority Rava spins a midrash that upholds both Avdimi's heteronomy of Torah obligation and Aḥa's autonomy. He interprets Esther 9:27 as a reference to the Jews' free acceptance not only of the post-Mosaic holiday of Purim, as the plain sense of the verse indicates, but also of the entire Torah already accepted under duress at Sinai. By so doing, Rava reaffirms in a new idiom—legal in metaphor, midrashic in form—the old theology of the Deuteronomistic literature already discussed: Jewry was already obligated by Torah when the choice was offered them, yet they freely and willingly chose the Torah and made it into an obligation binding upon them and their descendants for all time. The coercion at Sinai and the requirement that all generations of Jews will, like it or not, be bound by the ancient agreement represent the element of heteronomy. The Jews' choice to confirm this obligation many generations later, when no mountain was inverted over their heads, represents the element of autonomy in the dialectic of the theonomous life that is Torah. What is remarkable in this Talmudic passage is the way that the two poles that define the *biblical* dialectic of covenantal theonomy persist even though the *Talmudic* idiom for them is altogether different.

Leo Strauss, writing about Thomas Hobbes, suggests a definition of liberalism as "that political doctrine which regards as the fundamental political fact the rights, as distinguished from the duties, of man." Identifying Hobbes as "the founder of liberalism" so defined,[15] Strauss draws a connection between Hobbes's emphasis upon the right of self-preservation and his contractual theory of the state:

If the only unconditional moral fact is the natural right of each to his self-preservation, and therefore all obligations to others arise from contract, justice becomes identical with the habit of fulfilling one's contracts. Justice no longer consists in complying with standards that are independent of human will.[16]

The identification of justice "with the habit of fulfilling one's contracts" has substantial points of affinity with the ancient Jewish theology of covenant in both its biblical and its Rabbinic idioms. Indeed, if we bear in mind the importance and influence of liberalism in the North Atlantic world over the past three centuries, we begin to suspect that one motivation for the amount of attention focused on covenant in that world has been the affinities of this ancient theological idea with liberal political theory. In fact, much of this attention has had the effect, even if unintentionally, of recreating the Covenant of Sinai/Horeb in the image of modern liberal notions of civic obligation. In practice, this means stressing the autonomous element in the dialectic at the expense of the heteronomous, whose existence is often denied altogether. Consider this statement of a Jew, José Faur, about Exodus 19–24:

> As thus conceived, divine authority is not the effect of an Absolute Power who dictates His will to his inferiors, but of negotiation between two parties who are equally free to assent and dissent.[17]

Here Faur sets up a false dichotomy between heteronomy and autonomy, and elects the latter without qualification. He fails to see that Israel at Sinai is not "equally free to assent and dissent," but already owes her freedom and her life to the God with whom she has always been in an eternal covenant that was only announced and never negotiated. The same liberal bias is seen in this statement of a Christian, Ernest W. Nicholson:

> The concept of a covenant . . . is the concept that religion is based, not on a natural or ontological equivalence between the divine realm and the human, but on *choice:* God's choice of his people and their "choice" of him, that is, their free decision to be obedient and faithful to him. Thus understood, "covenant" is the central expression of the distinctive faith of Israel . . . the children of God by adoption and free decision rather than by nature or necessity.[18]

Nicholson does more justice than Faur to the heteronomous dimension of covenant. He puts Israel's "choice" of God in quotation marks and mentions it only after "God's choice [not in quotation marks] of his people." He then forfeits this advantage, however, by setting up a contrast between "adoption and free decision," on the one hand, and "nature and necessity," on the other, and identifying Israelite covenant exclusively with the former. This fits nicely with the Apostle Paul's argument that one becomes an Israelite through faith in the promise rather than through birth,[19] but this is not the position of the Hebrew Bible, and it is light-years away from the theology of covenant in the Pentateuch. A more accurate statement would be that those who stand under covenantal obligation by nature and necessity are continually called upon to adopt that relationship by free decision. Chosen for service, they must choose to serve. This is the paradox of the dialectic of autonomy and heteronomy. We can see the paradox clearly only if we resist the pressure to present the Torah as a species of liberalism. No statement of the autonomy and dignity of humanity can be adequate to this ancient Jewish theology if it fails to reckon with the difference made by the God who commands. The spiritual politics of the Hebrew Bible begins with duties, not rights, insisting that order is partly a function of the free and willing self-subordination of human beings to the God who continually creates a beachhead against the virulent and persistent forces of destruction.

12. Argument and Obedience

The dialectic of autonomy and heteronomy has relevance for Israelite theology beyond the specialized issue of the nature of covenantal service. It is, for example, the autonomy of humanity over against God that accounts for one of the most remarkable features of the Hebrew Bible, the possibility that people can argue with God and win.[1] As odd as this may seem in comparison with the New Testament and the Qur'an, for example, it is neither unprecedented in the ancient Near East (where the suasion of one god is usually performed by another) nor without continuation in post-biblical Judaism. In the Hebrew Bible the most eloquent instance of the justified human challenge to God is to be found in Abraham's response to YHWH's announcement of his imminent overthrow of Sodom and Gomorrah:[2]

[23]Abraham came forward and said, "Will You sweep away the innocent along with the guilty? [24]What if there should be fifty innocent within the city; will You then wipe out the place and not forgive for the sake of the innocent fifty who are in it? [25]Far be it from You to do such a thing, to bring death upon the innocent as well as the guilty, so that innocent and guilty fare alike. Far be it from You! Shall not the Judge of all the earth deal justly?" (Gen. 18:23–25)

The theological underpinning of Abraham's dramatic intervention is the assumption that God ought to behave according to certain generally agreed upon standards, even if he is *de facto* capable of violating them. In the soliloquy in which God decides not to destroy the cities without first informing Abraham, he identifies those standards himself: "For I have singled him out, that he may instruct his children and his posterity to keep the way of the LORD by doing what is just and right [ṣĕdāqâ ûmišpāṭ]."[3] These two terms, as we saw earlier, often denote the granting of an amnesty or reprieve.[4] God wants to see whether Abraham, the ancestor and prototype of the people of the archetypical amnesty or reprieve, the exodus, will plead that the same mercy be extended to the two corrupt and perverted cities about to be annihilated. Rising to the occasion, the patriarch plays on another sense of the term *mišpāṭ,* "equity, fair play": "Shall not the Judge [*šōpēṭ*] of all the earth deal justly [*mišpāṭ*]?" The grounds for the reprieve lie not so much in God's unmotivated mercy as in the blatant injustice of a sentence that falls upon guilty and innocent equally, as if YHWH were not the God to whom this distinction is paramount. Abraham's argument is that YHWH should combine mercy with distributive justice, sparing the whole city because of the innocence of a minority of its citizens. The argument is based upon the premise that there are certain norms that both partners in the discussion share, in this case, the norms of justice and generosity.

The assumption that God and human beings recognize the same values is hardly surprising. Most religions, upon rising to self-consciousness, present themselves to the world as the consummate articulation of universal values. What is surprising, in fact shocking, in Genesis 18 is that God may deviate from those values in practice, with no negative consequence other than a loss of reputation among people of conscience. Here, as a counterpoint to the assumption of shared values, we see the continual assertion of God's unlimited freedom, a freedom unlimited even by his own principles of justice and generosity. God's freedom from principle and his sovereignty over Abraham appear forcefully in his refusal to grant the point to Abraham at the outset, instead bargaining with him from fifty innocent to forty-five, then to thirty, twenty, and ten. He is, of course, testing Abraham's resolve: will the patriarch give up too easily? But he is also demonstrating his own sovereign freedom. The decision will be God's—Abraham can only argue and cajole—and this may be the point also of the mysterious refusal of Abraham to go from ten innocent to one, as his and God's principle requires. Perhaps he recognizes an inherent limitation upon any human being's right to question God and wishes to avoid the charge of hubris by stopping before he reaches the limit. In any event, it is surely that wish that accounts for the elaborate apologies with which Abraham prefaces other addresses after his initial outburst: "Here I venture to speak to my Lord, I who am but dust and ashes," and the like.[5] Those apologies capture the two-sidedness of the situation perfectly: they express both the *necessity* and the *absurdity* of a person's telling God what to do. They acknowledge both the justice of human protest against the dubious counsels of God and the inherent limitation upon the right of human beings to lodge such a protest.

If Genesis 18 represents the (qualified) autonomy of humanity over against divine decrees, we may take Genesis 22, the binding of Isaac, as the parade example of human heteronomy before the inscrutable command of God. For there the same Abraham, without protest or hesitation, obeys God's ghastly command to take his beloved Isaac, the son by the promise upon which Abraham has staked his entire life, to the land of Moriah to be slaughtered as a burnt offering by his father's own hand. Among Christian interpreters it is customary to see the "test" to which Genesis 22:1 refers as a test of Abraham's faith: he never doubts God's word that "it is through Isaac that offspring shall be continued for you,"[6] even when God's own command to slaughter and ignite his son seems to contradict it.[7] This nicely continues the general Pauline tendency to subordinate commandments to faith and fits well with Paul's specific reinterpretation of Abraham as a man of faith.[8] Without impugning the patriarch's exemplary faith, however, we can note that in the Torah he is also a man of the commandment, one who, in God's later words to Isaac, "obeyed Me and kept My charge: My commandments, My laws, and My teachings."[9] Indeed, in the context of this verse, it is Abraham's observance of commandments that enables the original promise of progeny, land, and blessing to be renewed for Isaac. Needless to say, the verse that depicts Abraham as a man of *mitsvot* and not only of faith is never quoted by Paul, but its theology is at least as relevant to the binding of Isaac in Genesis 22 as is the customary Christian view. God is here testing to learn whether Abraham's obedience is total or qualified, an enduring obedience or one that melts in the presence of a repugnant command, a command that contradicts his sense of justice, his paternal love, and even the divine promise itself. Here again the promise is renewed only when God has ascertained that, in the divine words to Abraham with knife in hand, "you fear God, since you have not withheld your son, your favored one, from Me."[10] Only then—when he has proven that he will obey even this command and not flinch from the slaughter of his own son, already lying bound before him upon the firewood on the altar—does God provide a ram for substitution. Promise leads to obedience, but obedience renews the promise.

Those two chapters of Genesis, with their contrasting perspectives on Abraham, present us as well with contrasting theologies of the divine–human relationship. In chapter 18 Abraham doubts, questions, argues, and even convinces God to back down from an extreme position. In chapter 22 Abraham demonstrates an absolute and unconditional obedience and as a result wins the reprieve for which he dared not plead. There is a telling analogy between these two chapters and the dimensions of covenant that I have been calling autonomy and heteronomy. Like the autonomous dimension, the theology of Genesis 18 assumes a large measure of validity in human judgment over against the will of God. Divine speech is, or at least can be, in the nature of a proposal that awaits human ratification. It does not demand immediate and categorical submission. Like the heteronomous dimension of covenant, Genesis 22 assumes a theology in which there is no defensible alternative to acceptance of God's will, and human dignity is a function of the completeness of conformity to the divine command. There are, of course, contextual differences between these two chapters, chief among them that in chapter 18 Abraham pleads on behalf of others, whereas in chapter 22 the sacrifice is to be his own: the reprieve he asks for is to be for others, *not* for himself. This granted, it is still the case that the two passages vary tellingly in their view of the right and capacity of human beings to understand and second-guess God.

As was the case with the dialectic of covenantal service, so here the inclusion of the two perspectives in the same Bible, indeed in the same patriarch, yields a subtle and nuanced theology, one that cannot be reduced to either component. By itself the theology of Genesis 18 would soon lead to a religion in which God's will had ceased to be a reality: the human conscience, having filtered out all divine directives that offended it, would produce a God that was only itself writ large, commendable human values practiced because they were right, not because God commanded them. In this highly autonomous theology, no room would be left for obedience, and the personal faithfulness to the suzerain which is the essence of covenant would play no role in the moral life. Left to its own, Genesis 22, on the other hand, would lead to a religion of fanaticism, in which God would be so incomprehensible that even the praise of him as wise or just would be meaningless: no act, no matter how silly or unfair, could be ruled out as the will of God, and faithfulness to him would be indistinguishable from mindless, slavish obedience.

Together, however, the two perspectives delimit a theology in which human judgment neither replaces the inscrutable God who commands nor becomes superfluous within the life lived in faithfulness to him. In this larger, dialectical theology, both arguing with God and obeying him can be central spiritual acts, although when to do which remains necessarily unclear. Not only is this dialectic close to the one that characterizes service in covenant, but it is also close to the dialectic of monotheism in the combat myth of creation, in which the consensual basis of kingship is both preserved and superseded. The presence of variations of this spiritual dialectic in narrative, covenantal, and cosmogonic texts suggests its centrality and its depth of rootage in the Israelite religious consciousness.

It remains to examine briefly the biblical text in which the ideas of the faithfulness required of human beings, the exercise of independent critical judgment by human beings, and God's creation of the world come together in the most painful way—the Book of Job. The theme of its first two chapters, the prose prologue, is whether Job's service to God is disinterested, or only his route to maximized self-interest. The only way YHWH can ascertain this is by accepting the Adversary's suggestion to "lay Your hand upon all that he has and he will surely blaspheme You to Your face,"[11] necessarily suspending in the process the correlation of sin and suffering. When the innocent victim humbly and submissively refuses to reproach God for his plight, the Adversary ups the ante: "Lay a hand on his bones and his flesh, and he will surely blaspheme You to Your face."[12] YHWH again agrees, but the pious sufferer still keeps faith with his divine tormentor, even resisting the enticement of his wife: "Should we accept only good from God and not accept evil?"[13]

In the prose epilogue YHWH restores Job and declares that he spoke the truth about God, as his three comforters had not.[14] It is hard to know what this truth is, because in the preceding verse Job had recanted, admitting that he had spoken "without understanding."[15] It has been argued that if we put the prologue and epilogue together, we have a tale in prose in which a pious and innocent sufferer, having heroically refused to question the justice of God despite the enticements of his wife and friends, is at last richly rewarded for his faithfulness under fire.[16] In any case, in Job 3 a very different note begins, as Job curses the day he was born and in chapter upon chapter portrays YHWH as an omnipotent sadist:

> [22]It is all one; therefore I say,
> "He destroys the blameless and the guilty."
> [23]When suddenly a scourge brings death,
> He mocks as the innocent fail.
> [24]The earth is handed over to the wicked one;
> He covers the eyes of its judges.
> If it is not He, then who? (Job 9:22-24)

In rebuttal his three comforters, and later a fourth, try a series of not altogether compatible arguments, but they all mostly maintain that suffering implies sin and that Job should drop his self-righteous claim of innocence, repent, and be restored by the just and merciful God in whom he has given up belief. If, as I think likely, the speeches in chapters 3-37 derive from a story different from that of the prose framework, there is, nonetheless, an exquisite irony in the received text: just as the comforters said, it is when Job submits and recants that he is restored (the epilogue), but he is innocent all the same, just as *he* said in answer to them (the prologue). In short, an innocent sufferer makes just claims against God and, upon submitting and recanting, comes to know anew the justice and generosity of his lord.

Between the dispute and the restoration comes YHWH's reply from out of the whirlwind:

> 2Who is this who darkens counsel,
> Speaking without knowledge?
> 3Gird your loins like a man;
> I will ask and you will inform Me.
>
> 4Where were you when I laid the earth's foundation?
> Speak if you have understanding.
> 5Do you know who fixed its dimensions
> Or who measured it with a line?
> 6Onto what were its bases sunk?
> Who set its cornerstone
> 7When the morning stars sang together
> And all the divine beings shouted for joy? (Job 38:2–7)

Never really addressing Job's charge of injustice, God changes the subject from ordinary experience to cosmogony. Again, the suspicion arises that chapters 38–41 presuppose a different story of Job, one in which the protagonist was not an innocent sufferer, but a Prometheus-like figure who challenged God's mastery of the world and claimed knowledge comparable to his. Even if this be so, in their present position chapters 38–41 attack Job not for his belief that God can be sadistic, inflicting unspeakable torture upon the most innocent of people, but for his insolence in expressing it. "Here I venture to speak to my Lord, I who am but dust and ashes" is Abraham's line, not Job's, at least not before four chapters of harangue from the mouth of God himself have wonderfully concentrated his mind.[17] The brunt of that harangue is that creation is a wondrous and mysterious place that baffles human assumptions and expectations because it is not anthropocentric but theocentric. Humanity must learn to adjust to a world not designed for their benefit and to cease making claims (even *just* claims) upon its incomprehensible designer and master. To make such claims is to throw off the yoke of obedience to God, to become like mighty Leviathan, whom God alone can tame.[18] The injustice of Job's experience is a powerful inducement to such disobedience, for it implies a grave flaw in God's design and mastery of the world. But in the prose epilogue, with its optimistic account of Job's restoration, we find the covenantal counterpoint to this severely heteronomous and theocentric idea of creation: open and unconditional submission to the God of creation grants humanity a reprieve from the cold inhumanity of the radically theocentric world. The recognition of God's inscrutable yet unimpugnable mastery is always painfully difficult—God has made things that way—but it does result in the good life in which God reinstates his justice and renews his generosity. Such is the comforting conclusion of a most disquieting book. With it, the frigid theocentrism of Job 38:1–42:6 is brought within the broad limits of the theology that has been the subject of our inquiry, as creation once again is made to testify to God's just and benevolent mastery over an otherwise fearsome and deadening reality. Though the persistence of evil seems to undermine the magisterial claims of the creator-God, it is through submission to exactly those claims that the good order that is creation comes into being. Like all other faith, creation-faith carries with it enormous risk. Only as the enormity of the risk is acknowledged can the grandeur of the faith be appreciated.

Notes

NOTES TO THE PREFACE

1. Ecclesiastes 12:12.
2. *The Tanakh* (Philadelphia: Jewish Publication Society of America, 1985). This book puts into one volume the previous volumes of *The Torah*, rev. ed. (1967), *The Prophets* (1978), and *The Writings* (1982), although with some small revision. I have taken the passages from the earlier three volumes.

NOTES TO PART I

Chapter 1

1. Psalm 97:5.
2. Psalm 93:4.
3. Yehezkel Kaufmann, *The Religion of Israel* (New York: Schocken, 1972), 60. (This is an abridgement and translation of his eight-volume Hebrew work, published between 1937 and 1956.)
4. Ibid., 21.
5. Ibid., 60.
6. Ibid., 25.
7. Ibid., 69.
8. A convenient translation is Alexander Heidel, *The Babylonian Genesis*, 2nd ed. (Chicago: University of Chicago, 1963), 18–60. See also the penetrating analysis in Thorkild Jacobsen, *The Treasures of Darkness* (New Haven: Yale University, 1976), 167–91.
9. Kaufmann, *Religion*, 25.
10. It is misleading to say, with H. W. F. Saggs (*The Encounter with the Divine in Mesopotamia and Israel* [London: University of London/Athlone, 1978], 62), that Apsu and Tiamat "were not born within the physical universe," because "they were born 'when the heavens had not been named, when dry land had not been called by name' " (*Enuma elish* 1:1–2). Marduk the creator, unlike YHWH, was born of the waters, and it is this element of theogony that is unparalleled in the Hebrew Bible.
11. See, e.g., Rashi to Genesis 1:1.
12. See the discussion of this verse in E. A. Speiser, *Genesis,* AB 1 (Garden City, N.Y.: Doubleday, 1964), 12–13. Speiser renders Genesis 1:1–3 thus:
    [1]When God set about to create heaven and earth—[2]the world being a formless waste, with darkness over the seas and only an awesome wind sweeping over the water—[3]God said, "Let there be light." And there was light.
    On the other hand, the familiar translation of Genesis 1:1 is defended in an

exhaustive survey in Claus Westermann, *Genesis 1–11* (Minneapolis: Augsburg, 1984), 93–98. Although Westermann's view of the verse as a late summarizing prefix is unlikely, it must be conceded that a resolution of this old controversy is probably impossible.

13. See Kaufmann, *Religion,* 68.

14. See Rashi to Genesis 1:26. It is important to remember that the "royal we" was not part of the vocabulary of kings or individual gods in the ancient Near East.

15. E.g., 1 Kings 22:19–23; Job 1:6–12; 2:1–6.

16. On Genesis 1:1–2:3, see Part II.

17. In rendering Psalm 82, I depart from the NJV, which obscures the polytheistic setting.

18. Rashi, for example, glosses *'ĕlōhîm* here as "judges," ibn Ezra as "angels." See Cyrus H. Gordon, *"'lhym* in Its Reputed Meaning of *Rulers, Judges," JBL* 54 (1935), 139–44.

19. See Karl Budde, "Ps 82 6f," *JBL* 40 (1921):41–42, and Frank Moore Cross, *Canaanite Myth and Hebrew Epic* (Cambridge, Mass.: Harvard University, 1973), 50–52.

20. See H. W. F. Saggs, *The Greatness That Was Babylon* (New York: New American Library, 1962), 364–67.

21. This departs from the NJV in order to bring out the likely precative use of *kî* here. See Mitchell Dahood, *Psalms II,* AB 17 (Garden City, N.Y.: Doubleday, 1968), 271.

22. Sense suggests "moon" as the translation of the obscure *mā'ôr,* which the NJV renders "the orb of the sun."

23. See Mitchell Dahood, *Psalms II,* 205–06; Cyrus H. Gordon, "Leviathan: Symbol of Evil," in *Biblical Motifs,* ed. Alexander Altmann; (Cambridge, Mass.: Philip W. Lown Institute of Advanced Judaic Studies; Studies and Texts III; Harvard University, 1966), 1–9; and John Day, *God's conflict with the dragon and the sea* (Cambridge, U.K.: Cambridge University, 1985), 4–7. The great programmatic study of this theme, of course, is Hermann Gunkel, *Schöpfung und Chaos in Urzeit und Endzeit* (Göttingen, Germany: Vandenhoeck and Ruprecht, 1895).

24. See the list in Kaufmann, *Religion,* 62.

25. Contra Saggs, *The Encounter,* 54–56. (See Day, *God's conflict,* 2–3.) Saggs's position seems to flow, in part, from a terminological decision to restrict "creation" to *creatio ex nihilo.* If we do so, it can be doubted that the idea of creation ever appeared in the ancient Near East. On this question, see now Richard J. Clifford, "The Hebrew Scriptures and the Theology of Creation," *TS* 46 (1985):508–12.

26. Kaufmann, *Religion,* 62.

27. See Day, *God's conflict,* 18.

28. See Otto Eissfeldt, "El and YHWH," *JSS* 1 (1956):25–37.

29. The question of the authority and potency of El in Ugaritic myth is a vexing one, perhaps irresolvable with the present available data. On this, see Otto Eissfeldt, *El im ugaritischen Pantheon* (Berlin: Akademie-Verlag, 1951); Marvin Pope, *El in the Ugaritic Texts,* VT Sup 2 (Leiden: Brill, 1955), esp. pp. 82–104; and Patrick D. Miller, "El the Warrior," *HTR* 60 (1967):411–31.

30. Day (*God's conflict,* 17) argues that "the fact that the Old Testament so frequently uses the imagery of the divine conflict with the dragon and the sea in association with creation, when this imagery is Canaanite, leads one to

expect that the Canaanites likewise connected the two themes." This argument, though formally circular, does point up the oddity of the absence of a cosmogonic theomachy in the known Ugaritic literature. Still, it is not proper to assume the existence of literature we do not have and to tie the biblical combat myth to Canaan at the expense of Mesopotamia, as Day does (e.g., p. 7). See Baruch Margalit, "The Ugaritic Creation Myth: Fact or Fiction?" *UF* 13 (1981): 137–45. Margalit is convinced that Baal's battle with Leviathan/ Yamm/Mot "has nothing whatsoever to do with cosmogony" (p. 140). The present evidence may support this, but it is difficult to imagine that Israel was unique in the west Semitic world in joining the two themes, especially given their linkage already in the *Enuma elish*. Richard J. Clifford is able to avoid the impasse by defining "cosmogony" as "the benign arrangement of the elemental forces to support human life." See his "Cosmogonies in the Ugaritic Texts and in the Bible," *Or* 53 (1984):183–201. The quote is from p. 201.

31. See Cross, *Canaanite Myth,* 13–75; 147–94.
32. See Genesis 1:6–7.
33. Genesis 9:1 and 1:28.
34. Genesis 8:20–9:17.
35. See Westermann, *Genesis 1–11,* 92; Richard J. Clifford, "The Hebrew Scriptures," 508–512, and "Cosmogonies," 184–188.

Chapter 2

1. Genesis 6:6–7.
2. Cf. Genesis 7:19–20.
3. Psalm 104:6–9 and Job 38:8–11. On the former, cf. Marduk's use of wind to distend Tiamat's belly and thus kill her in *Enuma elish* 4:96–100 (Alexander Heidel, *The Babylonian Genesis,* 2nd ed. (Chicago: University of Chicago, 1963), 40.
4. In "covenant" and "eternal servant," I have departed from the NJV in the interest of greater accuracy and in order to facilitate the ensuing connections.
5. As in Psalm 74:14.
6. See Mary K. Wakeman, *God's Battle with the Monster* (Leiden, Netherlands: Brill, 1973), 67. I dissent, however, from Wakeman's view that "the warring Leviathan is found in Job where there is no reference to the time of creation." It seems to me that YHWH's whole harangue in Job 38–41 is about creation. The point is that Job could never have conceived or produced a world such as this. The enormous attention paid to Leviathan (40:25–41:26) derives from the centrality of that aquatic beast in the drama of creation. Wakeman's separation of Leviathan here from creation invites the attack of H. W. F. Saggs in *The Encounter with the Divine in Mesopotamia and Israel* (London: University of London/ Athlone, 1978), 56–57. In truth, the elaboration of YHWH's capture of Leviathan within a context of creation makes Saggs's effort to separate the combat myth from cosmogony highly unlikely. On this passage in particular and the identity of Leviathan in general, see John Day, *God's conflict with the dragon and the sea* (Cambridge, U.K.: Cambridge University, 1985), 62–75.
7. Psalm 104:6–9.
8. See Jon D. Levenson, "Cataclysm, Survival, and Regeneration in the Hebrew Bible," in *Confronting Omnicide,* ed. Daniel Landes (forthcoming).

9. Genesis 9:1–17; Job 40:28.
10. Yehezkel Kaufmann, *The Religion of Israel* (New York: Schocken, 1972), 60.
11. Isaiah 40:2.
12. Isaiah 55:3–5.
13. See pp. 142–43.
14. Psalm 89:4–5; 29–38. On the Davidic Covenant, see Jon D. Levenson, *Sinai and Zion* (San Francisco: Harper & Row, 1987), 97–101. On Psalm 89, see also pp. 116–17.
15. See Richard J. Clifford, "Psalm 89: A Lament Over the Davidic Ruler's Continued Failure," *HTR* 73 (1980):38–47.
16. Frank Moore Cross, *Canaanite Myth and Hebrew Epic* (Cambridge, Mass.: Harvard University, 1973), 144.

Chapter 3

1. Cf. Hegel's "master–slave dialectic." According to Michael Wyschogrod (*The Body of Faith* [New York: Seabury, 1983], 8) "Hegel's understanding [was] that mastery is real only if the slave is a human consciousness whose conquest is worthwhile." See G. W. F. Hegel, *Phenomenology of Spirit* (Oxford: Oxford University, 1977), 111–19. The conquest of Leviathan is meaningful only to the extent that he is an opponent worthy of YHWH. It is the dialectic of opposition and worthiness which unlocks the inner religious meaning of the combat myth in the Hebrew Bible.
2. See Paul D. Hanson, *The Dawn of Apocalyptic* (Philadelphia: Fortress, 1975), 131–32, n. 84.
3. John Day, *God's conflict with the dragon and the sea* (Cambridge, U.K.: Cambridge University, 1985), 145–151.
4. *CTA* 4.VII 25ff.
5. Genesis 7:11. Cf. 8:2.
6. Day, *God's conflict*, 146.
7. Cf. Isaiah 54:9.
8. But the note to Isaiah 24:5 in the NJV does associate the "ancient covenant" with Genesis 9:4–6. Apparently the translators did not recognize the contradiction to the theology of Genesis 9 which the disaster of Isaiah 24 represents.
9. For reasons that will be apparent, it is preferable in this discussion to translate *billa* as "swallow" (rather than "destroy" with NJV) and to capitalize "Death" (unlike NJV).
10. *Enuma elish* 3:136–38, 4:1–2; Alexander Heidel, *The Babylonian Genesis* 2nd ed., (Chicago: University of Chicago, 1963), 36. See the Canaanite parallels in Day, *God's conflict*, 148–51.
11. See Sigmund Mowinckel, *The Psalms in Israel's Worship*, 2 vols. (New York and Nashville: Abingdon, 1962), 1.106–92; and Baruch Halpern, *The Constitution of the Monarchy in Israel*, HSM 25 (Chico, CA: Scholars, 1981), 61–109.
12. A convenient translation of the story can be found in Michael David Coogan, ed., *Stories from Ancient Canaan* (Philadelphia: Westminster, 1978), 106–15. See the discussion of the myth in Frank Moore Cross, *Canaanite Myth and Hebrew Epic* (Cambridge, Mass.: Harvard University, 1973), 112–20.
13. Ibid., 84.
14. See Leonard J. Greenspoon, "The Origin of the Idea of Resurrection," in

Traditions in Transformation, ed. Baruch Halpern and Jon D. Levenson (Winona Lake IN: Eisenbrauns, 1981), 284–87.

15. Cf. Daniel 12:1–3.

16. See Cross, *Canaanite Myth*, 156–63; and Greenspoon, "The Origin."

17. See n. 11, esp., Halpern, *Constitution*, 85–109.

18. Daniel 7, esp. vv. 11–14; see Day, *God's conflict*, 151–77.

19. This is true even of aspects of apocalyptic other than the combat myth that has been the subject of our discussion. Looking at the transformation of Wisdom Literature in the situation of political heteronomy in the Second Temple period, Jonathan Z. Smith astutely remarks: "Apocalypticism is Wisdom lacking a royal court and patron and therefore it surfaces during the period of Late Antiquity not as a response to religious persecution but as an expression of the cessation of native kingship." "Wisdom and Apocalyptic," in *Visionaries and Their Apocalypses*, IRT 2, ed. Paul D. Hanson (Philadelphia: Fortress; London: SPCK, 1983), 115. The essay first appeared in *Religious Syncretism in Antiquity*, ed. Birger A. Pearson (Missoula: Scholars, 1975), 131–56. Without denying the international currency of apocalyptic in Late Antiquity, I should point out that "the cessation of native kingship" in Israel first occurred in the sixth century B.C.E. The appearance of literature that might legitimately be called apocalyptic or protoapocalyptic (e.g., Ezekiel 38–39) in that century is not coincidence. It predates Jewish involvement in Hellenistic "syncretism." The genetic relationship of Wisdom to apocalyptic to which Smith draws attention is real, but it does not seem to have been a highly important ingredient until the Hellenistic period (e.g., Daniel).

20. See Hermann Gunkel, *Schöpfung und Chaos in Urzeit und Endzeit* (Göttingen, Germany: Vandenhoeck and Ruprecht, 1895). 173–398; and Adela Yarbro Collins, *The Combat Myth in the Book of Revelation*, HTR HDR 9 (Missoula: Scholars, 1976).

21. Revelation 21:1.

22. Ernst Käsemann, "The Beginnings of Christian Theology," *JTC* 6 (1969):40.

23. E.g., Jacob Neusner, *Judaism: The Evidence of the Mishnah* (Chicago: University of Chicago, 1981). On the methodological issue, see Hyam Maccoby, "Jacob Neusner's Mishnah," *Mid* 30 (May 1984): 24–32, esp. p. 26; and E. P. Sanders, *Jesus and Judaism* (Philadelphia: Fortress, 1985), 128. It must be stressed that the continuity of Amoraic *aggadot* on Leviathan and Behemoth with biblical, apocryphal, pseudepigraphal, and New Testament material is further evidence against the effort to describe Tannaitic Judaism by reference to its law code, the Mishnah, alone. See n. 34, this chapter.

24. See Hyam Maccoby, "The Greatness of Gershom Scholem," *Comm* 76:3 (September 1983):45: "The aggadah is the mythology of the Talmud, the embodiment of its abstract ideas in stories, picturesque, impossible, and wild. Only part of this aggadah, however—indeed, a very small part—is mystical in character."

25. See Irving Jacobs, "Elements of Near Eastern Mythology in Rabbinic Aggadah," *JJS* 28 (1977):1–11, esp. the bibliography and references throughout.

26. *b.B.Bat.* 75a.

27. See Coogan, *Stories*, 112.

28. See Rudolf Anthes, "Mythology in Ancient Egypt," in *Mythologies of the Ancient World*, ed. Samuel Noah Kramer (Garden City, N.Y.: Doubleday, 1961), 74.

29. An analogy with the Christian Eucharist as it was to develop over the centuries suggests itself.

30. The connection of the booth made of Leviathan's hide and the Festival of Booths is explicit in *Pesiq. Rab. Kah.* 187b (Buber ed.).

31. See Job 40:15–22. On the identity of this beast, see now Day, *God's conflict,* 75–84.

32. The background of this eschatological struggle between Leviathan and Behemoth can be found in *Pesiq. Rab. Kah.* 188b (Buber ed.).

33. Isaiah 51:4.

34. *Lev. Rab.* 13:3. Although this notion of the eschatological banquet prepared from the carcass of the slain beast appears in statements attributed to masters of the third to fifth Amoraic generations, it must be noted that the basic idea is pre-Rabbinic and appears in 2 Baruch 29:4, 1 Enoch 60:24, and 2 Esdras 6:52. The particular halakhic consideration of the *kašrut* of the meat, however, seems unique to the Rabbinic use of this old mythic notion.

35. On this concept of a new Torah, see Ephraim E. Urbach, *The Sages,* Hebrew (Jerusalem: Hebrew University, 1975), 275–78, esp. p. 276; and W. D. Davies, *Paul and Rabbinic Judaism,* 3rd ed. (London: SPCK, 1970), 71–73 and *passim.*

36. Leviticus 7:24.

37. See Ezekiel 38–39.

38. Deuteronomy 25:17–19.

39. Psalm 9:7.

40. *Tanh, ki tēsē* 11.

41. Ezekiel 29:1–7; 32:1–16.

42. Esther 3:1. Cf. 1 Samuel 15.

43. *Tanh, šēlah-lēkā* 15. The biblical quote is Ezekiel 36:27.

44. Jeremiah 31:31–34; Psalm 51:12.

45. On the two impulses, see Solomon Schechter, *Aspects of Rabbinic Theology* (New York: Schocken, 1961), 242–292; and Urbach, *Sages,* 415–27.

46. Deuteronomy 30:11–14.

47. IQS 3:20–25. The translation is from P. Wernberg-Møller, *The Manual of Discipline,* STDJ 1 (Leiden, Netherlands: Brill, 1957), 25.

48. See n. 43, this chapter.

49. IQS 4:18–19, from Wernberg-Møller, *Manual,* 26.

50. John J. Collins, "Patterns of Eschatology at Qumran," in *Traditions in Transformation,* ed. Baruch Halpern and Jon D. Levenson (Winona Lake, IN: Eisenbrauns, 1981), 365.

51. E. P. Sanders, *Paul and Palestinian Judaism* (Philadelphia: Fortress, 1977), 426–28; 543–49. It is not my intention to imply that Sanders himself exemplifies the misunderstanding to which his otherwise helpful dichotomy might give birth.

52. E.g., Matthew 25:31–46.

53. As in Numbers 20:14–21:35.

54. Here I depart from the NJV translation of *rā'* in Isaiah 45:7 as "woe," which although arguable, blunts the radicalness of the monotheism therein proclaimed.

55. See *b. Ber.* 11b: " 'Evil' is written, and we read 'everything' as a euphemism *(lišānā' ma'alyā').* "

56. See Exodus 7:2–5. It should not be overlooked that this hardening of Pharaoh's heart does not befall an innocent person. At the outset of his wickedness,

Pharaoh, like an addict upon his first indulgence, was free to choose the good instead, but then lost this freedom, as YHWH froze him in his evil posture.

57. 1 Samuel 16:14.
58. 1 Samuel 15:1–34.
59. On this concept, see Paul Ricoeur, *The Symbolism of Evil* (Boston: Beacon, 1969), especially pp. 151–157.
60. On God's responsibility for the Evil Impulse and its possible benefits to humanity, see *Ber. Rab.* 9:7.

Chapter 4

1. See Richard J. Clifford, "The Hebrew Scriptures and the Theology of Creation," *TS* 46 (1985): 508–512; and Richard J. Clifford, "Cosmogonies in the Ugaritic Texts and in the Bible," *Or* 53 (1984): 184–188.
2. Douglas A. Knight, "Cosmogony and Order in the Hebrew Tradition," in *Cosmogony and Ethical Order*, ed. Robin W. Lovin and Frank E. Reynolds (Chicago: University of Chicago, 1985), 142.
3. Ibid., 147.
4. Job 40:19.
5. Paul Ricoeur, *The Symbolism of Evil* (Boston: Beacon, 1969), 203.
6. See n. 11, chapter 3, esp. Baruch Halpern, *The Constitution of the Monarchy in Israel*, HSM 25 (Chico, Cal: Scholars, 1981), 85–109. In my view, scholars such as Mowinckel and Halpern make a convincing case for the centrality of the enthronement of YHWH in the Jerusalem cult and its early Israelite predecessors. Whether the enthronement was thought to take place on the New Year is, however, open to doubt and, in any event, not critical to the theological question.
7. On the idea of a theology of recital, see G. Ernest Wright, *God Who Acts*, SBT 8 (London: SCM, 1952), esp. pp. 33–58. Against Wright's position, it must be stressed that most of the time, God in the Hebrew Bible is doing nothing. The *magnalia Dei* are celebrated in part because of their rarity, in an effort to reactivate God's potential in times when he has allowed it to become sorely missed.

NOTES TO PART II

Chapter 5

1. Psalm 104:26.
2. Psalm 104:24.
3. Isaiah 27:1.
4. Such as the story of Atra-hasis, in which the birth goddess Nintur fashions humanity. See Thorkild Jacobsen, *The Treasures of Darkness* (New Haven: Yale University, 1976), 118.
5. See Umberto Cassuto, *A Commentary on the Book of Genesis* (Jerusalem: Magnes, 1961), 1. 50–51; and A. van der Voort, "Genèse 1, 1 A 11, 4ᵃ et le Psaume CIV," *RB* 58 (1951): 325.
6. Genesis 1:21–22.

7. Genesis 1:26-28.
8. See Kemper Fullerton, "The Feeling For Form in Psalm 104," *JBL* 40 (1921):51-56; van der Voort, "Genèse 1," 330-331; and Luis J. Stadelmann, *The Hebrew Conception of the World*, An Bib 39 (Rome: Biblical Institute, 1970), 33-34.
9. Genesis 1:3 and Psalm 104:1.
10. Genesis 1:9-10 and Psalm 104:5-10.
11. Genesis 1:11-13 and Psalm 104:10-18.
12. Genesis 1:14-19.
13. Genesis 1:3.
14. Psalm 104:19-23.
15. Genesis 1:20-23.
16. Psalm 104:27-30 and Genesis 1:29-31. Note that in both compositions humanity seems to be vegetarian.
17. Paul Humbert, "La relation de Genèse 1 et du Psaume 104 avec la liturgie du Nouvel-An israelite," in his *Opuscules d'un Hebräisant* (Neuchatel, Switzerland: Secretariat de l'Universite, 1958), 76. See also van der Voort, "Genèse 1," 331.
18. E.g., Genesis 6:13; Numbers 14:21; Isaiah 11:9.
19. Van der Voort, "Genèse 1," 332 (my translation from the French).
20. Psalm 104:24. See Hans-Jürgen Hermisson, "Observations on the Creation Theology in Wisdom," in *Creation in the Old Testament*, IRT 6, ed. Bernhard W. Anderson (Philadelphia: Fortress; London: SPCK, 1984), 118-34, esp. pp. 123-25.
21. On this, see van der Voort, "Genèse 1," 341.
22. The attempt of Fullerton ("Feeling," 51-56) to divide Psalm 104 into seven stanzas is artificial and unconvincing.
23. For a comprehensive review of the Sabbath in the Hebrew Bible, see now Niels-Erik A. Andreasen, *The Old Testament Sabbath: A Tradition-Historical Investigation*, SBLDS 7 (Missoula, Mont.: Society of Biblical Literature, 1972).
24. For the text, see *ANET*, 369-371.
25. See, e.g., James Henry Breasted, *The Dawn of Conscience* (New York: Charles Scribner's Sons, 1935), 277-310. It is difficult to imagine a modern historian more enamored of an ancient subject than Breasted is of Akhenaten.
26. John Wilson points out (*ANET*, 369) that the worship of the Pharaoh himself as a deity continued unabated under Akhenaten. The same and related points are made by Yehezkel Kaufmann in *The Religion of Israel* (New York: Schocken, 1972), 226, n. 6.
27. Sigmund Freud, *Moses and Monotheism* (New York: Vintage, 1939), 21-36. In fairness to Freud, he is keenly aware of the highly conjectural character of his reconstruction. See esp. p. 35.
28. Breasted, *Dawn*, 296.
29. See, e.g., William W. Hallo and William Kelly Simpson, *The Ancient Near East* (New York: Harcourt, Brace, Jovanovich, 1971), 269.
30. On this, see Aylward W. Blackman, "The Psalms in the Light of Egyptian Research," in *The Psalmists*, ed. D. C. Simpson (Oxford: Oxford University, 1926), 177-97; Georges Nagel, "À propos des rapports du Psaume 104 avec les textes egyptien," in *Festschrift Alfred Bertholet*, ed. Walter Baumgartner et al. (Tübingen: J. C. B. Mohr/Paul Siebeck, 1950), 395-403; Hans-Joachim Kraus,

NOTES / 165

Psalmen, BKAT 15/2; (Neukirchen-Vluyn, Germany: Neukirchener, 1961/
1968), 884–85; and, more recently, Stadelmann, *Hebrew Conception,* 31–33.
31. *ANET,* 370–71. The following citations are taken from this translation, except
that I have taken the liberty of modernizing the English grammar.
32. Psalm 104:2.
33. Psalm 104:21–22.
34. Psalm 104:25–26.
35. The only comparable instance known to me is the relationship of Proverbs
22:17–24:22 with "The Instruction of Amen-em-opet," an Egyptian Wisdom
composition. See *ANET,* 421–25; and William McKane, *Proverbs,* OTL
(Philadelphia: Westminster, 1970), 369–73.
36. Arthur E. P. Weigall, *The Life and Times of Akhenaton* (Edinburgh and London:
William Blackwood and Sons, 1911), 157.
37. See Breasted, *Dawn,* 367–68.
38. Ibid., 292.
39. Abraham Joshua Heschel, *God in Search of Man* (New York: Harper and Row,
1966), 46.
40. Breasted, *Dawn,* 292–93.
41. "Natural supernaturalism" is a term coined by Thomas Carlyle. See M. H.
Abrams, *Natural Supernaturalism: Tradition and Revolution in Romantic Literature* (New
York: W. W. Norton, 1971), 65–70.
42. Kaufmann, *Religion,* 226, n. 6.
43. See Nagel, "À propos des rapports," 401: "dans l'hymne à Aten, plus que dans
tout autre encore, le dieu solaire commande à toute la nature et il s'occupe
d'elle, il est donc bien en dehors d'elle."
44. Psalm 104:19–20.
45. This is not to imply that the process terminates, even within the Hebrew Bible,
with Genesis 1. See pp. 123–27.

Chapter 6

1. On the rationale for the traditional source–critical division between Genesis
2:4a (P) and 2:4b (J), see E. A. Speiser, *Genesis,* AB 1 (Garden City, N.Y.:
Doubleday, 1964), 15–16, and other commentaries. For reasons that will
emerge in this discussion, I regard the Priestly cosmogony as concluded with
Genesis 2:3. See n. 9, this chapter. Genesis 2:4 is best seen as someone's bridge
to the J material that follows.
2. *m. Abot* 5:1.
3. *b. Roš. Haš.* 32a; *b. Meg.* 21b.
4. Psalm 33:6 (my italics).
5. Gerhard von Rad, *Genesis,* rev. ed., OTL (Philadelphia: Westminster, 1972), 64.
6. See Werner H. Schmidt, *Die Schöpferungsgeschichte der Priesterschrift,* WMANT 17
(Neukirchen-Vluyn, Germany: Neukirchener, 1964), 169–73.
7. An example can be found in Schmidt, *Schöpferungsgeschichte,* 161.
8. Umberto Cassuto, *From Adam to Noah,* Hebrew (Jerusalem: Magnes, 1953), 5–6;
ET: A Commentary on the Book of Genesis (Jerusalem: Magnes, 1961), 1.13–14.
9. Contrary to Cassuto's claim (*From Adam,* 1.14), the two words for heaven (defined
as synonyms in Genesis 1:8) appear a total of twenty times, not twenty-one.

10. But "heaven" would appear twenty-one times (see n. 9).
11. Genesis 1:6–8.
12. Genesis 1:9, 12, 24, 31.
13. Genesis 2:2–3a.
14. Genesis 2:1.
15. Genesis 2:3b.
16. Aryeh Toeg, "Genesis 1 and the Sabbath" (Hebrew), *Beth Miqra* 50 (1972):291. Here is the breakdown:
    Genesis 2:1: *waykullû haššāmayim wĕhā'āres wĕkol-ṣĕbā'ām* (five words)
    Genesis 2:2a: *waykal 'ĕlōhim bayyôm haššĕbî'i mĕla'ktô 'ăšer 'āsâ* (seven words)
    Genesis 2:2b: *wayyišbōt bayyôm haššĕbî'i mikkol-mĕla'ktô 'ăšer 'āsâ* (seven words)
    Genesis 2:3a: *waybārek 'ĕlōhim 'et-yôm haššĕbî'i wayqaddēš 'ōtô* (seven words)
    Genesis 2:3b: *ki bô šābat mikkol-mela'ktô 'ăšer-bārā' 'ĕlōhim la'ăśôt* (nine words)
17. Genesis 1:2, 20–22.
18. Cassuto, *From Adam to Noah*, 6 (my translation).
19. This is not to claim, of course, that Cassuto, who attempted to do battle with the Documentary Hypothesis, would have accepted this position. See his volume *The Documentary Hypothesis and the Composition of the Pentateuch* (Jerusalem: Magnes, 1961).
20. For a succinct summary of reliable current thinking on the *akītu*, see Hayim Tadmor, "The New Year in Mesopotamia" (Hebrew), *EB* (Jerusalem: Bialik Institute, 1976), 7, cols. 305–11.
21. See pp. 10–13.
22. Jonathan Z. Smith, "A Pearl of Great Price and a Cargo of Yams: A Study in Situational Incongruity," in *Imagining Religion*, CSHJ (Chicago: University of Chicago, 1982), 101. See Smith's reinterpretation of the *Enuma elish* on pp. 90–96. His point that the negative confession of the Babylonian king during the *akītu* most likely reflects specific changes brought about by political heteronomy is correct and valuable, but should not be used to disqualify the general cosmogonic dimension of the ritual in earlier ages.
23. The possibility that the *Enuma elish* was recited on the fourth of every month (see Tadmor, "The New Year," col. 308) cannot logically be used as an argument against the importance of its role in the *akītu*. All this shows is that the significance of the epic was not exhausted by any one ritual occasion, just as the significance of the Babylonian *akītu* was not exhausted by its connection with the *Enuma elish*. One need not accept the whole myth-and-ritual scenario in order to see a large element of truth in it.
24. Ezekiel 40:1.
25. On this, see Walther Zimmerli, *Ezekiel 2*, Hermeneia (Philadelphia: Fortress, 1983), 345–47. On the ritual of the Day of Atonement, see Leviticus 16.
26. See *ANET*, 333.
27. Exodus 12:2–3.
28. Ezekiel 45:18–20, if one reads *baššĕbî'i bĕ'ehād lahōdeš* in v. 20 with LXX. Cf. 2 Chronicles 29.
29. Leviticus 23:24; Numbers 29:1.
30. E.g., 1 Kings 1:34, 39.
31. *m. Roš. Haš.* 1:1.
32. Roland de Vaux, *Ancient Israel* (New York: McGraw-Hill, 1965), 2.502–04.
33. See the calendar in Deuteronomy 16:1–17. It would, however, seem to be implicit in Deuteronomy 16:1 that Abib 1 begins the new cultic year. The

likelihood is that the Deuteronomic calendar intended Passover to be celebrated in the first week of this month and not in the third, as in Leviticus
23:5–8. On this, see Arnold B. Ehrlich, *Randglossen zur Hebräischen Bibel* (Leipzig,
Germany: J. C. Hinrichs, 1908), 1.312–13.

34. Exodus 23:16; 34:22.
35. Sigmund Mowinckel, *Psalmenstudien,* SNVAO (Kristiania, Norway: J. Dybwad,
    1921), 2.83–89, esp. pp. 83–84.
36. See Exodus 12:2.
37. *m. Roš. Haš.* 1:1.
38. See Frank Moore Cross, *Canaanite Myth and Hebrew Epic* (Cambridge, Mass.:
    Harvard University, 1973), 105, n. 48 and 123, n. 37.
39. Tadmor, "The New Year," cols. 306–07.
40. Deuteronomy 16:15; Leviticus 23:33–36. Leviticus 23:36 appends an eighth
    day to the Festival of Booths, but the fact that the sacrifices for this day do
    not conform to the pattern for the seven days of the preceding festival (Num-
    bers 29:12–38) demonstrates that the eighth day was partly a festival in itself
    and not altogether included in the Festival of Booths. See *b. Suk.* 47a.
41. Genesis 1:11; 2:6.
42. Genesis 1:12; Psalm 65:14. The debate is found in *b. Roš Haš.* 11a.
43. See *b. Roš. Haš.* 27a and *Lev. Rab.* 29:1 (and parallels).
44. Genesis 5:29.
45. Genesis 9:1–2; 1:28.
46. See Joseph Blenkinsopp, "The Structure of P," *CBQ* 38 (1976): 283–86.
47. Quoted from John Wilson, "Egypt," in *Before Philosophy,* ed. H. and H. A.
    Frankfort (Baltimore: Penguin, 1949), 60.
48. Ezekiel 28:2, 13, 14. See Jon D. Levenson, *Theology of the Program of Restoration of
    Ezekiel 40–48,* HSM 10 (Missoula: Scholars, 1976), 25–36.
49. Genesis 9:1–2.
50. Wilson, "Egypt," 60.
51. Exodus 40:2, 17.
52. Blenkinsopp, "Structure," 285.
53. J. B. Segal, *The Hebrew Passover* (London: Oxford University, 1963), 114–54.
54. Exodus 15:1–19.
55. Cross, *Canaanite Myth,* 131.
56. Exodus 14:21–22, 28.
57. I have changed the NJV's "will bring and plant" to the past tense in order to
    reflect the likely old preterite usage of the verbs here. See Cross, *Canaanite Myth,*
    125.
58. On this issue see Jeffrey Tigay, "Week," (Hebrew) in *EB* (Jerusalem: Bialik
    Institute, 1976), 7, cols. 468–69. See also William W. Hallo, "New Moons and
    Sabbaths: A Case Study in the Contrastive Approach," *HUÇA* 48 (1977):
    1–18.
59. Leviticus 23:24.

Chapter 7

1. 1 Kings 8:2.
2. 2 Chronicles 7:9. Cf 1 Kings 8:65, for which the MT seems to have been
   influenced by 2 Chronicles 7:9, as the LXX has not.
3. See Jon D. Levenson, "The Paronomasia of Solomon's Seventh Petition," *HAR*

6 (1982):135–38. The seven petitions are 1 Kings 8:31–32; 33–34; 35–37a; 37b–40; 41–43; 44–45; and 46–53.

4. 1 Kings 6:38.

5. Gudea Cylinder B, col. XVIII 19, and Statue B, col. VII 30. For ET, see George A. Barton, *The Royal Inscriptions of Sumer and Akkad* (New Haven: Yale University; London: Oxford University, 1929), 253 and 187.

6. Michael David Coogan, ed., *Stories from Ancient Canaan* (Philadelphia: Westminster, 1978), 103–04.

7. Exodus 35:3; 16:23.

8. L. R. Fisher, "The Temple Quarter," *JSS* 8 (1963):40–41.

9. 1 Kings 12:32–33. See Roland de Vaux, *Ancient Israel* (New York: McGraw-Hill, 1965), 2.499.

10. Ezra 3:1–6. See also 1 Esdras 5:47–55.

11. Whether this took place in 165 or 164 B.C.E. is still a matter of dispute.

12. *b. Šabb.* 21b.

13. 2 Maccabees 1:19. See also 1:18.

14. 2 Chronicles 30:1–20. See Solomon Zeitlin, *The First Book of Maccabees,* Dropsie College Edition; Jewish Apocryphal Literature (New York: Harper & Row, 1950), 53–54; and Jonathan A. Goldstein, *I Maccabees,* AB 41 (Garden City, N.Y.: Doubleday, 1976), 278.

15. James A. Montgomery, "The Dedication Feast in the Old Testament," *JBL* 29 (1910):29–40; and M. Liber, "Hanoucca et Souccot," *REJ* 16 (1912):20–29, esp. 24–26.

16. F. E. Peters, *The Harvest of Hellenism* (New York: Simon and Schuster, 1970), 284. Of course, the Hasmonean Chanukkah may have been advanced, in part, to displace a more general Feast of Lights marking the winter solstice, but if so, the new holiday was still only a recast and historically specified form of the old Temple reconsecration festival of biblical times.

17. See n. 40, Chapter 6.

18. Exodus 40:2, 17; Leviticus 9:1, 22–24.

19. Ezekiel 45:18–20, if one reads v. 20 with the MT. The LXX would suggest a temple-purgation ritual on both the vernal and the autumnal New Year's Days. See n. 28, Chapter 6.

20. See Mircea Eliade, *The Myth of the Eternal Return, or Cosmos and History,* Bollingen Series 46 (Princeton: Princeton University, 1971), 12–21.

21. De Vaux, *Ancient Israel,* 2.329.

22. Exodus 20:8–11; 31:12–17; Deuteronomy 5:12–15.

23. Peter J. Kearney, "Creation and Liturgy: The P Redaction of Ex 25–30," *ZAW* 89 (1977): 375. The seven speeches are Exodus 25:1–30:10; 30:11–16; 30:17–21; 30:22–33; 30:34–37; 31:1–11; 31:12–17.

24. Ibid., 375–78.

25. Exodus 27:20–21; 30:7–8; Genesis 1:2–3.

26. Exodus 40:17.

27. Kearney, "Creation and Liturgy," 381. The verses are Exodus 40:19, 21, 23, 25, 27, 29, 32.

28. Genesis 1:4, 10, 12, 18, 21, 25, 31.

29. Exodus 31:3; 35:31; Genesis 1:2. See Kearney, "Creation and Liturgy," 378; and Blenkinsopp, "Structure," 282.

30. See *b. Ber.* 55a: "Rabbi Judah said in the name of Rav: 'Bezalel knew how to

combine the letters through which heaven and earth were created, as it is written here [Exod. 35:31]: "He has endowed him with a divine spirit of skill [ḥokmâ], ability [tĕbûnâ], and knowledge [da'at], and there [Prov. 3:19] it is written: "The LORD founded the earth by wisdom [ḥokmâ] / He established the heavens by understanding [tĕbûnâ]," and it is written, "By His knowledge [da'tô] the depths burst apart [Prov. 3:20]." ' "

31. Joseph Blenkinsopp, "The Structure of P," *CBQ* 38 (1976): 276–78.

32. See Genesis 17:23; 21:4; Exodus 12:28, 50.

33. See the list in Blenkinsopp, "Structure," 275–76.

34. E. g., Leviticus 18:24–30.

35. See Blenkinsopp, "Structure," 280; and Moshe Weinfeld, "Sabbath, Temple, and the Enthronement of the Lord—The Problem of the Sitz im Leben of Genesis 1:1–2:3," in *Mélanges biblique et orientaux en l'honneur de M. Henri Cazelles* AOAT 212 [1981], ed. A. Caquot and M. Delcor (Kevelaer, Germany: Butzon and Bercker; Neukirchen-Vluyn, Germany: Neukirchener, 1981), 503.

36. Mitchell Dahood, *Psalms II*, AB 17 (Garden City, N.Y.: Doubleday, 1968), 247.

37. E.g., 2 Samuel 7:13; 1 Kings 8:13, 20.

38. Psalm 48:3.

39. Psalm 24:2.

40. See *BHK*. *BHS* does not list this variant.

41. Dahood, *Psalms II*, 247–48. His citation of Psalm 119:152 is quite persuasive on this.

42. De Vaux, *Ancient Israel*, 2.330.

43. E.g., Claus Westermann, *Isaiah 40–66*, OTL (Philadelphia: Westminster, 1969), 408–09.

44. See pp. 27–36.

45. Isaiah 65:17.

46. See Gösta W. Ahlström, "Heaven on Earth—at Hazor and Arad," in *Religious Syncretism in Antiquity*, ed. Birger A. Pearson (Missoula: Scholars, 1975), 68.

47. Genesis 14:19.

48. See pp. 8–10.

49. Cf. W. G. Lambert, "The Great Battle of the Mesopotamian Religious Year: The Conflict in the Akitu House," *Iraq* 25 (1963):190: "The Sea (Tiamat) was no doubt a small cultic structure in the Akitu house (probably a dais) and when the statue of Marduk was taken there, it was set on the dais to symbolize victory over Tiamat."

50. William Foxwell Albright, *Archaeology and the Religion of Israel* (Baltimore: Johns Hopkins, 1946), 147–50.

51. Ibid., 150–52. See also Michael A. Fishbane, "The Sacred Center: The Symbolic Structure of the Bible," in *Texts and Responses*, ed. Michael A. Fishbane and Paul R. Flohr (Leiden, Netherlands: Brill, 1975), 24, n. 43.

52. This was brought to my attention by S. Dean McBride.

53. Ezekiel 43:15.

54. *The Assyrian Dictionary* (Chicago: Oriental Institute, 1968), I, pt. 2.226–227.

55. Albright, *Archaeology*, 151.

56. Ezekiel 28:12–13, 14, 16.

57. E.g., Otto Kaiser, *Isaiah 13–39*, OTL (Philadelphia: Westminster, 1974), 267.

58. *The Assyrian Dictionary* (Chicago: Oriental Institute, 1977), 8, 476.

59. E.g., in Exodus 30:18 and 1 Kings 7:30.

60. Albright, *Archaeology,* 153–54. Albright does not seem to know the distinction in etymology of the two *kiūru*'s which the *Assyrian Dictionary* posits.
61. Ibid., 153.
62. Exodus 25:31–40; 1 Kings 7:49.
63. Carol L. Meyers, *The Tabernacle Menorah,* ASORDS 2 (Missoula: Scholars, 1976), 180.
64. Exodus 25:30; Leviticus 24:5–9.
65. Josephus, *The Jewish War,* LCL (London: Heinemann; New York: G. P. Putnam's Sons, 1928), 3.265 (book 5, section 5, paragraph 4).
66. *Bet ha-Midrasch,* 3rd ed., ed. Adolph Jellinek (Jerusalem: Wahrmann, 1967), part 2, 164–67.
67. Psalm 26:8.
68. Genesis 1:1; Psalm 104:2; Exodus 26:7. I have departed from the NJV translation of Genesis 1:1 in order to capture the sense that the verse had for the ancient darshan.
69. Genesis 1:6; Exodus 26:33.
70. Genesis 1:9; Exodus 30:18.
71. Genesis 1:14; Exodus 25:31.
72. Genesis 1:20; Exodus 25:20.
73. Genesis 1:27. In his "Sabbath as Temple: Some Thoughts on Space and Time in Judaism," in *Go and Study,* ed. Raphael Jospe and Samuel Z. Fishman (Washington: B'nai B'rith Hillel Foundations, 1980/5741), 304, n. 18, Arthur Green emends *bikbôd yôśĕrô* to *bakkābôd yĕsārô,* "in glory he created him," because he "can find no way of understanding the text as it stands." Although Green's emendation is defensible, it seems more likely to me that *kābôd* here is a gloss on *ṣelem* ("image"), one that lifts up the royal connotation of the famous crux in Genesis 1:26–27. On this, see pp. 112–17. The point here is that God endowed humanity both at creation and in the Tabernacle with some of his own awesome majesty.
74. Genesis 2:1; Exodus 39:32.
75. Genesis 2:3; Exodus 39:43.
76. Genesis 2:2; Numbers 7:1.
77. Genesis 2:3; Numbers 7:1. The passage is *Tanhuma Pĕqûdê* 2.
78. 1 Kings 7:51; Genesis 2:3. The translation of the latter verse has been changed from the NJV so as to bring out the interpretation of *laʿăśôt* of this midrash.
79. *Pesiq. R.* 6.
80. E.g., *b. Suk.* 53a–b. See Raphael Patai, *Man and Temple in Ancient Jewish Myth and Ritual,* 2nd ed. (New York: KTAV, 1967), 54–59.

Chapter 8

1. See pp. 66–68.
2. Deuteronomy 5:12–15.
3. Exodus 20:8–11.
4. See W. G. Lambert, "A New Look at the Babylonian Background of Genesis," *JTS* 16 (1965):297–98.
5. *Enuma elish* 6:8, 34, 51, 152, translation from Alexander Heidel, *The Babylonian Genesis,* 2nd ed. (Chicago: University of Chicago, 1963), 46–48.
6. *Atra-Ḥasis* 1:191, 243. The translation is from W. G. Lambert and A. R. Mil-

lard, *Atra-Hasis: The Babylonian Story of the Flood* (Oxford: Oxford University, 1969), 57, 60. The transliteration given of 1.243 there is "ap-ṭú-ur ul-la an-du-ra-[ra aš-ku-u] n."

7. Moshe Weinfeld, *Justice and Righteousness in Israel and the Nations*, Hebrew, Publications of the Perry Foundation for Biblical Research in the Hebrew University of Jerusalem (Jerusalem: Hebrew University, 1985), 6, *et passim*.

8. See Jon D. Levenson, "Poverty and the State in Biblical Thought," *Jud* 25 (1976): 230–32.

9. Exodus 23:9–12.

10. Exodus 21:2; Leviticus 25:44–46; Deuteronomy 15:12.

11. Exodus 19:5.

12. But see Genesis 9:25–27, which presents the Canaanites as cursed with slavery to the Shemites. This text may have served as an etiological rationale for the ineligibility of non-Israelite slaves for release in the Sabbatical or Jubilee Years.

13. Weinfeld, *Justice*, 2–4.

14. Ibid., 117–22.

15. See vv. 16–22.

16. Exodus 15:8.

17. See pp. 22–23.

18. *Enuma elish* 1:75. Heidel, *Babylonian Genesis*, 21.

19. *ANET*, 5. I have substituted "rested," the alternative given in the note, for "was satisfied," which appears in the text itself, in order to highlight the continuities presently under discussion.

20. E.g., Niels-Erik A. Andreasen, *The Old Testament Sabbath*, SBLDS 7 (Missoula: SBL, 1972), 182–83; Weinfeld, "Sabbath," 501.

21. Cf. v. 8 and 2 Chronicles 6:41.

22. Isaiah 66:1. I have substituted my own more literal translation for the NJV here. See pp. 88–89.

23. See pp. 84–85.

24. 2 Samuel 7:1. Here too the translation departs from the NJV in the interest of accuracy.

25. *m. Tamid* 7:4.

26. *b. Roš. Haš.* 31a.

27. Psalm 93:1.

28. *Abot R. Nat.* (Schechter edition), 3.

29. Exodus 20:8–11; Deuteronomy 5:12–15.

30. Mircea Eliade, *Myth and Reality* (New York: Harper & Row, 1968), 21–38.

31. Genesis 1:31.

32. Raffaele Pettazzoni, *Essays on the History of Religions*, SHR (Num Sup) 1 (Leiden, Netherlands: Brill, 1954), 32.

33. Genesis 1:31.

34. Andreasen, *Sabbath*, 185–86. See his discussion of the *otiositas* of God on pp. 174–82.

35. On this, see Phyllis A. Bird, "Male and Female He Created Them," *HTR* 74 (1981): 151, in which Bird points out that "there is no message of shared dominion here, no word about the distribution of roles, responsibility, and authority between the sexes, no word of sexual equality." On the other hand, her belief that in P "the cult which represents the culminating word or work

of God has no place for women in its service" (p. 156) is in need of qualification. See Mayer I. Gruber, "Women in the Cult According to the Priestly Code," in *Judaic Perspectives on Ancient Israel*, ed. Jacob Neusner (Philadelphia: Fortress, 1987), 35–48. Bird's belief that the royal institution to which Genesis 1:26–28 metaphorically points is exclusively male (p. 151) does not take adequate account of the actual role of women within the royal household. On this, see Roland de Vaux, *Ancient Israel* (New York: McGraw-Hill, 1965), 1.117–19.

36. See Claus Westermann, *Genesis 1–11* (Minneapolis: Augsburg, 1984), 147–55.
37. Rashi to Genesis 1:26.
38. Westermann, *Genesis 1–11*, 158.
39. See *Saadya's Commentary on Genesis*, Hebrew, ed. Moshe Zucker (New York: Jewish Theological Seminary of America, 1984), 257–58.
40. Genesis 1:28.
41. See Hans Wildberger, "Das Abbild Gottes, Gen 1.26–30," *TZ* 21 (1965): 259.
42. E.g., Psalm 89:10. Cf. v. 26.
43. On Psalm 8 see Wildberger, "Abbild Gottes," 481–83.
44. Ibid., 253–55, 484–88. See also Friedrich Horst, *Gottes Recht*, TB 12 (Munich: Chr. Kaiser, 1961), 224–26; and Bird, "Male and Female," 140–43. The following examples are my translation from Wildberger's German.
45. Wildberger, "Abbild Gottes," 253.
46. Westermann, *Genesis 1–11*, 153.
47. *ANET*, 417.
48. Wildberger, "Abbild Gottes," 489.
49. E.g., 2 Samuel 7:14 and Deuteronomy 14:1; Psalm 89:28 and Exodus 4:22. See Horst, *Gottes Recht*, 230.
50. See Jon D. Levenson, *Theology of the Program of Restoration of Ezekiel 40–48*, HSM 10 (Missoula: Scholars, 1976), 97–99.
51. Leviticus 22:8; Ezekiel 44:31; Exodus 22:30; Leviticus 17:15–16; Deuteronomy 14:21.
52. Leviticus 21:6 and 19:2; Exodus 19:6.
53. Psalm 89:2–3; 6–19 (cf. Psalms 47, 95–99); 4–5, 20–38 (cf. 2 Samuel 7:8–16); 39–52. See pp. 22–23.
54. James M. Ward, "The Literary Form and Liturgical Background of Psalm LXXXIX," *VT* 11 (1961): 322.
55. Ibid., 324. On the unity of Psalm 89, see also Jean-Bernard Dumortier, "Un Rituel D'Intronisation: Le Ps. LXXXIX 2–38," *VT* 22 (1972): 176–96; and Richard J. Clifford, "Psalm 89: A Lament Over the Davidic Ruler's Continued Failure," *HTR* 73 (1980): 38–47, esp. pp. 44–45.
56. Psalm 89:15 and 25. See also vv. 29, 34, 50, and Ward, "Literary Form," 331.
57. Psalm 89:10–14.
58. 1 Kings 1:32–2:12; 2 Kings 15:1–5.
59. This is surely connected with those traditions that conceive the *Urmensch* as a king. See Herbert G. May, "The King in the Garden of Eden," in *Israel's Prophetic Heritage*, eds. Bernhard W. Anderson and Walter Harrelson (New York: Harper, 1962), 166–76. For other old mythic motifs that stand behind this transfer of power, see J. A. Emerton, "The Origin of the Son of Man Imagery," *JTS* 9 (1958):225–42.
60. Leviticus 11:44. Cf. Deuteronomy 14:2.

61. Genesis 1:4, 6, 7, 14, 18.
62. Mary Douglas, *Purity and Danger* (London and Henly: Routledge and Kegan Paul, 1966), 53.
63. Leviticus 11:9–12.
64. Genesis 1:20–25.
65. Leviticus 11:2–8.
66. Leviticus 11:45.
67. Pp. 69–72.
68. Leviticus 23:2–5.

Chapter 9

1. Genesis 1:6–13.
2. E. A. Speiser, *Genesis*, AB 1 (Garden City, N.Y.: Doubleday, 1964), 9–10.
3. *Enuma elish* 1:1–2; translation from Alexander Heidel, *The Babylonian Genesis*, 2nd ed. (Chicago: University of Chicago, 1963), 18.
4. *Enuma elish* 4:96–100, 135–146 (Heidel, *Babylonian Genesis*, 40, 42–43). See W. G. Lambert, "A New Look at the Babylonian Background of Genesis," *JTS* 16 (1965):287–300, esp. p. 293.
5. Genesis 1:6–9.
6. See the discussion and critique in Lambert, "A New Look," 293–94.
7. E.g., Psalm 104:9; Proverbs 8:29; Job 38:11.
8. See Speiser, *Genesis*, 6.
9. Genesis 1:3.
10. Genesis 1:5, 8, 13, 19, 23, 31.
11. Leviticus 23:32.
12. Genesis 1:14, 18.
13. See Moshe Weinfeld, "God the Creator in Gen. 1 and in the Prophecy of Second Isaiah," Hebrew, *Tarbiz* 37 (1968): 122. As examples of night and darkness as characteristic of the function of evil powers, Weinfeld points to Genesis 32:27; Exodus 4:24; 12:13, 23; and Job 3:4.
14. Psalm 92:1.
15. *m. Tamid* 7:4.
16. Weinfeld, "God the Creator," 122–26.
17. Isaiah 40:18. Cf. 40:25 and 46:5.
18. Isaiah 40:14, 24; Genesis 1:26. That Genesis 1:26 relates a consultation of God the king with his cabinet has been suggested since Talmudic times. See *Ber. Rab.* 8:4.
19. Isaiah 40:28; Genesis 2:1–3; Exodus 31:17. In spite of these suggestive parallels, I cannot accept Weinfeld's contention ("God the Creator," 124) that the point of Isaiah 45:18 is that "matter was created in an ordered and organized form *ab origine* and had not existed in a condition of chaos" (my translation). Rather, it seems to me that the meaning of the verse is that creation transforms the chaotic wastes into areas fit for settlement. That is, the state of waste of the Land of Israel during the Exile is contrary to the creator's will and a defiance of the *telos* of creation itself.
20. The brackets around "by night" in the NJV have been removed because of the strong versional evidence for *hallaylâ* here.
21. Cf. Zechariah 14:6–7.

22. Isaiah 65:17.
23. Isaiah 56:3–8.
24. E.g., Isaiah 51:9–11.
25. Isaiah 40:28.
26. Yehezkel Kaufmann, *The Religion of Israel* (New York: Schocken, 1972), 60. See earlier, see pp. 3–7.
27. On the special priestly role in proclaiming the sanctity of the Sabbath, see Ezekiel 44:23–24.

NOTES TO PART III

Chapter 10

1. *Enuma elish* 2:122–129 (Alexander Heidel, *The Babylonian Genesis*, 2nd ed. [Chicago: University of Chicago, 1963], 29–30).
2. *Enuma elish* 3:138; 4:1 (Heidel, *Babylonian Genesis*, 36).
3. *Enuma elish* 4:5, 10, 14 (Heidel, *Babylonian Genesis*, 36, except that I have modernized Heidel's archaic second person forms).
4. *Enuma elish* 6:49–54 (Heidel, *Babylonian Genesis*, 48).
5. See Thorkild Jacobsen, "Primitive Democracy in Ancient Mesopotamia," in *Toward the Image of Tammuz and Other Essays on Mesopotamian History and Culture*, ed. William L. Moran, HSS 21 (Cambridge: Harvard University, 1970), 157–70, esp. pp. 163–169.
6. On the theory and practice of acclamation in both Mesopotamia and Israel, see Baruch Halpern, *The Constitution of the Monarchy in Israel*, HSM 25 (Chico: Scholars, 1981), esp. pp. 51–148.
7. Paul Ricoeur, *The Symbolism of Evil* (Boston: Beacon, 1969), 127.
8. I. Tzvi Abusch, "Merodach," in *Harper's Bible Dictionary*, ed. Paul J. Achtemeier (San Francisco: Harper & Row, 1985), 627 (my italics).
9. See pp. 17–25.
10. The translation departs from the NJV at the end of v. 2 for reasons laid out by Frank Moore Cross, "Notes on a Canaanite Psalm in the Old Testament," *BASOR* 117 (1950):21.
11. See especially Theodore H. Gaster, "Psalm 29," *JQR* 37 (1946):55–65. The earliest observation of the Canaanite roots of the psalm was that of H. L. Ginsberg, *Kitve Ugarit* (Jerusalem: Bialik, 1936), 129 ff.
12. Again, the translation departs from the NJV in order to bring out the full implications of *'elim* and *qōdeš*. See Frank Moore Cross, *Canaanite Myth and Hebrew Epic* (Cambridge, Mass.: Harvard University, 1973), 129, n. 61.
13. Exodus 15:13–18.
14. "Gods" in vv. 7 and 9 is a departure from NJV's pale and misleading "divine beings."
15. Exodus 19:5, 8.
16. The most exhaustive discussion is Dennis J. McCarthy, *Treaty and Covenant*, An Bib 21A (Rome: Biblical Institute Press, 1978). See also Jon D. Levenson, *Sinai and Zion* (San Francisco: Harper & Row, 1987), esp. pp. 23–80. The most recent

survey from a revisionist perspective is Ernest W. Nicholson, *God and His People* (Oxford: Oxford University, 1986).

17. E.g., Psalm 93:3-4.
18. E.g., Isaiah 14:9-14.
19. See Yehezkel Kaufmann, *The Religion of Israel* (New York: Schocken, 1972), 60 and 142-147; and Jon D. Levenson, "Yehezkel Kaufmann and Mythology," *CJ* 36 (1982): 36-43.
20. *ANET,* 204.
21. William L. Moran, "The Ancient Near Eastern Background of the Love of God in DT," *CBQ* 25 (1963):77-87.
22. Ibid., 80.
23. See Moshe Weinfeld, *Deuteronomy and the Deuteronomic School* (Oxford: Oxford University, 1972), 91-100, esp. pp. 92-93.
24. See Levenson, *Sinai and Zion,* 80-86.
25. *Sifre Deuteronomy* 346 (Finkelstein ed.). The biblical quote is Isaiah 43:12.
26. This is probably to be associated with the democratization of kingship and even divinity in Israel, as attested, for example, in Psalm 8 and Genesis 1:26-27. See pp. 114-16.

Chapter 11

1. See p. 160 n. l.
2. Michael Wyschogrod, *The Body of Faith* (New York: Seabury, 1983), 8.
3. Exodus 19:5-6.
4. Exodus 19:4.
5. Exodus 2:23-24; Deuteronomy 7:8.
6. Genesis 12:1-7.
7. Genesis 15:7; Exodus 20:2.
8. E.g., Leviticus 26:42; Exodus 32:13; Deuteronomy 9:27. See Jon D. Levenson, "On the Promise to the Rechabites," *CBQ* 38 (1976): 508-14.
9. See McCarthy, *Treaty,* esp. pp. 53-57.
10. Exodus 19:17.
11. Esther 9:27. I have departed from the NJV in order to capture the sense of the verbs appropriate to Rava's midrash.
12. *b. Šabb.* 88a.
13. David Novak, *Halakhah in a Theological Dimension,* BJS 68 (Chico: Scholars, 1985), 117-18. On the Rabbinic concept of theonomy, see also Ephraim E. Urbach, Hebrew, *The Sages* (Jerusalem: Hebrew University, 1975), 287-90.
14. *b. Ber.* 33b.
15. Leo Strauss, *Natural Right and History* (Chicago: University of Chicago, 1953), 181, 182.
16. Ibid., 187. On free choice as the defining characteristic of *religious* liberalism as well, see Eugene B. Borowitz, *Choices in Modern Jewish Thought* (New York: Behrman, 1983), 243-72, esp. p. 256.
17. José Faur, "Understanding the Covenant," *Trad* 9 (1968): 44.
18. Ernest W. Nicholson, *God and His People* (Oxford: Oxford University, 1986), 215-16 (his italics).
19. Galatians 4:21-27.

Chapter 12

1. See Yochanan Muffs, "Between Justice and Mercy: The Prayer of the Prophets," Hebrew, in *Torah Nidreshet: Three Interpretative Essays on the Bible,* ed. Abraham Shapira (Tel Aviv: Am Oved, 1984), 39–87.
2. See Joseph Blenkinsopp, "Abraham and the Righteous of Sodom," *JJS* 33 (1982): 119–32.
3. Genesis 18:19.
4. See pp. 103–6.
5. Genesis 18:27, 30, 31, 32.
6. Genesis 21:12.
7. Most famous, of course, is Søren Kierkegaard, *Fear and Trembling* (Garden City, N.Y.: Doubleday, 1954), composed in 1843.
8. E.g., Galatians 3:1–9; Romans 4:1–22. See Jon D. Levenson, "Why Jews Are Not Interested in Biblical Theology," in *Judaic Perspectives on Ancient Israel,* (ed. Jacob Neusner (Philadelphia: Fortress, 1987), 300–304.
9. Genesis 26:5.
10. Genesis 22:12.
11. Job 1:11.
12. Job 2:5.
13. Job 2:10.
14. Job 42:7–17.
15. Job 42:1–6.
16. See H. L. Ginsberg, "Job the Patient and Job the Impatient," VT Sup 17 (Leiden, Netherlands: Brill, 1966), 88–111.
17. Genesis 18:27; Job 42:6.
18. See Henry Rowold, "*My hw ? ly hw !:* Leviathan and Job in Job 41:2–3," *JBL* 105 (1986): 104–09.

Scripture Index

Job *(cont.)*
   155, 156; **38:2–7**, 155; **38:8–11**, 15,
   122, 159 n.3; **38:11**, 173 n.7;
   40–41, 49; **40:15–22**, 160 n.31,
   162 n.31; **40:19**, 31; **40:25–26**, 17;
   40:25–32, 16, 54; **40:28**,
   160 ch.2 n.9; **42:1–6**, 176 n.15;
   42:6, 155; **42:7–17**, 176 n.14

Esther **3:1**, 162 n.42; **9:27**, 175 n.11

Daniel **7:11–14**, 161 n.18; **12:1–3**,
   161 n.15

Ezra **3:1–6**, 168 n.10

1 Chronicles **21:1**, 44

2 Chronicles **6:13**, 94; **6:41**, 171 n.21;
   7:9, 167 n.2; **29**, 166 n.28; **30:1–20**,
   168 n.14

Author Index

MYTHOS: The Princeton/Bollingen Series in World Mythology

Jon D. Levenson / CREATION AND THE PERSISTENCE OF EVIL: THE JEWISH DRAMA OF DIVINE OMNIPOTENCE

Roger S. Loomis / THE GRAIL: FROM CELTIC MYTH TO CHRISTIAN SYMBOL

Bronislaw Malinowski (Ivan Strenski, ed.) / MALINOWSKI AND THE WORK OF MYTH

Louis Massignon (Herbert Mason, ed.) / HALLAJ: MYSTIC AND MARTYR

Patricia Cox Miller / DREAMS IN LATE ANTIQUITY: STUDIES IN THE IMAGINATION OF A CULTURE

Erich Neumann / AMOR AND PSYCHE

Erich Neumann / THE GREAT MOTHER

Erich Neumann / THE ORIGINS AND HISTORY OF CONSCIOUSNESS

Maud Oakes with Joseph Campbell / WHERE THE TWO CAME TO THEIR FATHER

Dora & Erwin Panofsky / PANDORA'S BOX

Paul Radin / THE ROAD OF LIFE AND DEATH

Otto Rank, Lord Raglan, Alan Dundes / IN QUEST OF THE HERO

Gladys Reichard / NAVAHO RELIGION

Géza Róheim (Alan Dundes, ed.) / FIRE IN THE DRAGON

Robert A. Segal, ed. / THE GNOSTIC JUNG

Jean Seznec / THE SURVIVAL OF THE PAGAN GODS: THE MYTHOLOGICAL TRADITION AND ITS PLACE IN RENAISSANCE HUMANISM AND ART

Miranda Shaw / PASSIONATE ENLIGHTENMENT: WOMEN IN TANTRIC BUDDHISM

Philip E. Slater / THE GLORY OF HERA

Daisetz T. Suzuki / ZEN AND JAPANESE CULTURE

Jean-Pierre Vernant (Froma I. Zeitlin, ed.) / MORTALS AND IMMORTALS

Jessie L. Weston / FROM RITUAL TO ROMANCE

Hellmut Wilhelm and Richard Wilhelm / UNDERSTANDING THE I CHING: THE WILHELM LECTURES ON THE BOOK OF CHANGES

Aryeh Wineman / MYSTIC TALES FROM THE ZOHAR

Heinrich Zimmer (Joseph Campbell, ed.) / THE KING AND THE CORPSE: TALES OF THE SOUL'S CONQUEST OF EVIL

Heinrich Zimmer (Joseph Campbell, ed.) / MYTHS AND SYMBOLS IN INDIAN ART AND CIVILIZATION